Surviving Sudden Loss
Stories from those who have lived it

Heidi Snow

Edited by Ariana Bratt

Copyright © 2012 by Heidi Snow

ISBN: 978-0-9854379-0-9

All rights reserved. No part of this book may be reproduced in any form or by any electronic or mechanical means, including information storage and retrieval systems, without permission in writing from the author, except by a reviewer, who may quote brief passages in review.

Self-published by the author

Dedicated to those who are grieving after the sudden loss of loved ones.

TABLE OF CONTENTS

Acknowledgements 3
Foreword *by Mayor Rudolph Giuliani* 5
Preface 7

Section 1 Introduction and Background of *Surviving Sudden Loss*
    Introduction *by Dr. Susan R. Snow* 11
    1 Heidi *by Ariana Bratt* 21
    2 To the Grief-stricken in the Wake of a Sudden Loss *by Heidi Snow* 23

Section 2 Heidi's Story and the Founding of AirCraft Casualty Emotional Support Services *by Heidi Snow*
    3 Michel and Me 29
    4 The Crash 39
    5 The Birth of ACCESS 57

Section 3 Stories of Sudden Loss
    6 Loss of my husband in 9/11 on United Flight 93 *by Lyzbeth Glick Best* . . .75
    7 Loss of my family in a private plane crash *by Elizabeth Spooner Norton* . .85
    8 Loss of my fiancé in a construction accident *by Julie Rudd* 93
    9 Loss of my daughter in 9/11 on United Flight 93 *by Catherine Stefani* . . .101
    10 Loss of my son in a motor vehicle accident *by Sharon Leighton* 113
    11 Loss of my husband in a private plane crash *by Mary Conklin* 121
    12 Loss of my brother and his family on Northwest Flight 255
       by Joan Pontante 131
    13 Loss of my baby to sudden infant death syndrome *by Lisa Brooks* 137
    14 Loss of my mother on TWA Flight 800 *by Dr. Lawrence Gustin* 143
    15 Loss of my fiancé in 9/11 *by Karen M. Carlucci* 149
    16 Loss of my mother to cardiac arrest *by Dr. Susan R. Snow* 157
    17 Loss of my husband on TWA Flight 800 *by Martha Rhein* 165
    18 Loss of my husband in 9/11 *by Monica Iken* 171
    19 Loss of my mother to sudden cardiac death *by Jane Begala* 177
    20 Loss of my father to suicide *by Seth O'Connor* 183
    21 Loss of my father in a private plane crash *by Rachel Courtney* 191

22 Loss of my son on Pan Am 103 *by Betty Capasso* 199
23 Loss of my husband in a private plane crash *by Veronica Campanelli*...203
24 Loss of my parents on Air France Flight 007 *by Nina Crimm* 209
25 Loss of my brother on Swissair Flight 111 *by Jack Karamanoukian* ...213
26 Loss of my father in a motor vehicle accident *by Andrew August* 219
27 Loss of my daughter in 9/11 on American Flight 77 *by Marion Kminek* .225
28 Loss of my parents on TWA Flight 800 *by Ned Brooks* 231
29 Loss of my daughter in 9/11 on United Flight 175 *by John Titus*.......237
30 Loss of my wife on TWA Flight 800 *by Stewart Mosberg* 241
31 Loss of my family in a private plane crash *by Richard Stanley* 247
32 Loss of my mother in childbirth *by Kiersten Stevens* 251

Appendix..255

ACKNOWLEDGEMENTS

We wish to acknowledge the generous contributions of those who shared their personal and painful experiences of grief and survival in the wake of sudden loss of precious loved ones.

The book is based on the cumulative experiences of AirCraft Casualty Emotional Support Services (ACCESS), so we wish to acknowledge Heidi Snow, its founder and executive director, as well as Mayor Giuliani and Governor Pataki for their instrumental roles in its founding. We acknowledge all those hundreds of generous individuals who support ACCESS as contributors, volunteer grief mentors, board members and volunteers for our charity events. We acknowledge Dr. Ken Druck for providing ACCESS volunteer grief mentor training.

We acknowledge Ariana Bratt, Heidi Snow and Dr. Susan Snow for interviewing contributors, transcribing the interviews, and writing and editing the stories.

Surviving Sudden Loss: *Stories from those who have lived it*

Mayor Giuliani is the most fitting person to write the foreword for *Surviving Sudden Loss* because of his unprecedented experience with the grief-stricken. His heroic response, reassuring presence and compassion after TWA, 9/11 and other disasters helped so many of us impacted by these tragedies. After my fiancé was killed on TWA Flight 800 and I was struggling with my grief, he guided me to a meeting that inspired me to found AirCraft Casualty Emotional Support Services (ACCESS). By joining our honorary advisory board and connecting me with people invaluable to the creation and growth of ACCESS, Mayor Giuliani played a pivotal role in ACCESS, which inspired this book.

—Heidi Snow

FOREWORD

by Mayor Rudolph Giuliani

I met Heidi Snow on a terrible morning in July 1996, just a day after TWA Flight 800 crashed on its way to Paris. Heidi's fiancé, French ice hockey player Michel Breistroff, was killed along with 229 others in that tragic plane crash off the coast of Long Island.

I urged Heidi to meet with family members of Pan Am Flight 103, which had been blown up by terrorists eight years earlier. I hoped that speaking to others who shared such a sudden and horrible loss would be of some comfort to Heidi.

She turned her meeting with those family members into AirCraft Casualty Emotional Support Services (ACCESS), a remarkable group that offers comfort and understanding to people who have suffered unexpected losses. Heidi's group pairs survivors so they can share their heartbreak with someone who truly understands their loss and can offer more than platitudes. Heidi also helps train airline staff so they better understand the grief process.

ACCESS was an invaluable asset after September 11, 2001, as those families were able to speak with ACCESS mentors about their pain. One woman, who was widowed on September 11th, remembers reading an article about Heidi years earlier, and was shocked to find herself joining Heidi to share her anguish after losing her husband. Heidi has started a club of mentors that no one wants the credentials to join. But in doing so, she has eased the path to healing for other survivors. ACCESS provides a poignant and sadly necessary role in our society, and it is essential that these families speak to each other so they remember a critical fact: that they must survive and continue.

Surviving Sudden Loss: Stories from those have lived it is an unparalleled collection of personal stories which captures the spirit of ACCESS that learning about another's journey through grief can provide comfort to others. It allows everyone to hear and to benefit from the voices and insights of those who have experienced grief in the setting of the sudden loss of a loved one.

PREFACE

This book is for everyone with loved ones (mothers, fathers, daughters, sons, sisters, brothers, husbands, wives, fiancés, dear friends and others) in their lives. Whether you have lost a loved one or not, these stories will touch you. They will inspire you to survive setbacks and to turn challenges and difficult situations into opportunities for positive growth, happiness and success. They will help you appreciate those whom you have in your life today and to strengthen your relationships. They will empower you to embrace every moment of every day with the people you cherish.

This book is specially dedicated to those who have lost loved ones suddenly and tragically without warning, and those who are helping them navigate and survive their difficult and life-changing journey through sudden loss.

I was inspired to write the book from my own personal experiences and from my interactions through AirCraft Casualty Emotional Support Services (ACCESS) which I founded after the loss of my fiancé Michel on TWA Flight 800. I found comfort in talking to others who had lived through a loss like mine years earlier. Through our 250 volunteer grief mentors, all of whom have survived the tragic loss of a loved one, ACCESS provides emotional support to those who have experienced a similar loss.

In *Surviving Sudden Loss*, we offer our own stories to comfort those who are now struggling with the unexpected death of loved ones. From our own experiences, we have learned that grief after sudden loss is a life-long journey with many common threads. The most important message is that each journey is unique, that lives are forever changed and that survival is possible after the most unthinkable and tragic loss of a loved one.

Heidi Snow, Founder and Executive Director
AirCraft Casualty Emotional Support Services (ACCESS)
www.accesshelp.org
ACCESS is a 501c3 nonprofit organization

Surviving Sudden Loss: *Stories from those who have lived it*

SECTION 1

Introduction and Background of *Surviving Sudden Loss*

Introduction

Every day millions of people say goodbye to loved ones as they leave for work, school, play, shopping, an evening out, a vacation or a business trip. They may never consider that death could separate them forever before they can see one another again. It is not even entertained as a possibility. The daily news demonstrates that unexpected death happens often, but the chance that it will happen to a particular person on a given day is very low. When we witness these deaths in the news, they are usually just interesting and sad events because the victims are strangers. We have compassion and would like to help if we could, but there are no direct emotional stakes. Statistically, these things happen to others. However, when sudden death strikes, it does so with 100% of its force on the victims and their loved ones. The statistics do not matter anymore.

Heidi Snow experienced tragedy from the perspective of the observer and the victim. As Heidi and her fiancé watched the coverage of the Florida ValuJet plane crash in May 1996, they were sad for those who suffered in its aftermath. As they watched those events unfold, they never conceived that one of them would soon die in a similar crash. It was an impossible outcome, but just two months later, their goodbyes and "I love you's" were their last moments together before his plane exploded off Long Island.

Eventually most everyone will be impacted by a sudden and unexpected tragic loss. There is no lingering illness and no warning that an accident, senseless crime, massive heart attack, or other unforeseen event will end a life and leave those behind in unfathomable grief.

Inspiration and purpose of *Surviving Sudden Loss*

Heidi Snow's world was forever changed on July 17, 1996 when her fiancé, Michel Breistroff, died in the crash of TWA Flight 800. This single event altered the course of her life and the lives of thousands of others left in unspeakable grief from the disaster. In the immediate aftermath of the crash, the American Red Cross, the airline, and other organizations provided crisis intervention to families and friends of the victims. However, after a few weeks, the disaster teams disbanded and the survivors dispersed. When

Heidi returned home, the initial shock subsided and her agonizing grief intensified. She was left all alone in her grief with no tangible future because all her plans were inextricably tied to Michel. Most people expected her to move beyond the loss after the funeral. She continued to find it hard to cope with what had happened, and desperately needed to find someone who understood the pain and utter emptiness she felt. It was difficult for anyone not personally affected by this kind of disaster to understand the extent of its impact.

Mayor Rudy Giuliani suggested that she attend a meeting of families who had lost loved ones in the bombing of Pan Am 103 eight years earlier. They understood Heidi's pain because they had lived it. Heidi was so inspired by these models of survival after loss that she immediately began setting up an organization to connect survivors of sudden death to those who had survived a similar loss years earlier. She was determined that no one should experience the loneliness, isolation and grief that she had suffered. She wanted others to have the opportunity to find encouragement and hope in the wake of their losses from those who had experienced it.

After receiving an enthusiastic response to her idea from hundreds of survivors from Pan Am 103 and TWA 800, Heidi founded the AirCraft Casualty Emotional Support Services (ACCESS). ACCESS is a nonprofit grief mentoring organization which partners those grieving from the loss of a loved one with those who have survived a similar loss years earlier. She formed a board of directors and an advisory board, which included New York's Mayor Rudy Giuliani and Governor George Pataki. Since its founding in 1996, ACCESS has grown exponentially. The organization has a 24-hour hotline and more than 250 volunteer grief mentors who have all lost loved ones unexpectedly in air disasters, and regularly trains crisis responders who work at airlines, companies and disaster response agencies interacting with the grief-stricken immediately following air disasters.

Surviving Sudden Loss embodies the philosophy of ACCESS, which is that those who have gone through the loss of a loved one have hard-earned gifts of survival for those just experiencing a loss. It is a collection of personal stories offering insights into surviving sudden loss told by those who have lived through it. The purpose of presenting these stories is for others to be able to realize, "That happened to me too. People responded to me like that too. I felt that way too. I am not alone. Since they survived, maybe I can too." They may be able to identify with one story or one aspect of several stories. This is key for the grief-stricken, especially when they feel it is too difficult to get through another day without their loved one because they hurt so much.

Introduction

These stories teach that others have survived catastrophic grief. Their personal accounts openly describe the horror that accompanied the news of their loved one's death. In their own words, they recount their lives before the loss, when they first learned of the loss, and how they reacted, coped and survived. They describe how it affected them days, weeks, months and years later, and they describe their hard-earned insights from firsthand experience with tragedy. The variety of reactions and coping mechanisms they demonstrate shows that there is no preset right way to react emotionally and to survive the loss of a loved one. Many reveal intimate details of personal struggles with pain and anguish that they would have otherwise kept private. They disclose them here in hopes that others might know how difficult it was for them and find comfort in learning how they survived.

In each of these unique stories, there are eighteen recurrent and common threads emphasized or mentioned to different degrees.

1) Life before the loss
The contributors to this book introduce their loved ones and their relationships. We can identify with the people they describe because we have parents, siblings, children, spouses and other loved ones whom we need in our lives. Before the loss, they do not even remotely entertain the possibility of the upcoming life-changing tragic events. From these stories, we realize how randomly and illogically death strikes. While fate chose them, someday fate could choose us or our loved ones.

2) The last moments together before the tragedy
Those left in the wake of sudden loss have vivid memories of their last interaction with lost loved ones. Their final interactions were final only in retrospect, so we can identify with these last moments because most of us part with loved ones temporarily on a daily basis. Whenever we say goodbye, there is no guarantee we will ever see them again.

3) Notification "No! It can't be!"
Suddenly life stops. All the contributors share how they first learned of their unbelievable losses. The news may have reached them in increments. When air disasters occur, for example, there is often knowledge of the missing plane or of the crash in the media before it is confirmed that a loved one was on the flight or died in the accident. If there are survivors, determining who survived can take a long time too. For example, one of our contributors hoped that a surviving toddler from a plane crash was her niece until someone else identified and claimed the toddler days later. Another lost her fiancé in 9/11,

but his death was only gradually realized from the knowledge that he went to work at the Towers that morning and never returned. No remains were ever found, so confirmation of his death painstakingly emerged only through the passage of time.

4) Still waiting for loved ones to return
From the earliest hint that loved ones might be lost, there can be hope for their reappearance. Their return is the only true remedy for the grief. Many wait for and look for their lost loved ones until the death is confirmed by word of mouth or by recovery of the remains. Some wait until the funeral or burial. Others keep a glimmer of hope alive for days, months or even years. The waiting is more than denial. It reflects ongoing hope to reverse the loss. Even when they know it is futile to keep waiting, they are not yet ready to accept the permanence of the loss. It is a coping mechanism that is very important to some throughout the grieving process. Heidi Snow looked for her beloved fiancé to emerge from the waters of the Atlantic off Long Island days after they called off the search for survivors from Flight 800. Weeks later, she walked the streets they had walked together hoping he would return to walk with her again.

5) The initial shock
After notification of the loss, many are stunned and shocked. They may appear to function normally as they notify others and make necessary arrangements. This is really just busywork consisting of robotic activities. It is a natural distraction which deflects or mitigates the onslaught of pain. The shock is analogous to that brief grace period a person has between seeing his finger accidently touch a hot burner and the sensation of pain from the burn. As shock subsides, the intensity of the pain increases.

6) Open questions
The sudden loss of a loved one is irreconcilable because there are so many questions that can never be satisfactorily addressed. Why did this have to happen to us? Why did our loved ones die leaving us in this terrible grief? In one of the stories, a young widow commented, "This 'who gets to live and who has to die' did not make any sense. It is almost like someone said, 'Okay. You, you and you, but you're gonna stay.'" We seek logic behind these baffling and inexplicable tragedies when there really is none. Nevertheless, we cannot help but ask.

7) Immediate plans change

While the loss of a loved one has far-reaching effects on the lives of those left behind, there is often a next planned rendezvous with the loved one which does not occur after the loss which can be the first overt manifestation of the loss. There might have been a plan for phone contact or a meeting at home or at the airport. Even in the setting of knowing about the death, when the anticipated follow-up interaction does not happen, there is additional disappointment with this corroboration of the loss. For Heidi, it was Michel's phone call from Paris the next morning when he would arrive at the airport. It was a big letdown and one of the earliest steps in her realization of the finality of her loss when his call did not come. For some, this evokes an initial blame for the lost one's failure to honor the agreed upon next contact. "She walked out the door and never came back," was the comment by one man whose wife died from a heart attack on her way to her doctor's appointment.

8) The vanishing future

After the loss, the world is never the same. The future devoid of the loved ones is filled with unanticipated and even paralyzing grief. Each circumstance previously associated with them reintroduces the loss and its associated pain. Holidays, such as the next Thanksgiving and the next birthday, are all painful reminders of a future presumed and anticipated to be celebrated with them. For parents, the future involved the growth and development of their children with birthdays, graduations, weddings and the birth of a new generation, now all gone. For children, the parents held the certainty of remembrances of their childhood and guidance and participation into their adulthood. For newlyweds and fiancés, there was an entire life planned together full of milestones to reach and to celebrate together. The futures of all those left in the wake of sudden loss are unexpectedly changed at nearly every turn. It is challenging to forge on with a future which must now exclude one of its main architects and vital participants.

9) Regrets

Most every story contains some aspect of regret or guilt. There are usually some expressions similar to "if only I had known!" and the assertion that slight changes in the circumstances might have removed their loved ones from harm's way. In Heidi's case, Michel had not felt well the day he left, and she could have suggested that he leave another day. In addition, had it not been for her, he would not have been in New York City to take that doomed flight. All these expressions of regret reflect the longing to turn back time to reverse the loss. Although they know it was an accident and there was no way to anticipate the chain of events leading to the loss, they entertain how reliving that day differently could have spared the lives of their loved ones.

10) Loneliness and isolation
After the funeral, the phone calls, visits and letters of condolence stop and society expects individuals to move on and forget about the loss at some level. Unsure of what to say and do, some may even avoid the mourners entirely. The world goes on and friends expect the grief to dissipate and the grief-stricken to normalize back to life before the loss. This expectation may force the grieving to suppress manifestations of their emotions. Even when there is a semblance of total recovery, there is often a tear behind the grieving person's smile. Even if they are surrounded by people who love them and want to see them recover, they may feel lonely and isolated when they do not feel free to share expressions of their pain. This personal sense of loneliness and isolation was the most important factor in Heidi Snow's founding of ACCESS. She wanted others grieving in the aftermath of an air disaster to have a safe place to share expressions of grief, and she found it in those who had survived similar losses years earlier.

11) Pain
Only those who have personally experienced the pain of suddenly losing a loved one can grasp its enormity. Even if the pain cannot be adequately portrayed with words, its depth and impact can be inferred from its effects and the reactions to it. Many have the pain, but are at a loss to define it in order to discuss and confront it. The attempts by others to describe their own pain and grief may allow those who have experienced a recent loss to say, "Yes, that is what I am feeling. I felt the same way and I am beginning to understand it now. I am not alone." This is especially important when the intensity seems unbearable, but they can see that others survived similar pain.

12) Self-doubt "There must be something wrong with me for still hurting so much after all this time"
There is a commonly held myth, even among some professionals, that it is abnormal for grief not to dissipate within some predictable or anticipated timeframe. One of the most important goals of these stories and of ACCESS is to dispel the feeling by the grief-stricken that there is something wrong with them for feeling whatever they feel. Imposing timelines on the grieving compounds their pain. The contributors to *Surviving Sudden Loss* describe ongoing expressions of loss and sorrow many years after their losses. They have found that their grief is a natural part of their lives and is intermixed with their joys. For example, out of TWA Flight 800, new close friendships

Introduction

arose in the setting of agonizing grief and loss. At the 15th anniversary memorial service, no one was afraid to cry and to remember loved ones. Each person's experience with grief is unique and not subject to typical societal expectations limiting its duration and intensity.

13) Rebuilding life in the wake of a loss
Many expect that time will heal all the pain, reverse all the effects of the loss, and allow life to proceed as if the whole thing never happened. However, some permanent changes after a loss are obvious. For example, children orphaned by air crashes may have new care providers, homes and schools. The widower married for fifty years suddenly has to dine and shop alone. In addition to these visible adjustments, the most difficult and challenging life changes may involve no immediate overt major changes in the daily routine. There may be emotional turmoil with grief affecting every thought process and interaction at home, at work and in the community that is very subtle and even imperceptible to an outside observer. At the 10th anniversary of TWA, a reporter asked a family member how long it took him to recover from the death of his niece. He replied, "Losing her was like losing part of myself, like an arm that never grows back, but I have learned to live with the loss." It is important to expect personal lives to remain forever changed. After the loss, most activities and experiences are associated with new emotions, insights and perspectives.

14) Survival is possible
Grief in the aftermath of horrific loss may be so overwhelming at times that survival does not seem possible. For everyone experiencing a sudden loss, no matter what the specific circumstances, these stories about journeys through grief can provide hope that they too can survive. One of our ACCESS mentors tells those seeking emotional support, "The truth is, you will get through it, but it is going to be a long road and it's going to be a difficult road."

15) A life-long journey
Many of these stories are recounted more than ten years after the deaths. Loss continues to impact lives even many years later. It is critical to see these ongoing effects to allay the frustrations of those who are told they should forget their grief and get on with their lives as if the tragedy never happened. The expectation of a full recovery in our fast-paced society creates additional anxiety and pain for the grief-stricken. People like to fix things, but grief cannot be fixed because the loved ones never return. It is a process and a journey which becomes a part of who we are, who we become, and how we live our lives.

16) Changed relationships and new friends

Sudden loss leaves the grief-stricken with permanently changed perspectives and priorities. They are different, so their relationships with others are not the same. Close friends may distance themselves when they do not understand or know how to react. One of our ACCESS volunteer grief mentors commented, "Some formerly casual friends became very dear, and some very close friends became totally distant and dropped out of my life." It is important for those in grief to know that others found themselves being treated differently than before their loss, and that they had to seek out and surround themselves with people who accepted them as they were.

17) Finding meaning in senseless tragedy and strength from adversity

We remain powerless to reverse the loss. Yet to survive it is a remarkable feat. It requires the development of strength and resourcefulness. There is a unique perspective gained as one ascends from the abyss of hopelessness and paralyzing grief. These stories illustrate the emergence of incredible powers of adaptation and coping during the often horrific journey through grief. By simply surviving their losses, the contributors to this book stand as models of human fortitude which they acquired out of necessity after their tragic losses. One of the most common experiences of the grief mentors in ACCESS as they support others is the realization of how far they themselves have come and how much they have learned along the way. These stories suggest that those who are now suffering from grief can likewise develop strengths from resources they do not yet appreciate within themselves. One woman who helps the grief-stricken through ACCESS commented, "I hope they look at me and realize I am no stronger than they are. And since I survived, they can say, 'If she could do it, maybe I can too.'"

18) Reaching out

As those who have survived their losses realize the special insights, knowledge and strengths they have acquired from their journeys through grief, many, including those who recounted their stories in this book, wish to share them with others experiencing similar losses. Heidi Snow founded ACCESS because she was comforted by the experiences of those who had lost loved ones on Pan Am 103 and wanted to reach out to others in the same way. Many stories in *Surviving Sudden Loss: Stories from those who have lived it* echo the experience of ACCESS volunteer grief mentors in noting that helping others is a means for them to understand how far they have come, as well as to emotionally support those who are now traveling a path similar to theirs.

Introduction

Surviving Sudden Loss is an unprecedented collection of 28 unfiltered firsthand accounts of grief and survival in the wake of the sudden loss of a loved one. The stories are presented by generous people who share intimate details of personal struggles following devastating losses. It was painful to resurrect some of the more horrific and tender moments, but they volunteered these hard-earned gifts to provide comfort as well as hope for survival to others just experiencing a most unimaginable death of a loved one.

The first section is dedicated to helping the grief-stricken realize that each journey through grief is unique. Through our own personal experiences with tragedy and hundreds and hundreds of interactions through ACCESS, we have learned that lives are forever changed in the wake of sudden loss. Relationships and priorities are never the same even though our society has expectations to the contrary. The grief-stricken need to embrace their own expressions of grief and embrace themselves as they are now in the wake of their losses. They need to seek out individuals who accept them as they are and their grief as it is.

The second section is Heidi Snow's story of hope following the loss of her beloved Michel. Her words are raw descriptions of her feelings in the wake of her loss. Acute disaster response teams provided temporary support, but they disbanded after a few weeks as her shock was wearing off and her grief intensified. Society expected her to be over it and to move on after the funeral. However, her entire future was entwined with Michel, so her future was gone while she was left in unfathomable grief. When Mayor Giuliani guided her to a meeting of families of Pan Am 103 which had crashed eight years earlier, she found comfort in learning that it was okay to grieve after the funeral and she found hope that she would survive her pain and grief because they had survived it. She had thought there was something wrong with her for continuing to grieve, but they were not afraid to cry after eight years. She immediately vowed that no one should have to experience the isolation she had felt. She asked the Pan Am 103 families at the meeting to formally help those with more recent losses like herself. Most everyone there, over one hundred, volunteered. This experience led her to found ACCESS, which is unique in that it not only pairs the grief-stricken with mentors who have survived earlier losses, but pairs them according to relationships lost. For example, Heidi paired a man who lost his wife and two young daughters on TWA Flight 800 in 1996 to another man who experienced a similar loss in 2011. ACCESS pairs mothers to mothers, sons to sons, daughters to daughters and so on. The other unique aspect of ACCESS is that their care, like the journey through grief, has no time limits. Some have sought out its resources of emotional support many years after their losses when they were finally ready to deal with their grief.

The third section of the book consists of insightful stories about the sudden loss of daughters, sons, mothers, fathers, husbands, wives, brothers, sisters, entire families, fiancés and others. These include United Flights 93 and 175, American Flight 77 and the Towers from 9/11, Pan Am 103, TWA 800, Swissair 111, other air crashes, sudden infant death, sudden cardiac death, car accidents and others. All the stories have the common thread of sudden unexpected loss, but beyond that, each person's grief and reaction to the grief are unique. This illustrates the theme of ACCESS that regardless of expectations of others, there is no set way to grieve and no one has the right to judge another's response to loss. The most important message from these stories is that no matter how deep and debilitating the pain, they all survived. They are models of hope of survival in the wake of the worst imaginable loss.

The appendix describes the work of ACCESS as a model of emotional support provided by those with the hard-earned credentials of experiencing a similar loss years earlier. It is the hope of Heidi and the entire team at ACCESS that those who read these stories will find comfort in their time of grief.

There is a classical approach to analyzing grief based on the classic 1969 Kübler-Ross stages of denial, anger, bargaining, depression and acceptance. This model and its spin-offs are sometimes interpreted as intolerant of grief beyond the funeral or other arbitrary points of reference. Those who do not conform are often perceived as wrong or even mentally ill. In fact, some propose that feelings be measured so that those of a certain intensity present more than six months after the loss be diagnostic of "prolonged grief disorder." Some propose that some grief should be classified in the psychiatric Diagnostic and Statistical Manual for Mental Disorders (DSM). The specter of standards for right or normal grief threatens the ability of individuals to accept themselves and their grief. Their feelings are not under their control, so if they do not comply with another's model, their only option is to think there is something wrong with them and to suppress their feelings because they fear they are invalid. It is important that they do not sense that they are being judged by some predefined standards. They need someone who simply listens and accepts them as they are.

The purpose of sharing these stories of survival following sudden loss is to help the grief-stricken accept themselves and their grief without guilt or anxiety. They may find great comfort in realizing that others were feeling what they are feeling and reacting as they are reacting.

—Susan R. Snow, M.D., Ph.D.

CHAPTER 1

Heidi
by Ariana Bratt

My sister's fiancé, Michel, told me that bagpipes rang in the day's festivities the morning of his graduation from Harvard. I was only five years old, but I had heard bagpipes before and sensed that their occasional discord and tone could signal something other than joy. My sister and he shared a future too bright to have anything cast a shadow before it. She was entering a promising career in finance and Michel was training with a professional hockey team. For the next two summers, he spent weeks with my family in Maine. He would effortlessly throw me into the air with his strong arms and carry me over the rough terrain of the woods on his shoulders.

Michel left to train and to visit his family in France. Heidi could not go with him because she was scheduled to take an exam. When they parted that day, they parted forever. He died in the crash of TWA Flight 800. I could not grasp this impossible outcome. I had seen him full of hope and life just days before. And now I was supposed to accept that he was gone forever. I watched my sister crumble. She wanted to join him under the ocean or sleep all the time so she could dream that he was still there. Her eyes were empty despite the tears as she gazed beyond me to something intangible and unreachable. The initial shock rapidly gave way to pain that I could sense was unbelievably intense and unremitting.

The President patiently heard stories from each of the mourners, including my sister. It struck me as odd that even the most powerful person in the world could not stay the pain in the grief site. I remember her panic as it closed and she left its relative security where the Red Cross and other organizations had provided information and support. Suddenly after two weeks, she was supposed to be over it and to move on with her life. I remember her quiet tears as JFK Jr. was married that September in a setting similar to the one that she and Michel had planned for their own wedding. She had met the couple in a New York museum and her photo on the beach after the TWA tragedy and the Kennedy wedding appeared in the same annual *Life Magazine* yearbook. Without imagining the tragic fate of the Kennedy couple in an air disaster only a few years later, she probably wished that Michel and she could emulate them.

She found comfort in talking with a group of people who had lost loved ones years earlier in the crash of Pan Am 103. Their survival gave her the first hope that she could survive and that there was nothing wrong with her for feeling the sorrow she had been told was supposed to vanish after the memorials and funeral. She could trust those who had experienced a loss similar to hers. While they helped her realize that grief can be prolonged and recurrent, they were the embodiment of survival after loss. She had to provide that same hope to others. She vowed that no one should go through the seemingly hopeless and endless pain and isolation she had experienced. That same year, she founded AirCraft Casualty Emotional Support Services (ACCESS), a national nonprofit organization that provides emotional support to those who are grieving from the loss of a loved one in an air disaster. The unique feature of all the volunteer grief mentors is that they, like my sister, have themselves experienced losses in air disasters in past years. They provide hope, guidance and inspiration to those who need it. My sister dedicates herself to a cause that was triggered by an event in her life which had been as inconceivable to her as it was to those she now helps.

Years have passed since I first learned that loved ones can disappear from my life without warning. One minute they are part of our daily routine, and the next minute we are left with only memories. Sometimes I envy others who are still as naïve as I was before Michel died because they can still trust that everyone will be there tomorrow. On the other hand, each time I see my family, I take a few minutes to express how much I enjoy them.

Heidi no longer regrets that she was not on the plane with Michel. She devotes herself to helping others through their grief and still often loses her composure as she recounts their last minutes together and the first agonizing months after his death. She has taught me that while the sadness and the memories can last a long time, there are always important ways to use experiences, even tragic ones, to help others.

While losses and disappointments are inevitable for us all, we can control their ultimate impact on our lives. Despite her painful memories, Heidi is one of the most positive people I know. She teaches me to concentrate on others rather than dwelling on my own problems. She is busy with others who, like her, have a unique ability to connect with the grief-stricken. As living examples of survival after a most painful loss, they offer special comfort and hope.

CHAPTER 2

To the Grief-stricken in the Wake of a Sudden Loss
by Heidi Snow

One of our greatest hopes is that the stories in *Surviving Sudden Loss* enable you to recognize that the intensity and duration of your grief is not under your control or that of anyone else. Each path following the sudden and unexpected loss of a loved one is as unique as the person who experiences it. Your grief is your own, and only you can appreciate it. No one can manipulate, define or predict its extent, its manifestations or its timing. There is no preset pattern or timeline. There are none, regardless of their experience or academic credentials, with the right to judge or evaluate what you feel. There is no right or wrong way to feel. Trust and embrace your emotions and reactions as you seek out those who accept your grief as it is and those who accept you as you are now.

When TWA Flight 800 exploded and crashed into the ocean, thousands of people mourned in its aftermath, but none of their experiences with grief followed the same exact course. Deriving a semblance of structure to grief provides satisfaction only to those conducting the analysis. Trying to force grief into some preconceived framework only evokes guilt and a sense of inadequacy for those in mourning. Imposing parameters may create anxiety, self-doubt and a perception that there is something wrong with them if their path is not in compliance with the expectations of others. The preoccupation with stages implies that the grief-stricken can adjust the timing and degree of their feelings. They are told, "According to this book and people who understand grief, you are supposed to be at stage B now, and in x number of days/weeks/months, you will proceed to stage C which should last y number of days/weeks/months." What they are really saying is, "I don't know how to deal with how sad you are. Instead, I will tell you what you should be feeling based on what others have concluded is right."

The ultimate frustration for many is that tragic loss is perceived to be like a disease from which one fully recovers. Yet no amount of time and no stage in the journey through life will bring back that person who was taken away. The loss is irrevocable, so lives are permanently changed. Our future and part of us are lost along with our loved one. For many of us, it is also the death of that trust that all of our loved ones, so exuberant with life, will be there tomorrow. We now become keenly aware that anyone can be cruelly wrested from us without warning. There is an increased appreciation for our remaining loved ones because we are acutely aware of life's fragility and uncertainty. It is important to grasp life now rather than to just assume we have plenty of time. For example, Michel and I spent as much time together as we possibly could. To many, his long trip from Paris to New England on Christmas Eve in 1995 for only twelve hours seemed excessive. Since we assumed there would be many more Christmases together, we could have deferred the visit to another year. I am so grateful that we spent it together because it turned out to be our last. Each of those hours is now a precious memory.

Well-meaning people often minimize another's grief with such comments as, "Don't feel sad. Time heals. You can find love again. They lived a good life." Feelings of love and loss are not determined by such platitudes. For example, one of our mentors lost her teenaged son aboard Pan Am 103. Because he was one of many children, people tried to comfort her by saying, "You are so lucky to have other children." What she heard was, "You surely should not feel all that much grief." It implied that her son was simply an interchangeable part of the family who could disappear with little consequence. She felt they were saying that she did not have a right to grieve as much as someone with only one child. Her devastation from the loss of her son was actually intensified in some respects. In addition to dealing with her own grief, she had to help all of her children with theirs. Those working with the grief-stricken need to accept and support another's right to react and to grieve in their own way. Attempting to minimize the loss invalidates their feelings and intensifies their pain.

It is inevitable that you will experience pain from your loss in your own way and on your own schedule. No one can manipulate that private realm within you which is not accessible to even your control. Unless you realize this, those who want to control or limit your grief may actually compound it.

My grief was, and is, a journey with unexpected turns and uncharted valleys. I was not a writer nor did I keep a journal before Michel died, but it was helpful for me to try to describe my feelings that were actually beyond words. I began writing my story on August 1, 1996 just two weeks after the crash. It was hard to write because the screen was blurred from my tears freezing in contact with the emerging stark reality of Michel's death.

My story consists of my own personal observations. The tone of my words and my reactions to my pain capture aspects of my emotional experience in

Chapter 2 To the Grief-stricken in the Wake of a Sudden Loss

the aftermath of Michel's death and provide some insight into my grief. You may identify with my story and the stories of others that describe a broad set of experiences and reactions to loss. They are not guides for your grief because there can be no how-to book on grief, but in demonstrating that everyone follows a different course after loss, they might help you to accept yourself as you are and accept your grief as it is.

All of us describe in our own words the awful life-changing event that we had never dreamed of in our worst nightmares. Though our stories are deeply personal and painful for us to recount, we hope they will help you get through another day in your journey. You may find solace in learning how others survived their own losses. Perhaps you will find that some of our experiences and feelings parallel your own and lend a voice to what you are going through. You can be reassured that you are not alone.

SECTION 2

Heidi's Story and the Founding of AirCraft Casualty Emotional Support Services
by Heidi Snow

CHAPTER 3

Michel and Me

Our Meeting

I met Michel in Martha's Vineyard one warm August evening in 1994. My closest girlfriend who lived in New York invited me. I had just returned home to Massachusetts from studying abroad and remember thinking, "I can't go! I have to unpack," but she convinced me to come as we had not seen one another for a while.

My friend nudged me as we simultaneously caught sight of the tall striking young man who began to enter our midst like a breath of robust fresh sea air. He stood apart from the already-scanned homogenous crowd of students.

I met Michel one beautiful magical summer evening in Martha's Vineyard.

Michel was walking down the steps from a restaurant by the beach towards a group of other college boys. He was adorned with a white T-shirt and beautifully tanned skin. His brown hair was blowing in the gentle ocean breeze. His face and arms were perfectly chiseled. In stature and appearance, he was the personification of the Greek god Apollo, whose statue I had just seen in Italy during my senior year abroad.

When he burst onto the scene and into my life, I was startled away from superficial conversation. My attention was immediately drawn to him as his gaze caught mine over the crowd, and the rest of the world around me blinked away. I found myself floating in his direction over my usual shyness. One of Michel's companions intercepted and introduced himself with a friendly "Hey!" I paused and partially recovered my senses enough to realize the impropriety of so directly approaching a stranger. We were less than a yard apart as Michel was talking to his teammates and glancing at me repeatedly and almost rhythmically. The innocence of chance then intervened to facilitate the meeting after all. Within fifteen long and seemingly interminable seconds, we were finally introduced by the same companion who had intercepted me earlier. Michel then introduced me to all his friends who surrounded him. He spoke in a charming French accent.

I found it impossible to concentrate on our conversation because of the intense magnetism between us. What we felt bore no relation to our overt exchange. We launched into small talk about where we went to school and where we were from and so on. Beyond words and body language, something picked up strength in the reciprocal communication between us. We were getting to know each other, but not from the simplistic and one-dimensional data we exchanged. We were drawn together in part from the curiosity about the enormity of what we clearly both sensed between us. Our instincts knew it at once, but we had no perspective or context in which to place it. Later he commented that it was best expressed in the lyrics from *South Pacific*:

"*Some enchanted evening, you may see a stranger across a crowded room and somehow you know, even then, that somewhere you'll see her again and again... Some enchanted evening when you find your true love, when you feel her call you across a crowded room, then fly to her side and make her your own!*"

The feeling was so intense and unprecedented for us that we were reeling from its effect and had to separate in order to recover our poise and equilibrium. I recognized some Tulane girls from my sorority I had not seen in two years. Michel's companions coaxed him to come with them, but he pulled away leaving them staring, silent and visibly perplexed. We found our gazes riveted again and again to one another's. There was a private aspect to our relationship that began at that point. We were so captivated with one another that we often lost track of the rest of the world.

We went to the beach with my friends. As the others ran into the chilly black waves of the Atlantic, he held back commenting that he did not like the dark water. We held hands in the cool summer breeze while unseen waves noisily and persistently tried to claim the sand between us.

He asked me for my number. He did not write it down but remembered it. The next day, he called me from the Vineyard. Although his phone kept disconnecting, persistence triumphed and we talked for three hours through the din of background laughter and noise. That began a permanent trend in our lives together. Each time we were apart, we were sustained across the miles by phone. We talked about all things and nothing. Later when we recalled those first phone conversations, neither of us could remember what we said. Across the wires, we were fastened on the nuances of sharing the various aspects of our lives and exploring each other's minds in the ritual of two beings exposing their vulnerabilities, establishing trust and learning about each other. We missed no opportunity to talk together. It was as if we had to atone for all the years we had spent apart.

As a new college graduate, I was working in finance but was unsure what I wanted from my future. For the first time since I was five, I was not a part of that first-day-of-school fall ritual. School and classes had been a reliable format upon which I had built friendships, arranged my schedule, and set my priorities. Now I sat in my family's colonial home, which had evolved into an empty shell of my past. I had grown up within its walls and beneath its ceilings, but my family had moved to Texas in the middle of my senior year in college when my mother took a directorship in a Texas hospital. Now the house had so many large empty rooms and spaces that even my loneliness felt dwarfed.

A New Life

Michel and I found joy in every conversation and moment together. When we met, he was a Harvard senior and I was working in finance in Boston.

The freedom from routine beyond work left me with a large void upon which I could begin to inscribe an adult life. As I was setting my course, there was Michel standing like a beacon before me. I saw him again several days after we first met. I visited him at Harvard where he was a senior and played ice hockey, and we began a daily ritual of being together. In between, we talked endlessly by phone about animals, people, anything and everything. We had long conversations that overflowed with the joy of two minds and souls finding gleeful interactions unperturbed by anything beyond. The transformation in both our lives transcended traditional relationships we had known in the past. In all the clutter of words, there was a wonderful specter emerging. Even in between phone calls and meetings, we were warmed by something.

Michel and I spent every moment we could together.

We never tired of being together. Even when we thought we were too tired to meet, nothing could put to rest that continuous yearning to simply be together. We rented movies and played pinball. When we played tennis, he would patiently show me how to play better. My little sister, barely four, would sometimes come with me, and we three would hang out together in the dorm. We ate egg and cheese sandwiches every morning, and we ate at Chef Chow's in Harvard Square each Sunday.

For both of us, there had been relationships with all

the same accouterments of long walks, romantic dinners, talks of commitment and so forth. On the surface, they were the same conversations and activities from our past, but the surface did not matter. Michel and I together had something that dwarfed all that. We grew more and more amazed with the capacity of our togetherness to make the ordinary things of daily living extraordinary. We talked about all the things we wanted to do. We could say anything to one another. We unveiled our deepest dreams, aspirations and fears in unmitigated sharing. There was no filter, so everything was said. Some of his comments troubled me and now haunt me. He used to tell me, "I don't think I'm going to live a very long life." I would protest, "Why would you say that when you are so strong and healthy?" I dismissed his remarks because I did not want to entertain them. I now hope he did not understand their premonition.

Michel and I knew we belonged together from the first moment we met. It seemed that nothing could ever separate us.

Like the adage, "Life is what you are experiencing when you are planning something else," we found that love happened while we were discussing the weather. He recounted that he came to recognize how greatly he loved me as we sat together in a theater watching *Terminal Velocity* that first winter. The new feeling had defined itself. We were like children making out the colors of the prism in our first rainbow and suddenly replacing the concept with reality. The words and the descriptions were imperfect compared to the perfect rainbow emerging. It had begun the moment we had first seen one another that night in August, but neither of us could make it out then. Now it was defined and unmistakable in its entire splendor. We were unconditionally in love and there would be no dreary unfulfilled days in our future.

Michel was a Harvard hockey player so we enjoyed skating together.

I was working for Putnam Investments and he was a Harvard senior and ice hockey star. We were apart for the whole day when I worked in Boston, but we would call one another four or five times, which was unprecedented in the time before cell phones. He would pick me up at the subway station after work every day. It seemed that he always had something for me. I especially remember the irises, which he frequently brought because he knew I liked them.

I was with him every day whenever I was not working and he was not in class or playing hockey. Sometimes I would go to class with him and he would

Chapter 3 Michel and Me

Michel and I sometimes escaped the city to ski in New Hampshire.

draw sunflowers and write "I love you" on the soles of my running shoes. We would sit in the balcony of the classes among statues and draw caricatures of professors and communicate by making faces. We would ride double on his bike. He would push his notebook up into the front of his sweatshirt to free up both hands to steer. Sometimes we got away from the city to ski with my brothers in New Hampshire.

He always commented that he loved awakening to the traditional bagpipes on graduation day at Harvard. After graduation, Michel went to Europe to begin his professional hockey career and I moved to New York where I worked and studied for my finance examinations.

Before my first trip to see him in France, we had been apart for a few weeks while he had been training for the upcoming hockey season. We were excited beyond belief to see one another. He was so handsome in his blue sweatshirt. I wore a long white and gold floral sundress with a measly jacket. I was chilly when I deplaned, but within seconds he embraced me. He was warm and strong like no other. I was at once safe, protected, and at home within his arms in this new place.

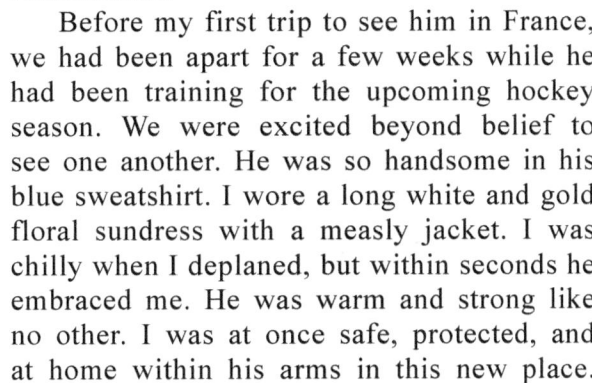

Michel and me in France. We missed no opportunity to be together and were planning a future in which we would never be apart.

He lifted me off my feet, and we hugged each other so tightly that it seemed that nothing could ever pull us apart. He set me on the ground. We stared into one another's eyes and exchanged smiles. We embraced again and then stepped back. We had not yet said a word, both fearing that this long-awaited meeting was not really finally happening. He then whispered into my ear, "I love you."

Michel and I lived our lives in terms of one another. No matter how many miles separated us, there were phone calls at least twice a day as our spirits leapt across all barriers to connect. My life away from him could be filled with parties and new acquaintances in a city brimming with opportunities, yet to complete a day and to be ready for the next was to hear from the man who loved me unconditionally. Whenever possible, Michel came to New York City to be with me. We jogged down the city streets and sat on Central Park benches. We dined at restaurants that became our favorites. We had the flu together and we shared our joys.

The summer of 1996 had begun early for us. Michel came over from

Europe in the spring and we were together for months. In early summer, Michel and I went to Maine where I had spent all of my childhood summers. We went fishing with my eleven-year-old brother in my cousin's fishing boat at Pine Point and ate at my aunt and uncle's clam shack. We hiked down into thick woods with him carrying my six-year-old sister on his shoulders as easily as if she were a feather. We spent much time at our family camp on the pristine waters of Sebago Lake where we loved watching the sunset from the screened porch.

As we were leaving Maine and passing through the tollbooth into New Hampshire, Michel abruptly blurted, "Heidi, I have a feeling I am never going back there again." I was upset and incredulous as his statement was so out of context and contrary to everything we had experienced since we met. Even though I knew it was not the case, I reflexively responded with the only rational cause for such an outcome. I asked if he was worried that we were going to break up. He replied, "No, that is definitely not it. I just feel that I am never going to see all those people again." And we left it at that. There was no rhyme or reason or any conceivable explanation for his overt thought. I wondered at it. I passed it by my mother and my girlfriend. It was left without any rationale being offered.

Our Last Trip Together

We would have a lifetime together, but for now I was studying for my Series 7 finance exam and working at a hedge fund. Michel was playing for a professional hockey team and preparing for the Olympics in Europe. He insisted that we get away from New York City and do everything we could together before he returned to Europe to train for the upcoming hockey season. The summer in New England was in full bloom, but he wanted to get away from the dark waters of the Northeast. We headed to Key West. We rented a convertible and used our video camera to tape our conversations as we stood together by all the different scenery. We wanted to etch all these moments together into our memories. We were living each day as if there would be nothing to outshine it. One night we were still in our bathing suits at 8 p.m. when everyone else was all dressed up. There were outdoor shows everywhere including fire-eaters. Michel carried me on his shoulders so I could see over the crowd. Then he effortlessly and gently carried me over the sharp shells so they

Just before Michel left for Europe, we went to the turquoise waters of Key West. We never suspected that anything would interfere with our future together.

would not hurt my feet.

The next afternoon was perfect. The ocean was calm with its waves just quietly lapping the beach. We sat under an umbrella staring beyond ourselves across the glossy ocean surface which led infinitely into the horizon. We saw specks that were probably boats. People must have been walking past us, but everything besides the water, the sand and the horizon was invisible now. We were entranced together as one from the love between and within us. It seemed there was no earthly force capable of coming between us.

Michel had to go back to Europe to train with his hockey team, and I still had to pass my exam in New York, so we had to be apart for just a little while.

Our Last Day

It was overcast the morning of the day he left. We passed a maternity store. Michel commented that he would never want me to wear black when I carried our child someday. He said I should wear bright and cheerful colors. Suddenly he stopped me and held me close. With a transient uncharacteristically disturbed expression, he said that he had often envisioned me as a beautiful bride, but that he could never see himself beside me. He said he finally had to share it because it was a dream he had over and over again. I reasoned, "Perhaps he was the observer in his dreams and, like the photographer taking the picture, simply out of range." It was still disquieting.

Michel and me in Paris. Michel carried a framed enlargement of this photo aboard the plane.

I kept a big picture of us in front of the Eiffel Tower in my room. He wanted to bring it with him. I told him that he had enough to carry, but he insisted that he needed it next to him. The six hours of video of our time together were never duplicated. He conveyed a desperate need to keep them with him, and he carried away the last recording of our voices and moments together.

We found it harder than ever to say goodbye. Although we had parted many times before, this time it was filled with heartrending overtones. As his car drew away, he blew me a kiss and tears ran down his face. I had never seen him cry before. There had been sorrow at our partings. There had been utter disappointments for yet another separation, but there had never been a tear in his eye. The men in my life did not cry. My grandfather never cried, yet I had seen a tear when his face was buried in his hands as my grandmother lay dying.

How could I reconcile this tear when I had seen no other men in my life cry except with the loss of their paramount love? I lay frozen on the bed and awaited the phone call that would come in the morning as soon as he arrived in France.

Before he boarded his plane for Paris, he called me from the airport and said he had seven minutes before he had to board. He insisted that we specifically plan our future together. He said, "Heidi, we need to plan our lives together so we never have to be away from one another again. I need to be with you always. I want to marry you." I thought it didn't need to be said. It was presumed. I said, "Of course, Michel. I want that too." He asked, "You promise that you will be my wife?" I said, "Michel, I promise." He recounted that I would meet him in Germany when I passed my examination. He would find me a wonderful job there. Eventually we would compete against each other on Wall Street. The wedding would be on an island surrounded by light blue water next summer. There would be a few very close friends and family, and he named his best man. At the final boarding announcement, he pleaded for confirmation that seemed unnecessary because we had both already acknowledged the plan. There was an urgency in his voice in those last minutes to fix the details so that it was not only a specific and clear vision, it was a certainty. The nuances and reflections of our lives together going forward were permanently etched within us both now. Just before he hung up, he poured forth that beautiful song, "I love you", as he had so many times before. Now it was almost forlorn and less confident of the morning to come. When he hung up, I was paralyzed and warmed only by the now too distant plan to hear his reassuring voice again. Our life together was flowing along beautifully. Our present and our future were together. There would be a wedding near warm turquoise water. Most importantly, we would be together again soon.

> I wrote, "The future was so bright, so unbelievably bright! We had spent nearly every moment together for the past few months. We had to say goodbye that day because he was traveling to Paris. He called from the airport and we talked right up until he boarded. We talked about our love, our future and our marriage. It was all perfect. We both carried the same image as he boarded the plane, which I see now as a cave that swallowed him up along with all that was beautiful in life."

For now, everything seemed so drab. I ran along the same streets that we had jogged on so many days in the past. Now I could see the dirt and the dreariness. I returned to my room and looked out the window for the car that had taken him. It was no use. I called my mother and told her about our parting and recounted how important it would be for her to find the time from her busy schedule for our wedding. I did not convey our plans in the appropriately exuberant context because I felt so lonely. I thought it was because he had gone away, but he had gone away before. The doleful tone was new. I took a nap to pass some of the time that I must wait. He would call as soon as he arrived at the airport in Paris.

CHAPTER 4

The Crash

When I heard about the TWA crash, I tried not to remember the vivid red TWA ticket that Michel had in his hand as he left. I wanted it to be another airline so it would not be his plane that had crashed.

My phone rang harshly in the dark. My mother said, "Michel wasn't going to Paris when he left tonight, was he?" I said, "He was. Why?" She responded, "There has been a plane crash. A plane blew up. It was TWA Flight 800." Suddenly everything stopped. My life stood still, but I responded confidently, "Maybe it wasn't TWA that he was taking." I vividly remembered the bright red TWA ticket in his hand, but it had to be a different airline. I knew that when Michel said his final "I love you", he was boarding, but maybe he had not made the flight. He stayed on the phone so long that maybe he missed it. There was not 100% certainty that he got on the plane or that it was a TWA flight that he boarded for Paris. My parents began calling TWA to learn whether Michel had actually boarded that plane, but the line was perpetually busy. I remember calling American and some other air carriers hoping that he had changed his flight.

I had to make a call that I didn't want to make. Before there was official confirmation that he was on the roster, I called Michel's family in France in the middle of the night to let them know there was a possibility that he was aboard the plane. Unwillingly in my heart, I already knew the unspeakable truth. His sister screamed and I knew I could never comprehend his family's pain since I could not perceive my own. Making that call was one of the hardest things I have ever done.

"It's Over"

I lived with a couple, Annie and Steve. I was shaking as I knocked on their door. When Annie saw me standing there, her first thought was that I had been mugged or harmed in some way. I managed to tell them what was happening and that my parents were unable to get through to the airline to confirm the details of the flight roster. Steve kindly went directly to the airport in person to view the manifest. He returned all too soon with confirmation that Michel's name was on the list of passengers that boarded. I called my mother at about 2 a.m. and said, "It's over." I called my older brother Corey. I didn't know what to do. My girlfriend came over to stay with me. I told my mother that I needed her to come right now. She took the first flight out of Houston in the morning carrying photos of Michel from last Christmas to give me.

I remember someone saying to me that first night or the next day, "You'll get over it. It will just take time." I thought, "Over what?" I could not fathom what he was saying. There was just shock from that time forth.

The fires of the wreckage of TWA Flight 800 on the black waters of the ocean resembled hell itself and abruptly gave meaning to Michel's fear of dark water.

I stared at the crash scene on TV. It was black water punctuated with fiery pools that resembled hell itself. I remembered the many conversations with Michel about his fear of dark water that I had wondered at. In our first moments together, he had explained it as he evaded the waves on Martha's Vineyard. He had even left me wading in the water alone while he walked in the sand parallel to me. Just before he left, he had insisted that we vacation in Florida, rather than on the nearby northern beaches in the peak of summer. This was why we were getting married near turquoise water. As we had flown back from Florida, we talked about the what-ifs of a plane crash. He said, "At least we would die together," and commented that he hoped it would be over land because he feared the water. And there it was! The dark water! His fears now blazed and flickered like ugly neon signs over my dilapidated life. I could see his dreaded vision of the wreckage burning in those black Atlantic waters, those waters under which he now lay somewhere torn from life. He was so strong, and yet he somehow knew the promise of the threats that beckoned to snatch him so prematurely away. How did he know? Why did he still go? Why did he construct such a clear image of the future if he was just going to take it with him into that water? Perhaps the message of the promise had been so profoundly engraved that nothing could ever taint it, let alone erase it. He had taken it beyond human tampering.

My favorite flowers were irises. The most recent ones from Michel were still in water sitting in a clear vase on my bureau. I had put them there to replace the framed picture of Michel and me that he had carried with him on the plane. I would keep them there until he returned from the water.

Hope

There were life rafts floating in the water. The press announced that they were looking for survivors. Perhaps he was at a local hospital. I thought, "Michel is so strong that he will of course survive. He cannot possibly be gone." That was unthinkable. And so I waited with hope for Michel's return. One of the priests who rushed to the hospital that night said, "I hurried to comfort the survivors. I waited, but they never came." Like him, I waited for Michel to be found and brought back to me, but the next morning they called off the rescue operation to pursue one of recovery. But there was still hope. Any minute he would walk through the door covered with seaweed. He had been knocked unconscious, but had found his way back to me.

We did not say goodbye forever. We said goodbye only for those hours before he would arrive in Paris and could call me. We trusted the future. We trusted that we would always be together. We made promises to one another that we had to fulfill. That call had to come.

> I wrote, "Dark storms had always been followed by sumptuous sunshine. Michel and I sat rocking on the screened porch so many mornings with my little brother and sister just weeks ago on Sebago Lake in Maine. I remember the earth-shattering thunder and lightning when the dark footprints of rain and ominous brown clouds would waltz across the glassy lake. The wind would descend noisily and the sharp fire-like wind-driven drops would spatter everywhere. Almost as soon as it began and as we were just putting words to the fear it invoked, the wind and rain would cease and the sun would come out seemingly brighter than ever, leaving only a small memory to punctuate an otherwise beautiful day. How I long now to again feel the cool wind, sharp rain, lightning and thunder venting into my life, so I can feel the even more beauteous sunshine in the wake of this most disastrous storm! Michel and I could sit together and forget the horrific experience. This tempest, however, has pain that feels eternal and intense beyond any comparison, but I still hope it will suddenly dissipate to be forgotten in the splendor of even greater togetherness. The relief never comes. There is no respite from the growing anguish."

Dreams

Every time I would drift into sleep, Michel was alive. He came to the door breathless and wet from the sea. He was fine. Before I could study his face, he was holding me. Then I would awaken and pain would pierce into my very being causing such agony that I would fade back away from it into shock even as I walked and talked.

Over and over again I dreamed that just as he was about to board, I rescued him by imploring him to stay off the plane and come right back to me because we had both felt an unusually intense uneasiness over this parting. There had been a dark aura lurking over that entire day. We both sensed a sinister presence which we would not take time to acknowledge in our desperation to make the most of those last hours and minutes together. We should have known it was a premonition and heeded its warning, but we attributed our foreboding to the pain of separation.

> I wrote, "For now when I dream, he is always alive, but when I wake up I see flowers of sympathy reminding me that the nightmare will not disperse with daylight. I know he will reemerge. He is so strong that he cannot die. I saw life rafts on the dark fiery sea. He probably is disoriented and clinging to a rock some place. He will show up at the door anytime with sandy disheveled hair and tattered clothes. They say he is not ever coming back. I cannot imagine forever."

I had to go back to reverse our separation. I dreamed we were in the plane together, but I had not seen the plane meet the sea and take him away. I miraculously landed in a tangled bush of thorns. Between lapses into unconsciousness, I could feel scorching fragments of broken glass and water in my eyes that mercifully spared me the sight of the wreckage and the bodies. Suddenly we were together and all the physical limitations were obliterated. Our love could no longer be ravaged by time. In being together under the sea, we could be forever entwined and young.

> I wrote, "Our life together was perfect and our future was going to be perfect. Like the maiden in 'Ode to a Grecian Urn', it will now be forever untainted by the reality of living. 'Forever wilt thou love, and she be fair! Ah, happy, happy boughs that cannot shed your leaves, nor ever bid the spring adieu.'"

Consciousness was a nightmare from which I could not awaken. In all the dreams I had after the crash, he never came to me with acknowledgment that he was gone. He should have said, "Heidi, I am leaving you and I am sorry to leave you. I want (or I don't want) you to go on." I know why he didn't say that. He had done it before he died in accepting that he could never place himself next to me on our wedding day. Despite that knowledge, we set our wedding plans and our future together precisely in those last minutes before he boarded. He was the one who took them with him on the plane to be dropped, like the videos of us together, into the ocean.

Why?

Michel and me with my sister on his shoulders in front of the Christmas tree in Maine on his last Christmas.

The what-ifs reprimanded me. There were so many circumstances that had to align to place him on that exact flight. If we had never met, he would not have left from New York City. He did not feel well when he left, so why didn't he postpone his trip? When he called before he boarded, why didn't I insist he come back? It would have been so easy to delay the trip or to miss the flight or something or anything that would bring him back. Why did he have to go away and never come back? How could I live our dreams by myself? So much more than Michel died in that dark water. The life

Chapter 4 The Crash

together punctuated by the beauty of the wedding and all the children and so many other celebrations were all gone.

> I wrote, "Every Christmas our widely dispersed family condenses in Maine at my grandfather's house to share memories and to catch up on the new growth of spouses and children. Bringing Michel to my Christmas there last year was an acknowledgment of my ultimate trust in his acceptance of me. I had never brought anyone with me before. After he flew in from Paris, he attended our Christmas Eve service and quietly sat on the piano bench the next morning as he watched me and my family unwrap gifts. He played with my little sister who was so drawn to this spirited athletic man who could so easily pick her up in his strong arms. I had to get him back to Boston in the early afternoon, but we spent hours at the terminal together that Christmas day and his last. It was supposed to be the beginning rather than the end of our sharing the festivities of life together."

I wondered how different it might have been had I only known. Then I remembered that even those who know they are dying or watching a loved one die feel somehow cheated even when others assert it is for the best, an end to the suffering, or the right time.

The First Days after the Crash

The large five-story house in Manhattan became a morgue from the moment of that phone call heralding the tragedy. The air was so cloying that the end of each breath was filled with a heaviness that seemed to add weight to my sorrow. The dark wood of the study and living room cast a dreary pall upon the entire house and us.

I didn't really sleep. I couldn't eat. I don't remember anything except the pain that stabbed me whenever I opened my eyes or tried to fathom the reality of his going away forever. Every time a nerve began to awaken, it seared, sent fire into my heart and burned any sensation back into oblivion. Any appreciated stimulus triggered more hopelessness that the relentless growth of the pain would not abate. If only the weight would just kill me so the pain would be gone. Michel and I would be together looking down and feeling sad for the people in grief.

> I wrote, "There is a redeeming God because at least when the unspeakably cruelest loss occurs and love is torn away from your adherent soul, you are in shock. Just hours before, we had held one another and exchanged tearful goodbyes with an anticipated separation of days. Abruptly the separation is forever. I cannot grasp the concept of forever. Any prolonged separation is still too painful to even consider. It would have been so much easier if I had been beside him in the plane. I am paralyzed and powerless now to follow him into the water. Instead, I stand in the dark with no orientation and react only from habit."

I wore his robe. I hugged the stuffed tiger he had brought me. The irises he had given me sat in their vase of water. They were so brittle that they could easily break and lose their similarity to the living plants they were when Michel handed them to me with a kiss just two short days before. Their dead vessels no longer welcomed the water of life into their dry leaves. The water, which once extended their life, was becoming a murky substance that ate away at their stems. I would protect them until Michel came back.

> I wrote, "Where is Michel? Is he on the ocean floor waiting to be taken out of the water? It would feel so much better if I could just understand where he is right now or just know for sure what has happened to him. Why doesn't he tell me? Michel would often make insightful comments that I would ask him to write down. Now I am listening, but I cannot hear him. We love each other too much to not hear one another, especially at a time like this."

I knew him so well that I know exactly how he would have reacted if he had not been on the flight. Just a few months earlier, we sat stunned and mute watching the horror of the ValuJet air disaster unfold in the Florida Everglades. He would have held me and been awestruck by the enormity of the TWA disaster as we watched the ocean lit only by those fires reflecting in the still night water. We would have sighed at being unable to help or to fully appreciate it.

Because our motives were geared to enriching one another's lives indefinitely, he would not do anything to separate us, including dying. It was still inexplicable that he did not call me the next day. We cared for each other too much for him to just steal away from me and evaporate. Michel is the only person who could pick me up from the devastation, cool my eyes, lighten the breath-stealing burden, and help me move beyond it all back into the sunlight. He would have protected me from the pain as Sir Lancelot shielding me from a fiercely plunging sword. He alone would be my comforter, my umbrella from the glare of suffering and my lift over the sharp rocks. He is the one person who would never abandon me like this.

It was painful talking about Michel but I needed everyone to know about him. Photograph by Harry Benson.

Annie asked me if I wanted to talk about Michel. I said, "Of course." Yes, I would tell the whole world about this wonderful, compassionate, brilliant, athletic and understated hero who loved me unconditionally. Before he died, we did not depend on anyone else. The distractions of life beyond us were simply gifts to bring to one another for discussion and enrichment. He said that I was his mirror and he mine. Without him, the image he reflected of me was gone, so I had to bring him back by any means. There had been such an innocence in our trust in the future we had planned so vividly with such conviction. There was a naiveté, at least on my part, about its vulnerability to tragedy.

I talked to the reporters that came over to the house. I wore the same dress I was wearing when I met Michel. I wore the shoes he had given me and the

Chapter 4 The Crash

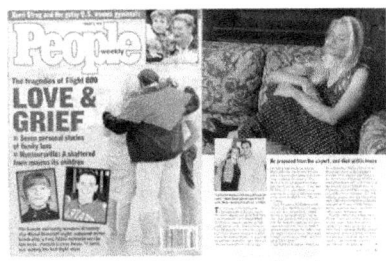

Coverage of the TWA crash in People Magazine. *I wanted the whole world to know about Michel so he would live on.*

flowing hairstyle he loved. No one else knew that. It remained between us. For now, I had to be the figment of a living person speaking for us both. They were asking me questions I could not answer. On *Larry King Live*, he asked, "How are you dealing with it, Heidi?" The right answer was, "I am not yet dealing with it and will not deal with it for a very long time." I said something when they asked me questions. I do not remember what I said because it wasn't really me speaking. It was that formal creature who comes out to greet people at the door when another lies inside in such anguish that he cannot receive callers. There were no words for the cries from the intermittently comatose dying waif within. The conversation, however robotic and uncensored, helped drown out those occasional moans that would rise up from those depths. I appeared calm and followed all the social proprieties of polite rhetoric.

Gathering at the Grief Center

I was instructed to go to the JFK Ramada Inn to receive information about the crash. I arrived at the front entrance alone early in the morning, but I was not allowed inside because I was not officially next of kin. I pleaded with all the TWA representatives, but was again turned away. I still did not understand why I was not allowed inside. I explained that I was the only person who could identify his personal belongings and describe what he was wearing so they could find him. I explained that I was desperate for any information and that his family was still in France.

Finally, after I had been at the front door for close to an hour in tears, a sympathetic police officer understood my situation and appeared with a blue pin, which provided me admission. I am so grateful to him to this day for understanding the importance of my being with the others to receive information regardless of my official family status. That hour of being held outside and having to justify my grief was very frustrating. I was the last person to see him, hold him, talk to him, and plan our future together, yet I had no official right to any information or to mourn with the others.

We went to the beach near the last piece of land over which the plane had soared unworried with 230 passengers and crew. I mechanically recounted the memory of Michel and me meeting on the beach in front of this ocean. I wore the dress I had worn that night. I floundered in the sand and squinted into the sun and at the horizon which remained empty. The wind blew harshly

Surviving Sudden Loss: Stories from those who have lived it

forcing sand into the torment.

My brother Corey, my mother and I went to meet his family at JFK. As we waited in a public area, reporters clung to us. We showed them pictures and told them what needed to be said so everyone could know about Michel. Maybe through the sheer number of outcries about him, there would be such a huge uproar of appeals to heaven that, as in *It's a Wonderful Life*, he would be saved and come back to me. Surely his bright future and the devastation left in the wake of his loss were more than great enough to justify his return. I was appealing to every force I could solicit. When I spoke of him, I was really saying, "Please, just please, don't let it be so! Michel, come back to me because only you can rescue me from this anguish." But nothing happened. Nothing changed. I was like the mother pleading on TV for her murdered son to return, hoping against all odds that he was watching and just forgot to come home even after his bloody shoe and bicycle were found in an abandoned junkyard. At least the appeals were out there and they could be answered someday like the note in the bottle cast onto the ocean or the lost letter found and delivered years later.

Just a few days after the crash, I went to the beach closest to where the plane crashed off the coast. I hoped to find Michel, but all I found was an angry ocean and sharp wind-driven sand.

Michel was young, strong and full of life.

Michel took this photo of me and it was his favorite. He set it on the top of our stack of photos just before he left for the airport.

I wrote, "The person who will always see me through times like this and will guide me through this inconceivable tragedy is not here. It cannot be. I need him. He has always been here since we first met. I talk about him and show pictures of him. I go on *Larry King Live* and tell the whole world about Michel. I tell the papers. I tell anyone willing to listen about this wonderful man and about us. He cannot die. Look at this picture and look at his face. Look at him! He is strong and young and his eyes are full of life and love. Look at this picture of me! It is the one he placed on top of our stack of photos. When he snapped the photo, he captured the love in my eyes. It is his favorite and it is still there and the love is still there. Just hours ago, he was warm and we embraced and we promised each other a life together. But he did not call the next morning. There is an ever-looming shadow as I wait and wait and wait. He still does not come back to help me through this and to end this hell on earth. I cry out, 'Michel, I love you so much!' There is no response."

It was raining as someone escorted us from the crowded airport to a bus that took us back to the hotel lobby. I had a book of pictures to give

Chapter 4 The Crash

to Michel's family and they gave me a picture of Michel playing hockey. Mayor Giuliani was with us and had seen the photos. He commented on Michel's striking resemblance to his father. I provided Michel's family with the wonderful things he had said about them and the details of his final months, weeks, days, hours and even minutes. The reunion was still missing the only bond between our families. Michel was missing and our families were separating.

At the Ramada, we had dinner at a long table. We talked, but we were just a stunned group of people robotically taking the food and placing it to our lips while venturing words that we would forget. The food had no taste, and all our conversation flowed beyond our ability to process it. I had no feeling because the gash in my spirit was still so fresh that it had not begun to bleed. For now, it held the anticipated anguish that would sear beyond belief when the shock let down its imperfect yet protective guard.

Later that night, I remember watching the news with my mother. Everything was about the crash. We collected the newspapers. There was nothing else to do. There was no sleeping, but there was a surreal state while I lay there in that little bed with oversized white comforter amidst the scattered newspapers. I didn't sleep, but I dreamed. We were together outside and above the tragedy looking down with awe. Somehow he was there just enough to satiate the immediate need, but not as before when he had so brilliantly lit the deepest corners of my life. Now it was different because we were not growing and planning the dream we had so vividly envisioned.

He died with our clear vision of our unscathed future that for him can never be tainted with daily problems, illness, aging and suffering. Michel would be forever my fiancé as he was when he boarded the plane. I would forever be his chosen bride as he had fixed the vision before he died. The wedding on that island in a coral sea would never be denigrated by the glare of reality. He would always be the handsome, strong, caring, loving, brilliant man who would walk me through life on a plane above the sordid world. Now I would have to watch its fruition die and the dream fade as I took the dreary steps to bury it. Emptiness and sheer loneliness were left in its place. There was nothing. I had never seen such darkness that stretched on indefinitely without any hope.

For hours, my brother or my mother would hold me. They wrapped their arms around me as I crouched in the corner slouched under total despair. The trickle of tears was never followed by relief. Instead, it was followed by ever more pain. Gradually numbness would set in again and I could stand and resume the semblance of the life which I no longer felt.

> I wrote, "I am simply left here with nothing. I can see and I can talk, but I am just a pair of eyes and a mouth with no life behind them. Whenever reality begins to take shape from the darkness, it is a veil so heavy that I sink onto the floor and cry."

Beyond the blankness, sheer habit guided me in the day-to-day rituals of greeting and propriety. It was reflexive and reactive and maybe not always appropriate. There was little mentation left for orchestrating conversation and action when all of my energy was consumed with the growing void. People brought sandwiches and juice, but I could not eat even though I wanted to be polite.

> I wrote, "The pain is unremitting and unbelievably intense. My friends are all around me, and my family is here too. I am curled up in the corner trying to stave off the barbs filling the emptiness. They tell me that they took turns embracing me, but I could not feel anything except a searing unimaginably intense burning. My eyes search beyond the world now for those of Michel. The world before me is empty except for the pain. When I become numb to one level of pain, it inevitably increases beyond that which I can endure. There is no hope of emergence. It is too deep now. Michel is the only one who can take away that ache, that ever-increasing bottomless ache."

We went back to the Ramada each day. We wore little colored buttons that distinguished us from the armies of reporters who waited with cameras and microphones at every entrance to the hotel behind police lines. They were so anxious to talk to anyone who would stop. Inside everyone was concerned with their own loved ones, but Michel had to be remembered for the special person he was. Though it was painful, I would always try to talk to the reporters outside because they were vehicles to tell others about him in hopes of bringing him back. His body had not yet been found, so maybe if everyone knew what he looked like, they would find him.

More bodies were brought from the ocean each day. A priest who was in the morgue to bless those from the sea choked back tears as he described how he stood in for us in that place where we could not be. He assured us that for that time, the dead became his own children, parents, and loved ones. Every so often, a hearse would appear in front of the Ramada. Simultaneously another table would empty in the grand ballroom that usually hosted weddings and parties celebrating life. The next day we would read about another funeral.

Inside the large ballroom, there were briefings by the NTSB and other agencies involved in the recovery of our loved ones.

There were briefings by those monitoring and directing the recovery, identification, autopsies and investigation. We were seated at a big round white linen-covered table with throngs of other families. I guess we talked. I do not remember. We were mere reflexes responding in place of the people we were before our losses. We may have talked about the pain, but it was beyond description because we were still numb. There may have been words and mannerisms signifying anger, joy, trust, distrust, hate and love, but we could never express what was within us because it was unavailable to our senses. We were reactive and unwittingly insincere in anything beyond our silence.

> I wrote, "I am so busy. There is something robotic about the activities in the days after a death. Someone told me, 'It is sweeping up the hearth and putting love away that will not be used again until eternity.' I was a woman with a bright future in love with a beautiful man. Now I am a woman and that is all. The other essential part of me, that love and that hope, has no place. I go through the motions. I wear the dress he loves the most so he will see that nothing has changed. My family is there at the grief center and his family arrives. They bring me the photo album I gave him on his last birthday. It was supposed to be his last birthday until the next one, but now there will not be a next one. We never knew. We are busy talking about DNA, scars and the distinguishing features of Michel. Our talks are interrupted by new discoveries about the crash and new sections of the plane recovered. There are announcements over the loud speaker, but the graphic details are only in the main room so the children do not hear. They are out in the lobby and in the children's rooms filled with toys from FAO Schwarz. Children are in playrooms where no child wishes to have justification for entering. They are there because their parents or siblings died. They have paid the dearest admission price."

My little brother Arin and me on our way to the memorial service on the beach. His youthful presence was reassuring as he just naturally accepted me as I was.

The next day my mother and I picked up my eleven-year-old brother Arin at the airport. Arin was one of those rare creatures with an undemanding presence who was always there for me. He had enjoyed following Michel and me around in Maine just weeks before the crash. He arrived with a smile and it was refreshing to be with him. With his sweet childhood innocence, he was so unencumbered by expectations that he just naturally accepted me as I now was.

The Memorial Service

All the preparation for the memorial service was mechanical with the dressing, the taxi to the grief site and boarding one of the buses in the caravan taking us to Smith Point Beach on Long Island. Arin sat next to a man who had lost his entire family. We found our way to the chairs facing the beach and the podium. There was an impressive number of uniformed servicemen representing all the agencies involved in the recovery mission, clergy of all denominations

The TWA memorial service was impressive and represented all of the agencies involved in the recovery effort as well as dignitaries and clergy from all the countries of origin and denominations of the victims.

and dignitaries from the fourteen countries of the victims.

The memorial service on the beach for all the victims was extremely difficult because Michel had not yet been found and it was hard to accept that he was never coming back.

I placed a rose and a picture of Michel and me in the boat to be taken to the crash site in the ocean.

After the memorial service, I walked into the surf on the beach closest to where the plane crashed and where Michel was last known to be.

The bagpipe music sorrowfully resounded reminding me of his graduation day. It was a cruel contrast. Now, rather than signaling the launch of a bright new future, it announced an end to his hopes and untold anguish for those left behind.

I put a rose and our picture together inside a white boat as we descended the wooden stairs to the beach. Michel's family and I embraced by the water's edge. We were all mourning, but still incredulous of our loss.

I walked over to the water and into the surf knowing the ocean would not deliver him up. The cold water was no panacea to my desolation. My brother pranced around me sensing that he needed to give me space. I embraced myself. The Mayor asked if the service had helped and I know what I should have said. He genuinely cared and I felt warmed by his ongoing support and concern, but none of the pain had dissipated despite his sensitivity and the grandeur of the service. The grieving spirit inside reached out and snatched away the proper "yes" and instead uttered a heartfelt "no". It was reacting to the simple fact that Michel was still not there and his return was the only thing that could have helped. After this blunt but honest response, I now heaped guilt onto my grief. I know he understood that I was too preoccupied with missing Michel to acknowledge how much I appreciated his reassuring presence and overt expressions of reaching out to help in every way he could.

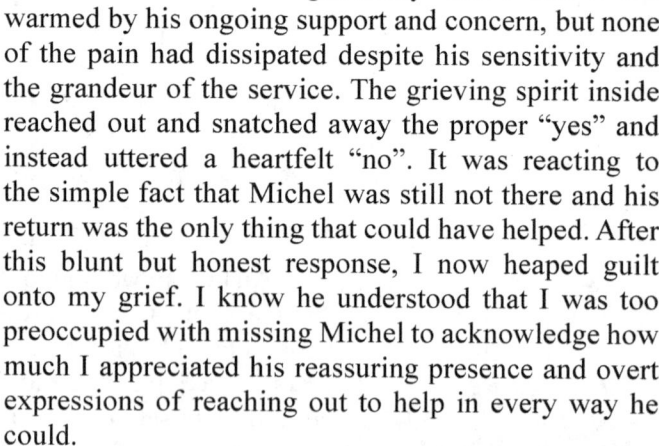

The boat was launched into the waves with my flower and our picture for Michel to see somehow. I longed to communicate with him one last time to let him know I still loved him, how much I missed him, and that he had to return because he was the only one who could get me through this. He was not only the love of my life, he was my best

Chapter 4 The Crash

The boat with my flower and our picture carried a message to Michel that I was waiting for him on the beach.

friend and confidante to whom I should have been able to turn at a time like this. About two hundred yards from shore, the wooden white rowboat met a larger boat that carried wreathes and our flowers and gifts to the crash site eight miles into the horizon. How incredibly small my one rose and picture were among the heaps of flowers. Even the larger boat seemed to shrink in the enormity of the ocean and sky beyond the beach as it disappeared from view.

Suddenly I looked around to find the beach abandoned. Everyone else had given up the vigil on the beach. I reluctantly left behind the hope to connect with him that day. On the way to the bus, I paused at the site that had been brimming with memorial activities only an hour earlier. The podium was empty and all the people and chairs had vanished. The scene was as disappointingly expectant and devoid of purpose as my life without Michel.

As I left the beach after the memorial service, I paused at the empty podium and stage which had been overflowing with people just an hour earlier. I reluctantly left behind the hope to connect with him that day.

Maybe the Most Powerful Man in the World Can Help

After Michel's family returned to Paris, I went back to the Ramada Inn one last time eight days after the crash. President Clinton met with us and my brother stood beside me as I spent many minutes talking with him about Michel. I gave him photos and was certain that he could do something to help bring Michel back if anyone could. He now knew how much Michel was missed by me and his family. I had him write a letter to Michel's family. He wrote, "I am so sorry for your loss. Our divers are out trying hard to find your son. God bless you." Years later, my girlfriend and I were in a crowded event with President Clinton. He clasped my hand warmly as he looked me in the eye and said, "Heidi, how are you doing?" The way he compassionately referenced my

My brother stood beside me as I talked with President Clinton, who listened thoughtfully as I told him about Michel.

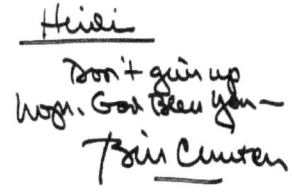

I met with President Clinton. After we talked, I asked him to write a letter to Michel's family in France and he wrote a note to me which said, "Heidi, don't give up hope. God bless you."

51

loss meant so much. He had met hundreds of grief-stricken individuals from TWA, but after all those years, he remembered my name, my face and Michel. I was glad I had been strong enough to approach him about Michel. My loss touched a person who dealt with everything going on in the world and met thousands of people every year. That validated my belief that Michel would live on in everyone who learned about him.

> I wrote, "There is a memorial service at Smith Point Beach. There are bagpipes and very important people including the Mayor, the Governor and heads of everything. There is a Coast Guard boat going to the crash site. I send out a photo of Michel and me so he will know I am on the beach waiting. I am hoping that Michel can follow the trail of roses and will come running to me because I need to talk with him. I wait and am the last to board the bus. Michel's family returns to Paris on none other than TWA Flight 800. The President meets with us and we give him a picture of Michel. Maybe the most powerful man in the world can do something to help."

It meant so much to me that my friends from high school came long distances just to be with me after Michel died.

Michel's family with me embracing on the beach after the memorial service. This photo ran on the front page of every newspaper in the country and appeared in many magazines. Although we were not identified, my friends had recognized me.

After I Leave the Grief Center

After we left the grief center, Arin, my mother and I stopped in Massachusetts to meet up with my close network of friends that I had known since elementary school. After college, they had dispersed and were now busy with their emerging lives.

They had seen me on TV and with Michel's family embracing on the beach in a photo which had, unbeknownst to me, run on the front page of every major newspaper in the country. They had recognized me even though we were not identified. They took the time to travel great distances to be with me. We remembered happy childhoods of sleep overs, birthday parties, dance recitals and proms. Between the discussions of years past, I saw them intensely looking at me and almost studying me. It was a palpable attempt to embrace what I was feeling over the conversation. Everyone there explicitly offered and wanted to do anything they could to help me deal with my loss. Just their being there was enough.

I went to Martha's Vineyard to the exact same place where Michel and I had first seen one another. I was hoping to recapture the magic of that cherished memory that only he could embody. I went to the spot at the water's edge upon which we had stood and talked so long on our first evening together. There was nothing there. All the enchantment had flown into the Atlantic Ocean aboard that doomed flight.

I visited the places in Maine we had frequented together. I gazed at the same pea-green bikini in the storefront that we had laughed at only weeks earlier at the seaside resort. The beach was full of people milling over the firm cold sand. We had not noticed them before, but now they stood out as meaningless scenery against which nothing mattered. The depths of the cold dark ocean at the end of the pier seemed more cold and bottomless than ever.

> I wrote, "The world is not the same. The park benches where we sat, sidewalks where we strolled, and stores and restaurants we frequented together are now empty and sad. The world is empty and lonely. I need Michel. I ask a girlfriend to take me to Martha's Vineyard to the restaurant and beach where I met him to look for his youthful strong figure and bright eyes. I walk on the shores in Maine. Just weeks before we were fishing there and we walked along Scarborough River. It was beautiful, but is now desolate. There is nothing there anymore because he is not there. Everything that was so full of joy is gone. In its wake is something worse than death. There is no sense being here without him. I look beyond the horizon into the shadows to find him and to bring him back, all in vain."

I went to Sebago Lake and sat in my Aunt Marion's dark lake house. She and Aunt Ruth labored over their jigsaw puzzle and traded superficial talk about the weather. They did not know what they should say, so they avoided the whole thing. There is a certain amount of respect for and acknowledgment of grief when the topic is avoided. It allows the afflicted the option of bringing it up or talking about something else to distract from the pain. Had they acknowledged it, I would have cried or I would have said, "I'm fine," with the same disingenuousness of a dying person saying he is fine.

> I wrote, "I am still desperately trying to reclaim the relationship that has been cruelly severed. The utter silence from him now leaves me feeling so isolated. Until we are together again, all I can do is summon every memory I have of our lives together onto these pages. It is all I have because he did not call me the next morning after he left as he had promised, and he did not call the next day or the next, and now it has been weeks. Telephone communication had sustained us across the miles when we were separated until we would meet again. We never made plans for the contingency when even phone contact would be interrupted. Now I am forced to settle for something far inferior to bridge this new great abyss between us that is trying to keep us apart. The memories flow with a welcomed respite that lasts only long enough to raise me to a higher place and set me up for the next disappointment and greater fall each time I take stock of the empty world without him."

The Funeral

About five weeks after the crash, they said Michel was found sitting next to a twelve-year-old boy in the bottom of the ocean still fastened into his seat. I went to the cremation somewhere in Queens where there was a casket, but the rest of the memory was mercifully evanescent. There was a service in the Harvard Memorial Church which Michel and I had frequented. He had told me how proud he would be to bring me there for college

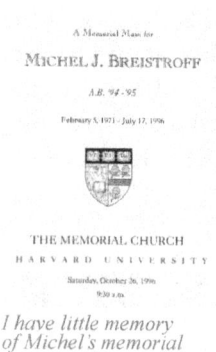

A Memorial Mass for
MICHEL J. BREISTROFF
A.B. '94-'95
February 5, 1971 - July 17, 1996

THE MEMORIAL CHURCH
HARVARD UNIVERSITY
Saturday, October 26, 1996
9:30 a.m.

I have little memory of Michel's memorial service at Harvard because at that time it was too painful to process such an overt expression of the finality of his death.

I remember the warmth of my friends coming to Michel's memorial service.

reunions and to introduce me as his wife. There was so much pain to the ceremonial finality of his death that its details were lost in the same abyss from which he would never return. I was going through the motions.

The service was a distraction. I remember the richness and warmth of having all my girlfriends of years past assembled there simply to accompany me at this most desolate moment. At the Harvard chapel, when Michel and I had been spellbound and awed by the names of all the young people who had died, he had commented that he wanted to be buried under a tree so he could make things grow. That comment seemed so remote and irrelevant at the time. There was a tree planting in the courtyard on campus near his dorm, but I heard his ashes were being sprinkled in the Charles River. When I saw the tree a little later, I felt no connection between the tree and Michel since he was not there to grow with it.

I wrote after the funeral, "I leave the grief center. Weeks later, they find him still in his seat in the water. There is no hope now. It is finally really over. He sat there for weeks and I could not help him. No one could help him. I remember seeing the video of Jackie Kennedy reflexively moving a portion of her husband's scalp back into position. It must have been some relief to know or be there to see it all unfold. I could not see anything. Did he suffer? Did he feel pain? I know only that he boarded the plane happy with a large picture of us tucked under his arm. Maybe if I had been there, I could have at least held him as he died. Perhaps I could have reached over to prop up his head, kissed him just once more, and said goodbye when I knew it was really the last goodbye. I envy those who are there for the death scene to know what happened, and they envy me that I do not have the final death images burned into my memory. I envy those who see their loved ones die because they immediately know without a doubt that they are alone. They envy me for my gradual realization that Michel is gone."

My friends returned to their lives. My mother gave up her directorship to work part-time to make herself more available to me, but school had already begun for my younger brother and sister in Texas, so my family had to leave. I was left alone to return to New York. My entire future had been bonded to Michel. Once in France, he would have called the next morning, I would have joined him days later after my finance exam, and we would have planned our days entirely based on our being together around his hockey schedule. Now my future was gone and Michel was gone, but our love was not gone.

Chapter 4 The Crash

> I wrote, "I just want to fade back into the past where Michel and I held one another. My heart hurts. Everything is painful. My family and friends want me back the way I was when I was full of hope and happiness and life. The future can be trusted now only to be devoid of Michel and full of pain. I am in a world without Michel where I do not want to be."

There are death scenes in old movies of the dying resting comfortably in a luxuriant bed with extra illumination and a beautiful countenance created with a softening lens. Loved ones gather around as profound lessons and requests are exchanged. After the last scripted sentence, the dying one stops breathing, and the group gasps an "Oh, no!" in unison and begins sobbing. After a few minutes, they get on with their lives. Michel's death had no resemblance to these morbidly idyllic scenes. First, I was not there with him. Second, when it was over, there was no life for me to resume since mine was inextricably intertwined with his.

Michel died and that is all. He was gone and I was still here as a vessel of the void left in the wake of his death. All of my grieving would have been mercifully avoided had I gone too, but who could then celebrate what would have been? Who would tell of his past few years, his last months, his last few days and minutes? Who would remember the man beyond the boy, beyond the son, beyond the brother, beyond the student, beyond the hockey star, and beyond the friend? Who would know the last words he uttered before he boarded and what he wore and why he wore what he wore. I packed his socks. I packed everything and touched everything he carried onto the plane. Who would know if I could not tell? Who would remember if I did not remember? The last months of our lives were summarized on six hours of video. He took those videos with him on the plane. I will never know what happened to them. In me lives the last bastion of those beautiful last few months. They are part of me.

The person who dies may enter some grand immortality, but for those left behind, it is nothing but loss and suffering that continues indefinitely. Michel specifically promised to be with me in every action, in every phone call, and in every conversation. He promised and I trusted. He would be with me if he possibly could because I knew his immitigable strength of character and commitment. Any potential anger at him was supplanted with the deep sorrow and tears of disappointment and frustration that we could no longer be together the way we planned.

> I wrote, "It is a blur, and yet the free-fall of my life's dreams to the lowest place possible should have been memorable. It has been weeks since I last saw him and even as I write this, I feel that part of me is still plunging fast."

We had never realized how quickly and mercilessly we could be taken away from one another. The dreams had been set to concrete plans and were as good as done. Nothing had come between us before, but now we were suddenly torn apart. It raises the question of why bother to ever again trust anyone to be there tomorrow despite vows and promises. After Michel died, most everyone did leave. The only people I let into my daily life were special in grasping the uncertainty of tomorrow and appreciating the gift of those present in our lives today.

Someone said, "Heidi, you're young and have your whole life ahead of you." I thought to myself, "What life? Michel is my love, and my future is joined with him and now he is gone." I could not go on with the life we had planned together. That life and that future were never to be lived.

> I wrote, "What I feel is not what they say I should feel. I should be over it, but I am not. Beyond the loss, the worse thing for me is the expectation that after the funeral I should resume my life as I had planned. That plan is now hollow. Its very substance and all my experiences, all my joys and all my achievements were to be with Michel. That was part of our life together and it now holds nothing for me."

For a while I could study for my finance exam. I passed the test, but it did not matter because Michel was not there to tell. He had confidence that I would do well, but without him to complete the celebration, it had no meaning. There was no sense in any of it.

> I wrote, "I want our life back. We have a right to our future. There is no one to understand that I will always miss Michel and that I do not want to go on without him. No one wants to see me cry any more. They want to see the old me, someone who is no longer here. I cannot accommodate them because Michel is no longer here. The new me, the hopeless, devastated and lonely woman with all her dreams crushed, is one that nobody, not even I, wants to know. I smile, but I am crying inside. I walk, but I am really an amorphous heap of sorrow and pain. The days stretch on without any relief. The pain is intermixed with guilt for continuing to feel so sad and hopeless. I no longer hope for the return of the joy. I just hope for an end to the pain."

CHAPTER 5

The Birth of ACCESS

Like thousands of loved ones of the 230 people who perished on TWA Flight 800, I was left in unspeakable grief and torment and my life was changed forever. As the initial shock subsided during the first weeks and months, the agony intensified. In between, there was utter desolation. My future was with Michel, and without him there was nothing. My friends expected a smooth day-to-day improvement towards recovery. Long after they thought I should be over it, the days and endless empty nights continued relentlessly. There was no one with true perspective about what was happening to me.

Finally, after looking for an air disaster support group in New York City to no avail, I called Mayor Giuliani's office. He advised that I might benefit from meeting with the friends and families of the victims from the 1988 Pan Am 103 bombing over Lockerbie, Scotland. They sent a man who had lost his brother in the crash to bring me to their meeting in Albany.

I remember thinking, "I hope they accept me even though I am not from Pan Am." When I walked in, a woman reached out to me and just held me. She started to cry and then I started to cry, but it was okay. It felt safe because I could just tell that she understood. She offered that everyone in the group felt a connection with all of us from TWA 800. I met a woman who had lost her fiancé. Without my having to explain anything, she just knew. It exemplified the importance of being around other people who "get it". For the first time in months, I did not have to apologize for my tears. It was okay for me to still grieve nearly two months later and well beyond the funeral. They were still grieving and supporting one another after eight years.

They were living examples that at least some people survive the emotional devastation of having loved ones ripped from their lives. They had survived, so I felt somehow that I could make it too even though it still hurt so much. During the years of grieving and healing, they had acquired knowledge about survival which they generously shared. It was okay for me to diffuse my pain among those whose backs had grown strong over the years from bearing a loss similar to mine. Maybe I too would grow strong enough to bear the impact of seeing my future with Michel shattered in that explosion off the shores of Long Island. For now I could share my grief with those who accepted me even if I could never again be the person I was before my loss. The Pan Am 103 survivors knew how to embrace me along with my sorrow because they had learned to embrace their own. They accepted the fragments of my former self because they were once like that. They knew there was no recovery. This validation removed my guilt over knowing that I would never be the same.

I realized that many are impacted every year by the loss of loved ones in air disasters. I knew the news coverage ending with the funeral leads the survivors into the false belief that when they continue to suffer, there is something wrong with them. After months of solitary torture, I finally found help. I wanted others to have the support that it took me too long to find and that others may never find.

I realized that the help they gave me could be extended to all the others left behind after Flight 800. They needed the opportunity to talk with people who had already experienced a similar loss. These survivors helped make the grief less frightening, isolating and hopeless. That was the moment when the idea for an organized support network for friends and families of victims of air crashes was born. I was so timid, but I somehow mustered the courage to get in front of the group to ask if they would be willing to talk with others affected by more recent air disasters. They met the concept with such enthusiasm that there were over a hundred volunteers from this one organization who signed up to support the grieving after air crashes. I still have the sheet of paper upon which everyone wrote down their information, which later became the ever-expanding volunteer base of ACCESS.

Since that day with the Pan Am 103 group in September of 1996, I have worked tirelessly to fulfill my vow that no one should ever have to go through the desolation, loneliness and sense of utter abandonment I experienced after leaving the TWA 800 emergency grief site. I recognized the need for access to long-term emotional support from those who had already survived the sudden loss of a loved one.

Pairing Grief Mentors with Callers according to their Relationship Lost

The Pan Am group's support of survivors from TWA Flight 800 inspired me to found AirCraft Casualty Emotional Support Services (ACCESS). From my experience, I knew how important it was for survivors to have the inspiration and support of those who had lost loved ones in prior air disasters. I wanted to do everything possible to facilitate their emotional support, and that included matching them with grief mentors who shared their specific type of loss. The idea of pairing grief mentors to callers with similar relationships lost was born from my direct personal experience and my observations of what others found most helpful in dealing with their grief. For example, a woman with four children who lost her husband on TWA found it especially comforting to talk to a woman with children who had lost her husband years earlier on Pan Am 103 and had already dealt with the challenges of helping her children through their grief and all the changes they suddenly faced from the loss of their father. Grief is a common tie for everyone who loses a loved one suddenly, but there are collective logistics among women left with young children to raise alone, among children who lose their parents, and among fiancés, spouses and significant others who lose the love of their lives. Through the Pan Am group, I met two women who had lost their fiancés years earlier and had already dealt with some of the issues specific to my loss. We had all experienced sudden death indiscriminately taking away our loved ones as we were just setting out to begin careers and marriages. Their stories had a special significance for me because they had lived through a loss similar to mine when I still thought it was impossible. This showed me the importance of having a model of survival from a similar type of loss. That is why ACCESS pairs mothers to mothers, spouses to spouses, children to children and others based on relationships lost. Matching the grief-stricken seeking our emotional support to the most appropriate mentor was my goal from the start and is a distinctive feature of the grief support provided through ACCESS.

Turning the Concept of ACCESS into Reality

In the fall of 1996, as I began putting ACCESS together, my heart was dedicated to my mission. At times when it seemed so overwhelming that I wanted to give up, the same intense pain that threatened to cripple me spurred me on and made me even more adamant to persevere. I kept visualizing how many people could be helped by the realization of my concept of free and unfettered access to a trusted and confidential person who truly understands their losses.

Everyone I asked about beginning a nonprofit guided me to others who might be able to help. All the implementation was up to me while I was struggling with my own grief. I missed Michel every minute and I was still in disbelief that he was permanently gone from my life. One of my friends introduced me to a lawyer who helped me tackle the initial paperwork. At that time, just months after Michel's death, I was hitting a wall in my grieving process and frustrated by the mounting logistical challenges unfolding before me. I was the epitome of the lost souls looking for the very help that I was seeking to provide others. I was in tears as I entered his office. He was very sweet and patiently listened as I tried to formulate the mission of ACCESS. He donated much time from his busy schedule to help me. Later he became an active board member and an integral part of ACCESS.

In my ongoing quest to help others, I met a person who ran a nonprofit in New York City. He reinforced my knowledge about the complexities in setting up and maintaining a nonprofit. He recommended that I find somebody involved with a nonprofit focused on death and grief, such as the founder of MADD. She and I met at her home, where we created the mission statement for ACCESS and wrote grants. She forced me to face up to a lengthy list of challenges that I had to overcome to convert my vision into reality. The grim statistics of nonprofits succeeding beyond their earliest phases were enough to make most people quit, but that was not an option. Although I said to myself, "How can I do any of these things? I don't even know where to begin," I knew I would succeed because I was so determined to help others deal with their grief.

I was invited to speak about my loss at conferences and other venues related to air disasters, grief and sudden loss. Retelling my story kept reinforcing in me the importance of having an organization in which people could freely discuss their feelings and talk about their loved ones in a safe nonjudgmental environment with someone who really understood. Sharing my story about Michel helped me make it through the day, and I grew more confident each time I spoke. As I met more and more people who wanted to help with ACCESS, and as more people came together to launch it, the need and the concept made even more sense. I saw its potential ever more vividly each time I had the opportunity to touch another person who was grieving.

I remember being invited to meet our first major ACCESS contributor at his office in New York. Kerry Felski had lost his in-laws in the United Flight 232 crash seven years earlier. He explained that he was accustomed to fixing things and felt helpless when he could not make his wife's and children's pain go away. From his personal experience, he recognized the importance of ACCESS. He provided some of the resources to launch it and to help it thrive. He met with me every few months to make sure that I was not discouraged and helped me with my own grief along the way. He always said, "We will need your organization going forward because unfortunately these accidents continue to occur. Heidi, we need to be sure that ACCESS is prepared and there at all times."

On September 1, 1998, after several years of informally carrying on our mission, we had a board meeting to launch our website. The very next day, Swissair 111 crashed off the coast of Nova Scotia en route from JFK

Chapter 5 The Birth of ACCESS

to Geneva. ACCESS launched into action. I was so glad that we had our response plan in place. We assembled our grief support materials and wrote personal condolence notes to the loved ones of each of the victims. I just knew how much I would have appreciated people reaching out to me who understood and had "been there".

At the Swissair 111 grief site where the families gathered, it was as if time had rolled back to 1996 because the parallels to TWA Flight 800 were remarkable. The faces were eerily familiar. I recognized the same expressions of periodic sorrow, pain, shock and anger from the early days at the TWA grief site. I knew how quickly and how dramatically their lives were changed. I knew their need for hope. At a Swissair memorial service, as at TWA's two years earlier, I witnessed the closeness of so many bonded by horrific losses who just days earlier had been complete strangers. ACCESS partnered with the American Red Cross and the airline so that the bereaved had our contact information for a safe and confidential place to turn when they went back home.

We immediately began receiving requests for help on our website and helpline. The incredible volunteers from Pan Am 103, TWA 800 and other previous air disasters came forward. We began pairing mothers who lost their children on Swissair to mothers who had lost children on Pan Am and TWA. We paired siblings to siblings, spouses to spouses and so on. All of our volunteer grief mentors generously shared the perspectives and insights they had acquired from their own experiences. While it was helpful to have the comfort of others suffering in the wake of the same accident, our ACCESS mentors had traveled the same road ahead of them and were models of survival after loss. This aspect of emotional support helped. We received dozens of testimonials about the significant impact of our volunteers after only a few weeks. The concept worked. We had the same response through our work with the EgyptAir 990 crash out of JFK a year later and again with Alaska Airlines 261 in 2000 and with 9/11. With these and other large air disasters, I made appearances on behalf of ACCESS on the major television networks to let people know about our services. In between these large air disasters, we had many calls from private and small commercial and military air crashes.

Kerry was the first to call me after Swissair and Alaska Airlines crashed. I was so grateful to be able to tell him that we had the resources we needed thanks to his support and his belief in us. On September 11, 2001, I was very shaken. I had a conference scheduled with the Port Authority at the World Trade Center at 11 a.m. ACCESS immediately became very busy reaching out and fielding calls. In addition, Kerry's office was in Tower Two. When I did not immediately hear from him, I thought, "There is no way that he could be among the thousands lost. He always helps others and will want to help everyone now." I was unbelievably relieved to learn that he had survived. He lost everything in his office, but told me that he would "most miss the collection of thoughtful handwritten thank you notes" that I had sent him as he helped me begin the important work of ACCESS. He said he had saved them because they were so meaningful to him.

Heidi's mentor Kerry on the 10th anniversary of TWA Flight 800. Sadly he died the following year in a car crash.

Kerry would sometimes go to conferences and TWA memorials with me. When I was speaking about ACCESS in DC, I saw Michel's parents in the audience. I remember looking at them and crying while I was still at the podium. I just knew that they were in such deep pain. Even though we shared the loss of Michel, we each had our own grief and different ways of dealing with it. They lived in a different country and spoke a different language. Kerry knew that it was important to bring us together, so he arranged to take us all out to dinner. Additionally, he invited a friend who spoke French fluently. She translated the stories Michel's mother told me and everything I said to them. This was an important step in my grieving process.

Kerry always made himself available when I was confronted with a dilemma involving ACCESS or my own loss. He was one of those rare individuals always there to help in overcoming any obstacles. He said, "We are all bound together through our losses no matter what the particular incident." I last saw him at the 10th anniversary of TWA Flight 800 in July 2006. One morning I called his office to catch up with him. When I asked for him, all was silent on the line. Then a woman explained that he and his wife had just died in a car accident after taking their daughter to college. I thought, "How could that happen? How are his children going to survive?"

Heidi Snow and Mayor Giuliani at the dedication of the TWA Memorial.

I am so grateful for all the insight and courage he gave me to succeed with ACCESS. He touched me and so many lives through ACCESS with such grace.

I continued to find more and more amazing people who wanted to support ACCESS. Mayor Giuliani and Governor Pataki joined our advisory board. They both knew people lost aboard Flight 800, so it was close to their hearts. I had first met the Mayor fewer than 24 hours after Michel was killed. He was sitting with me in the green room as we prepared to go on *Larry King Live*. He was busily preparing his upcoming schedule

Chapter 5 The Birth of ACCESS

Governor Pataki with Heidi Snow at the groundbreaking of the TWA Memorial. He supported the mission of ACCESS.

Heidi Snow presented Governor Pataki with the ACCESS Humanitarian Award.

Heidi Snow at the TWA Flight 800 Memorial on the 15th anniversary of the crash. The flags in the background reflect the fourteen countries of origin of the 230 victims. The plane went down in the sea just off the coast of the Memorial on Long Island.

Heidi Snow and Governor Pataki on the 10th anniversary of TWA Flight 800. Governor Pataki spoke at the memorial service.

with his assistant, but he took the time to talk with me and to hear about Michel. It was early on and I was still in utter shock. I do not remember the words we exchanged, only his kind, sympathetic and heart-filled tone. Later we were together at the grief site and at the memorial service. He was with all of us from the time TWA Flight 800 went down, and he knew each of us and the names of our lost loved ones. He was instrumental in my grief process and my founding of ACCESS. Not only did he guide me to the fateful Pan Am 103 meeting that led to the founding of ACCESS, but he hosted some of our early board meetings in his offices.

We presented Governor Pataki with the ACCESS Humanitarian Award. He wrote in our newsletter, "I want to thank everyone involved with ACCESS for the wonderful and important work you do…One of the most important things we can do in life is to give a piece of ourselves to lighten the burden of others." He also spoke at the memorial service on the 10th anniversary of TWA Flight 800.

At the 15th anniversary of Flight 800, I walked around the beautiful Memorial in front of the sea where Michel died. I remembered the joy that ended so abruptly that night, the grief that followed and my journey so permanently affected by his loss. There were close friends everywhere. It seemed ironic at some level that the warmth and friendships we enjoyed were bought at such a dear price as sharing tragic loss. In my own life, I met my husband through his work with ACCESS and we have two precious little girls. My loss taught me to cherish each day with them and to squander no opportunity to tell them how much I love them. That care and appreciation extends to all those who help in the mission of ACCESS and all those who suffer in the aftermath of loss.

I was so honored to read the names of the victims of TWA Flight 800 along with ACCESS grief mentor Dr. Larry Gustin. As we stood at the Memorial and remembered each of our loved ones who had died, we cried that they were no longer beside us, but we felt their presence as we joined together in the ceremony. Our sorrow resonated with one another's. We had pride for surviving and found new hope for brighter and brighter futures.

Heidi Snow and Larry Gustin reading the names of those lost on TWA Flight 800 on the 15th anniversary of the disaster. The service overlooked the sea where the plane crashed.

I recognized the need for ACCESS as a result of my own experience with sudden loss. I wanted others to be spared the isolation and loneliness I had felt. Now I am joined by so many people in that same mission. ACCESS consists of hundreds of people who contribute their funds and volunteer their time to be grief mentors, board members and to help with our mailings, charity events and other efforts, which ultimately allow us to provide emotional support to the grief-stricken. Each of them has come to participate in ACCESS through different paths.

Some of our generous volunteers supporting the mission of ACCESS to help the grief-stricken by raising funds at our annual charity golf event.

I met one close friend when she called ACCESS for help after losing her father in a plane crash. She is an attorney who donates much time and hard work towards making ACCESS available to those needing its services by being on our board, grief mentoring the bereaved, and spearheading our charity events. Another long-time friend began our largest ongoing annual charity golf event, which we always hold during the anniversary of 9/11. He has dedicated his time and resources to establishing and maintaining this tradition as well as being on our board.

Brad Burlingame, who lost his brother on 9/11 in Flight 77, with Heidi Snow and former 49er Gary Plummer at our annual ACCESS charity event.

An editor of a major daytime television series donated her talent to produce a professional video of personal stories from those who lost loved ones that reflect the important work of ACCESS. We share these stories at our sensitivity training workshops for agencies and companies that are with the bereaved following a sudden loss, such as crisis response teams, airlines, medical examiners, and the American Red Cross.

Grief mentor trainer Dr. Ken Druck and Heidi Snow at an ACCESS mentor training session.

Shortly after Flight 800 crashed and I was beginning to put ACCESS together, I met Dr. Ken Druck. He is a psychologist and a noted author and speaker on grief who had lost his 21-year-old daughter in a bus accident. He generously offered to share his own experience with grief and his extensive clinical expertise to train our volunteer grief mentors. He has been magnificent in assisting us to provide the best emotional support possible.

Given our focus on air disasters, it is ironic that I have met some key people in ACCESS on planes. I do a lot of flying for conferences and meetings related to ACCESS. When people ask me what I do, I usually offer, "I will let you know when we land." That starts a conversation. Most people comment that they are so glad to know that ACCESS is out there just in case.

I met my husband when he donated his time and expertise to create the ACCESS website, which required our spending many hours together. He respected that dating was very far from my mind, but our friendship evolved and we were married six years later.

Many who have been instrumental in our mission at ACCESS came to us after hearing or reading about our work with major air crashes. For example, some became involved after reading a large piece about ACCESS in *The New York Times* following EgyptAir 990. A woman called who had lost her father in a mid-air collision forty years earlier when she was only eight. She explained that she had felt a kinship to the mourners from TWA Flight 800. For the first time in all those years, she began to confront her grief and was so glad that ACCESS was available to her. A man who had lost his father in the same accident at the same age and a woman who had lost both parents in an air crash about the same time at the same age called after reading our article. In addition to providing them with mentors, we brought all three of them together to share their experiences. Both women became grief mentors and joined our board.

Volunteers at the annual charity golf event supporting the mission of ACCESS.

I could never do justice to all of the people who make ACCESS possible. With the help of our dedicated volunteers, I can work to be sure that ACCESS continues to operate and has the funds it needs because hundreds of people rely on our emotional care for hope of survival

Heidi Snow and San Francisco Mayor Willie Brown, who cut the ribbon at our inaugural ACCESS charity event in San Francisco.

after terrible life-changing losses. Our largest annual charity event is held in San Francisco each year over the anniversary of 9/11. The first year, Mayor Willie Brown cut the ribbon at the inaugural event. Mayor Gavin Newsom joined our honorary advisory board and later declared the day of our event "ACCESS Day" in San Francisco. Hundreds of volunteers from the community come out to support our mission as ACCESS continues to grow. I enjoy planning charity events, writing grant proposals and speeches, and working with our board, our volunteer grief mentors and all of our wonderful volunteers and supporters. I continue to oversee the months of preparation for our charity events, as well as our grief mentor trainings, newsletters and our all-important grief support network. The most immediately rewarding part for me is being the first point of contact for the callers to determine the most appropriate grief mentor.

Sharing our Experiences with First Responders

We at ACCESS share our unprecedented collection of firsthand knowledge from surviving our losses to train those who have contact with the grief-stricken in the immediate aftermath of air disasters. I regularly travel across the country and have been as far as the Middle East and New Zealand to train disaster response teams.

Each time we train airline and other crisis response teams, it reinforces in me the importance of our sensitivity training. It is very helpful that some of their training is by someone who has experienced loss in an air disaster. I have dedicated much time to interviewing the loved ones of air disaster victims in their homes and jobs around the country to present these individuals on video to help prepare crisis response teams. Some of the responders know what to say and what to do, but they are not sure how to say it and how to deal with the emotional turmoil of the bereaved. In the Middle East, I remember a first responder timidly asking, "How do we say hello to the victim's family that we are assigned to?" In our training sessions, I have found that a lot of people are anxious about dealing with those in grief. Arming them with what to do and say helps them gain the confidence they need to best respond to the bereaved.

It always amazes me, but doesn't really surprise me, that grief after sudden loss is so universally felt. Anywhere I share personal stories of loss using my own experience and those in our videos, there is not a dry eye in the room. They identify with our losses or realize how incomprehensibly sad

Chapter 5 The Birth of ACCESS

it would be to lose their own loved ones.

How ACCESS is Unique

ACCESS connects our community of volunteer grief mentors, who have themselves experienced the loss of loved ones in air disasters in years past, to individuals more recently experiencing grief from similar relationships lost. Before ACCESS, loved ones of air crash victims did not have formal ready access to mentors who had survived similar losses. There were two main sources for emotional support beyond friends and family. The first was mental health professionals, and the second were peer organizations from a specific incident. For example, we who lost loved ones on TWA Flight 800 bonded to address the issues surrounding the specific crash and to create a memorial, but we were all starting from the same point. Both professionals and peer groups can be very useful, but a unique bond and genuine trust is established between one who has taken a similar journey years earlier and one just beginning.

During the last ten years, there were over 12,500 deaths from air crashes. The emotional after-effects for those left behind are devastating and debilitating. ACCESS bridges those grief-stricken survivors in need of emotional support with mentors who have survived similar losses. When it seems like there is no hope of moving beyond the pain, seeing that someone else has survived through the years can be more reassuring than a professional adroitly mapping out stages of grief, or than meeting with others who have also just suffered a loss. It is easy to find comfort and hope in words from someone who has already lived through a tragedy similar to your own.

Many years after attending that Pan Am 103 meeting and beginning to pair the grief-stricken with those who lost loved ones years earlier, ACCESS has grown to include hundreds of volunteer grief mentors and has answered over a thousand calls for help. All of our mentors are members of an unenviable community of people who have experienced the unexpected and devastating loss of a loved one in an air disaster. Since they were able to create new lives in the wake of their grief, they have helped hundreds of people find hope that they too can survive their losses. One caller from Swissair 111 wrote, "I appreciate ACCESS more than I can say. I was crushed and nothing was helping until Heidi assured me that she had been like that too. After listening to me, my mentor said, 'I lost my daughter too.' With those simple

ACCESS volunteer grief mentors, who have all lost loved ones in air disasters, gather in New York City for training to help others who have more recently experienced losses.

67

words alone, I knew she understood everything I had been going through and everything I had been feeling. I don't know how to express how much it meant to me to finally not have to explain anything. She had experienced the same despair facing her daughter's empty room and she helped me see beyond my tears. She is doing okay and I know now, thanks to her, that I will probably be okay too."

Remembering Along the Journey through Grief

Each time I speak and recount that emotional devastation and that hopeless and lonely early part of my journey, my eyes well up as the ache reasserts itself. At the 15th anniversary of TWA Flight 800, tears flowed abundantly as I touched Michel's name on the wall at the Memorial site and stood again on that beach.

Heidi's sister placed a picture of Michel next to his name on the wall at the TWA Flight 800 Memorial on the 10th anniversary of the crash.

The same year that Michel was killed, JFK Jr.'s wedding to Carolyn Bessette lightened the shadow that hung over my life. At least someone was living a part of our unrealized future by marrying in the same island setting that Michel and I had envisioned for our own wedding. A beautiful photo of the couple graced the cover of the 1996 *Life Magazine* yearbook, while tucked inside the same magazine was a somber photo of me and two other women who lost fiancés on Flight 800. We had gathered at the beach closest to the crash site standing stunned and sad in the surf one fall day in 1996 as a photographer captured our expressions. I remember how the gloom muted the otherwise vibrant colors of the flowers we clutched as we gazed out toward the horizon above the ocean where their lives had ended. To the outside observer, the inclusion of our story of loss in the same edition as JFK Jr.'s wedding was a cruel contrast, but I felt that our dreams were somehow honored in their wedding. On July 16, 1999, I was bracing myself for that dreaded next day, the third anniversary of Flight 800. Suddenly I learned that JFK Jr. and his wife were killed in a private air crash. It immediately took me back to those first moments and days after Michel was killed. The loss

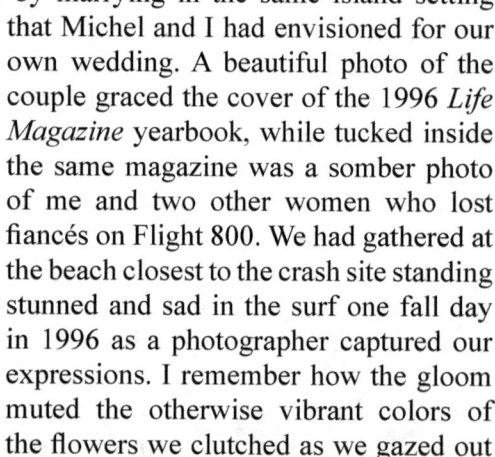

Shortly after Michel died, JFK Jr. was married in a seaside setting similar to that which Michel and I had planned for our own wedding. Within the same Life Magazine *featuring their wedding on the cover was the story and photo of the three of us who lost our fiancés on TWA Flight 800. Photographs of fiancées and Kennedy couple by Harry Benson and Susan Ragan respectively.*

Chapter 5 The Birth of ACCESS

became as painful and fresh as in the beginning. I found myself in front of a camera at Fox News being asked my perspective on the grief that lay ahead for the Kennedy family in the wake of the young couple's death. Not only could I comment on their immense pain, but I could feel it myself.

On 9/11, I felt that my entire journey through grief from Michel's death was beginning all over again. The fireballs in the World Trade Center Towers brought back the horror of the images of the burning wreckage of TWA Flight 800 on the surface of the Atlantic Ocean. I remembered the thousands left grieving in the wake of TWA. Mostly I remembered the children at the TWA grief site sequestered away in playrooms and sheltered from the graphic details about recovery of bodies. Now in 9/11 the faces of those children were multiplied for me by thousands, but they had no shelter from the avalanche of images in the news of bodies falling from the Towers. Everyone knew about the thousands of people who died on the planes and in the buildings, but I knew at once about the thousands worried at home and glued to the TV as they wondered if their parents, children, spouses and other loved ones were safe. It was difficult for me because I so keenly sensed the unprecedented scope of the loss felt by the loved ones left behind. I knew about the pain they were already experiencing and how much harder it was going to be for them when that immediate shock subsided because I had been there before, and now I felt I was back there again.

The specific loss that was most difficult for me personally was the death of Father Mychal Judge, my spiritual mentor in the wake of TWA 800. Like many who suffered in the aftermath of TWA 800 five years earlier, Father Judge was my guide and a constant reassuring presence at the TWA 800 grief site. He would often hug me. I remember him saying softly, "God is smiling having received Michel." He prayed for me, "May God fill you with courage, calm your discomfort and take away your grief." He ministered to all of us at the TWA grief site regardless of our denomination. I remember how sad I was as more bodies were being brought to the morgue each day from the TWA 800 crash. Father Judge assured me he would be there to bless Michel when they found him. He led the ecumenical TWA 800 memorial service after the crash and was present at many of the support meetings I attended in New York. He called me every year before the anniversary of TWA just to let me know he was thinking of me. He was always there at the TWA anniversary at Smith Point. Suddenly as I watched the coverage of 9/11 in disbelief, I saw them carrying the lifeless body of Father Judge, the first victim recovered from the ruins of the Towers and that special person who would have been invaluable to all of us dealing with the enormity of the tragedy of 9/11.

When 9/11 happened, ACCESS was ready. We had already responded to a number of major air disasters and hundreds of smaller plane crashes and we knew our model worked. Further, unlike many other support groups, our mission was specifically geared to those affected by 9/11 because we served those who have lost loved ones in air disaster related tragedies. With our response procedures in place, we immediately began fielding calls from and providing bereavement care to those who lost loved ones both in the buildings and aboard the planes on 9/11. Our grief mentors at that time had personally experienced the loss of loved ones in private plane crashes and aboard Pan Am 103, TWA 800, Swissair 111, Alaska Airlines 261 and EgyptAir 990. We matched our trained grief mentors with callers based on whom they had lost. We paired a mother who lost her son in Tower Two to a mother who had lost a son on Pan Am 103, and we matched spouses to spouses, siblings to siblings, children to children, parents to parents and so on.

Although there was a huge outpouring of help for the grief-stricken following 9/11, the support that ACCESS provided in 9/11 was like no other. ACCESS was the only one whose mentors had all personally previously suffered and survived similar losses. In addition, many of the resources available to those after 9/11 were temporary. Since our commitment has no time limits, we were there for them as long as they needed our help.

It was wonderful to see our work filling such an enormous need. At the same time, I was experiencing the impact of 9/11 through what it brought up for me personally from TWA and through talking to those left desperate in its wake. It was sad beyond words for me. The events of 9/11 were so horrific and reminiscent of my own loss that I almost wanted to turn off the TV and hide beneath the covers, but that could not stave off my need to help all those left in utter despair in its wake. In addition to answering the calls for help, I met with those suffering from 9/11 informally and at support groups. I appeared on major television networks to let people know about our services. Helping those affected by 9/11 was bittersweet as it always is at ACCESS. It is a positive thing to provide our services and share our experiences with those who are freshly experiencing similar losses, but it is never easy to see others going through that pain because we have all experienced it and appreciate its enormity.

Jack Grandcolas, Heidi Snow, Sean Penn and Rachel Courtney at a 9/11 meeting in San Francisco. Jack lost his wife Lauren in United Flight 93 on 9/11. Rachel is an ACCESS grief mentor who lost her father in a private plane crash.

Many of our volunteer grief mentors came to us after losing loved ones in 9/11. A mentor who lost her husband in Flight 93 on 9/11 wrote about her work with ACCESS, "It is a privilege to use what I have learned from my experience

ACCESS volunteer grief mentors at a training session in San Francisco. All of our mentors use their hard-earned experiences with grief to help those struggling with more recent losses.

to help others in their time of need and their time of crisis. I am grateful to Heidi for starting ACCESS. Before ACCESS, there were no organizations dedicated to this vital aspect of surviving a tragedy. I remember reading Heidi's story and she was just becoming engaged. My fiancé asked, 'Why are you interested in this?' I thought, 'This person was just getting engaged and that is where I am.' I could not imagine losing him before we were married and had our daughter. Then fast forward five years, and Heidi and I are sitting across from each other discussing our losses."

At our mentor training sessions, it is remarkable to see all of the faces of those bereaved from prior sudden losses together in one room. As their loved ones boarded those ill-fated planes, they never could have imagined that their parents, children, siblings or spouses would be bonded to the loved ones of fellow passengers. Our losses were the most horrible experiences we could have ever imagined, but except for them, all these warm and generous people would never have met.

The kindness of others has touched me most over the years as ACCESS has grown. It is heart-warming to see so many people generously volunteering their hard-earned knowledge and resources to help others through their losses by serving as grief mentors, board members, supporters and contributors. I have the privilege to associate with these remarkable people. Our grief mentors come forward simply because they themselves remember how hard it was for them to get through each day. They travel long distances to attend training workshops and open their hearts to those in need without any tangible reward or recognition. It is a precious honor to be joined with so many compassionate people in the mission to make grieving easier for others. Despite how intensely I wish that my own personal loss that provoked the founding of ACCESS had never occurred, I am lucky to be associated with individuals of such noble caliber.

SECTION 3

Stories of Sudden Loss

CHAPTER 6

Loss of my husband in 9/11 on United Flight 93
by Lyzbeth Glick Best

Jeremy and Lyzbeth Glick on their wedding day.

I lost my husband Jeremy Glick on 9/11 on Flight 93. We had met in ninth grade and were high school sweethearts. He was 31, and we had been married for five years. Our daughter was just eleven weeks old and he was a doting father to her. We valued our time together and our time with our family and friends. He was a national judo champion and very active in sports. He worked from home, so we were usually in constant contact with each other. When he was traveling, it was not unusual for us to speak to each other a dozen times a day by phone for just a quick "Hello, I love you". He was a sales representative for a company in California, and on 9/11 he was flying there for a business trip.

I replay that last week of my life with Jeremy like a film. The Saturday before September 11, I had to go into New York City for some training because I was going back to work. I called Jeremy periodically throughout the day and was excited to get back because it was the first time I was away from him and the baby for a full day.

Jeremy with infant daughter Emerson.

September 9 was a rainy Sunday. The baby was almost three months old and I was sleeping a little bit better. Jeremy and I enjoyed lying on the couch watching movies. We talked about what a beautiful place we were in our lives. That is a blessed memory to carry because we were so focused on what was good at that moment. On Monday Jeremy had a meeting in New York and was flying out for a business trip. Since he was going to be gone for a few days, I decided to go to my parents' house in the Catskill Mountains, which is about a two-hour drive from our home in New Jersey. When I woke up that morning, Jeremy said, "Take your time getting ready and I will get the baby up and ready to go." He dressed the baby and fed her a bottle. We took a little walk. Then I remember so clearly his carrying the baby's seat to the car and waving goodbye as we pulled away. I had two small dogs and the baby in the car driving to the Catskills. When I had to stop at a rest area and was juggling the dogs and the baby, I thought to myself, "How do single moms do it?" I had no idea that right around the corner fate was going to turn me into a single mother.

Jeremy Glick.

Jeremy called me at 5 p.m. on Monday to say that his flight was cancelled. He decided to take the first flight out from Newark in the morning. He was sad because the baby and I were now in Upstate New York and he missed us already. I said, "Take the opportunity to get a good night's sleep."

The baby was up quite a bit that night at my parents' house. When Jeremy called around 7 a.m. and my dad told him that I was still sleeping, Jeremy told him to not wake me up. He said, "No, just tell her I will call her when I get to California." I got up around 8:30 a.m. with the baby. It looked like a beautiful day, which I called a "wedding day" because it was that type of day that you would want for your wedding. The sky was really blue, and I had such excitement because I was going to have the whole day to go for a walk. I loved that time of year in September when the weather was turning to fall.

I turned on the TV and saw that the World Trade Center was on fire. As I sat down to nurse the baby, my thoughts went to all the people who could be in that building and reasoned that since it was before 9 a.m., maybe there were not yet many people at their desks. I thought about that as a blessing as I tried to minimize the situation.

Then I saw the second plane hit. It was weird that a second plane hit in the same day. I wanted to watch the news as I moved from room to room, but my parents were turning the TV's off. They were nervous, but I could not imagine why. I was not thinking Jeremy's plane was in danger because I assumed the crashed planes came from JFK and he was flying from Newark. I thought his plane was just still in the air.

At 9:32 a.m., the phone rang. It was Jeremy. My mom answered and said, "Thank God, Jeremy. We have been so worried about you." I immediately ran into the room. I knew something was wrong. Their faces told me. I grabbed the phone and he told me that his plane had been taken over by three hijackers wearing red headbands and that one of them had

Chapter 6 Loss of my husband in 9/11 on United Flight 93

something strapped to him like a bomb or claimed that it was a bomb. My initial response was to panic. I can remember holding the phone to my ear and shaking uncontrollably. Then there was just something very reassuring. It is hard to explain. We started saying "I love you" to each other. We said it for what seemed like ten minutes. The phone call was only twenty-seven minutes or so. For a few minutes we breathed together and we collected each other.

Then I thought, "Okay, what do we need to do to get him off this plane? This is not going to happen!" He said, "I do not want to die. I think I am going to die." I said, "No, just put a picture of me and the baby in your head and think good thoughts. Breathe. We are all going to be okay." He said, "If something happens, I want you to be happy in your life. I will respect what decisions you make. I love you."

After we said what we needed to say personally to each other, it was really a mission of how he was going to land that plane. We went into planning mode. He was going to do what he needed to do. He already had a lot of information from other people who were making phone calls. As we talked, I recounted to him everything I was watching on the TV. He started asking questions. He asked me if it was true that there were planes crashing into the World Trade Center and if I thought his plane was going to crash there. My initial response was just astonishment because it was so bizarre to see those two buildings on fire as my husband was telling me that he was part of this. It did not seem real. I said, "The plane's not going to go there." When he asked why, I explained, "Well, there is really nothing left." He asked me what he should do. I asked him if they had guns. He said, "No, they have knives. Okay, there are three guys as big as I am and we are going to take a vote. What do you think I should do?" I said, "You know what you need to do to attack the hijackers." He said, "Okay, I am going to leave the phone here and I am going to be right back."

At that point I gave the phone to my father and went to the bathroom and just collapsed. I got sick and then my dad took the phone outside. Days later, my dad said that he had heard a series of screams and then there was nothing. Then it sounded like a roller coaster and then he heard another series of screams. Then the line went dead.

Jeremy had told me where he was. He said they had turned around and were in Pennsylvania. I asked him if he thought they were going to land in Philadelphia, but he didn't know. I grabbed my pocketbook and asked Mom, "Do you think I should go to Philadelphia or should I go to Newark?" She said, "No, I think you need to stay here." It had been a reflexive idea and I immediately realized, "You are right. I am nursing a baby. I cannot go." The next thing I knew, an emergency response team was at the house because my mom had called 911. I was in shock or going into shock. My response to them was, "Get out of my way." They were taking my pulse and telling me I needed to sit down. They asked if I needed medication. At that point, I was completely not accepting any of it. I sat on the couch like a catatonic. I let nobody come near me. I just sat there. At some point the minister came over from the church and said there were survivors. I said, "Oh! Okay." He commented, "There were thirty-three people on the plane and if there are survivors, Jeremy will be a survivor."

It seems that whenever anyone has lost a loved one in a plane crash, there is always hope that they somehow survived. I went through every possible scenario. "Okay, he is burned. Well, what is life going to be like for him if he is burned? How will I care for him? Maybe he has lost his legs. That is not so bad. He is still there. He is in a wheelchair. We will deal with this together." In my mind, he had to survive this crash. I was waiting for the phone to ring. I knew he was going to call me. Then a couple of hours went by. I remember walking into the kitchen to get a glass of water. I collided with my father. He was crying and he hugged me. I looked at him in disbelief and said, "You think he is dead?" He knew he was dead. I just could not believe that I woke up on September 11 to a beautiful day with a beautiful new baby, and now they were telling me that my husband was dead. From then on, I do not remember the next day or two until formal events started to happen. It is probably good that I cannot remember. There was numbness. People came to the house and the FBI came to ask questions. That was okay. It felt good to talk about what happened. I had knowledge to share with them from our last phone call.

United Airlines called at some point on 9/11. I answered the phone. A man told me that Jeremy was on the flight. The whole thing was so foreign to me. I thought, "Who is this person calling me? How did he get my number?" I was not even able to process what he was saying, but I knew. I knew my husband had died because we had been on the phone with him. I think I said, "You know you are not giving me any new information." I got off the phone with him really quickly.

I can remember the first morning after 9/11. I had slept, so I had forgotten for a few hours. In just waking up, it was all back. I woke up just wailing and screaming because the pain was so fresh. My best friends came to see me. I am lucky that I have a lot of close friends. I remember one girlfriend saying, "Today is day one. This is the worst day. Tomorrow will be day two." That did not mean much at the time, but it did later. Another friend had lost both parents in childhood. She advised, "Get out of bed quickly. Do not stay in bed. The longer you stay in bed and think and remember, the harder it is going to be." I got out of bed.

Chapter 6 Loss of my husband in 9/11 on United Flight 93

My daughter was in her crib. She looked so innocent sleeping there. It was a blessing that I had a daughter because it felt like I had lost everything else. I just cried and thought, "She is going to know only a sad mom. She has lost her father who loved her, and now she is going to have a mom who is screwed up." That thought didn't last long because another then suddenly clicked into my head, "You know what? I am going to get better for her!" I stayed with my parents for a few months, which was good. They took care of me and helped me with the baby. Without them, I would not have fed myself or taken a shower. They really helped me with the day-to-day things such as remembering to pay my bills. I was incapable of doing anything that had to do with logistics. Thankfully my uncle was there to handle such details as going to my house to get Jeremy's brush for DNA and calling the dentist for his dental records. My girlfriends came to help with the baby. After about four months, it was time for me to move back home and to be independent again.

We were very fortunate that Flight 93 crashed in the very small town of Shanksville. It is a very strong community with people who really cared about each other and us. They treated us as family and welcomed us. We were invited to the crash site about a week after 9/11. I was very afraid to fly, so the airline sent limousines and town cars to take our family to Pennsylvania. It was good meeting other family members right away and sharing information. We wanted to know what others had heard in their phone calls. Since I had received a phone call from my husband, I had a lot of answers for those who had not received phone calls. Getting the family members together in a supportive environment after the crash was instrumental for gathering information.

The Red Cross was always with us when we went out to the crash site in Shanksville. I felt like I was suffocating around them and needed to get away from them whenever I could. I really did not want anybody telling me how I was going to be feeling in those early months. United Airlines sent two young women to our house to provide grief counseling. They could not possibly understand what I was feeling and they could not possibly say anything to make me feel better. They told me that I would be going through four stages of grief from a textbook. I am sure United's intentions were good and right for some people. It was not the right help for me.

It was really hard to get information about what had happened. My only helpful contact for that first year was the Shanksville coroner. He answered my most morbid questions. He was available if I needed to cry even at three in the morning. I would call him day in and day out. Still, years later, I feel that if I ever needed something, I could pick up the phone and call him. He was really instrumental in helping the Flight 93 families because he was very sensitive and protective of us. He was a small-town coroner who was given a big job and he rose to the challenge.

In the first few weeks and months, I did not want any information about Jeremy's remains. I wanted to picture Jeremy nicely asleep. At that point, I could not even imagine what had happened to him. Four months afterward, I had to get the death certificate out. The cause of death read "blunt fragmentation". I called a friend and asked, "What is blunt fragmentation? What does that mean?" I was trying to imagine how it could apply to Jeremy. But he did not know either. In February, I flew out to Pennsylvania and met with the coroner. I wanted to know everything. I asked him what they had found. He said that there were just really small pieces of remains. I worked with that, but it was a difficult process. Not having remains prolonged my grief process.

Jeremy's remains were finally identified and sent directly to the funeral home in May. At 31 years of age, I had to pick out a casket for my husband. We had a memorial service shortly after 9/11, but we had another one in May to bury his remains. Months later, I asked one of Jeremy's good friends what the remains were. He said, "There were just a few teeth." Now I really needed to disconnect my thoughts from his body and redirect them to his spiritual remains. It was important for me to think he went to heaven immediately. We have a gravesite that I visit, but I do not feel he is there.

The return of his personal things was handled in as sensitive a way as it could have been. I was notified before they arrived. After I received them, I waited for a time when I had the privacy I needed and when I felt that I was in the right place to go through them. I got back his date book. Some pieces were burnt, but I wondered how it had survived at all. All of his entries in his date book stopped after September 11. I got part of our credit card that had Jeremy's name on it. He had used it to make the phone call to me from the back of the seat, so it was something that he had touched while he was calling me at the last minute. It took my mind back to the unimaginable and made me ask, "What were his last moments like? Did he suffer? What was going through his mind?" It is part of the grieving and healing process to get something tangible back. It is part of creating an interpretation of what happened.

I started my grief process while caring for a newborn. It was really just about getting up every day, making it through the day and doing the same thing again the next day. I find an analogy that is kind of ironic that reminds me of how to grieve with a child. The oxygen masks in airplanes are first applied to the adults and then to the child. As a mother, I learned that I had to breathe first to survive so I could then care for my child. Surviving parents need to take care of themselves and get the help they need, whether it is

Chapter 6 Loss of my husband in 9/11 on United Flight 93

joining a support group or seeing a personal counselor.

I had a lot of support. If there is any blessing in 9/11, it is that I was not alone. I was not the only widow. I found strength in communicating with other people who had similar stories. The United Way put me in touch with a support group of mainly 9/11 widows. It was an incredible group of young women with small children. We could relate to each other and discuss our special problems, such as being up all night alone with a child with an earache. I remember the first time our daughter said "Mama." She did not say "Dada", so when I heard other children say "Dada", it would break my heart. Jeremy did not get to see her crawl or walk for the first time, so all those events were really bittersweet for me. It helped that I could share these experiences with our widows' group. I received advice from them and it sometimes just helped to have someone there to listen to me. There was something unique about going into a room in which I did not have to explain myself.

No one from the 9/11 support group tried to put a quick Band-Aid on me, but my girlfriends sometimes discussed, "How do we make Lyz feel better? Let's do this for Lyz to take it all away." What I really needed was to cry and scream, "I am sad. I am hurting. I am broken." I allowed myself time to grieve and to get the emotions out and to go through the motions and the whole process. I did not wake up one day and find it was all better. I still cry. I still go into my closet and scream about the injustice of it all. Only people who have been through it can understand.

The most helpful thing for me was having people just hug me and cry with me. It was not what people said that was most important to me. It was what they did. Grieving people are not likely to ask for things they need because they are just trying to make it through another day, but they are appreciative of things that are given. I did not know what to say when someone said, "What can I do for you?" It was more helpful when someone just did something. There were people who brought chicken Parmesan, walked my dogs, mowed my lawn, and just did so many things. My brother's company sent me a basket of diapers, wipes and formula. These were things that I needed for the baby when I just could not imagine getting to the store. I really was not thinking about eating. When my baby started eating baby food at six months, I was too exhausted and had no interest in eating at all, so I would just eat baby food with her. People brought dinners over and those dinners were very helpful because I was not up to getting anything myself.

Everybody deals with a loss differently. Different things help different people deal with tragedy. Ultimately, to me, it was most helpful to concentrate on making myself strong, whole and healthy in order to provide a positive environment for my daughter to grow up in. Years later, I am doing that. I am on the road, but it is definitely a journey.

I look back now and I think, "Thank God my life is not like that anymore." I cannot think of anything more horrific than those first weeks and months. For the first year I was mostly going through the motions of trying to survive. The second year I was trying to rebuild my new life. I was miserable until I finally decided, "No matter how miserable I am, he is not coming back. If I am happy, he is not coming back. Which way do I want to live my life?" It took me a long time to allow myself to be happy, and I did it mainly for our daughter. It involved giving myself the freedom to move on with my life and even to be open to love again. My relationship, marriage and love with Jeremy were unique and nothing can change that. Years later, our anniversaries and his birthday are still important. Our anniversary is August 31, his birthday is September 3 and then there is September 11. That time of year is always difficult for me. I like to keep a quiet profile during those two weeks. Over the years I have had to learn to deal with those trigger events so I do not fall off the deep end. Some days I walk that fine line between staying afloat and going back to that time of awful pain.

I am remarried and I have another daughter. I do not know where I would be without my current husband who is completely supportive and very understanding because he was Jeremy's best friend. He watched the Towers fall, so he deals with his own trauma from his own loss from 9/11. It is very comforting that he is able to listen and be a really supportive presence. If I say I am feeling very anxious and panicky, he gets it. Our relationship was a gradual progression several years after 9/11. It was a very natural relationship in that he knew my trauma and had been by my side through every step along the way. He was a big part of my healing, and the person I could call at three in the morning when I was lying on the bathroom floor thinking life could not go on without Jeremy. We have some guilt in being happy again because we both miss Jeremy so much in our lives. I have the gift that Jeremy called me from the plane and said, "I need you to be happy," so whenever I doubt myself, I remember those words.

My daughter was only eleven weeks old when Jeremy died. In some ways it is a blessing because she did not have to grieve at the same time I was dealing with my own grief. In our house, Jeremy's name is a household word. It is a natural thing. I am very fortunate that my new husband was Jeremy's best friend because he shares stories about him with my daughter. She was about two when she realized that she had lost her real father. She is lucky to have a mother who is working through her grief. She is very comfortable going to the cemetery, and I took her out to the memorial in Shanksville when she was five.

Since Jeremy died, I have become a more compassionate person. I count

Chapter 6 Loss of my husband in 9/11 on United Flight 93

my blessings more than I did. I am able to not sweat the small stuff because most everything in life that can be viewed as a potential setback seems ridiculously insignificant when the worst thing that could have possibly happened to me has already happened.

At the ACCESS grief mentor training, I listened to the stories of others and thought, "Wow, that person lost a whole family!" I realized that I could find a way to deal with the cards that I was dealt. I have learned that we grow in life to meet challenges and to deal with pain. Until I began going through this tragedy, I did not know the strength I had. I needed to focus on the moment to help overcome the grief. I am able to be more present in my life and to really live life to the fullest.

ACCESS lends such a helpful hand because there is something about having been in the same shoes as another. I can sit next to another widow who is just holding my hand and saying nothing while she simply lets me cry. That might be all I need.

ACCESS is a necessity. The airlines should all get involved with promoting it because they cannot do what ACCESS does. They are not able to offer the insight and sensitivity that a mentor from ACCESS can bring to the table. I know that because I would not be where I am today had it not been for being with others who already had been through what I was going through. At ACCESS I learned even more about myself and my own loss from hearing the stories of others. I will always be thankful for the opportunity to connect with others that have gone through a similar experience. There is just something unique and touching in talking with others who are like me, whether it is a day after the crash, six months after the crash, or ten years after the crash. I recognize a need to give back because in my tragedy so many people came out to help me. There were more people than I could ever thank. It is a privilege to use what I have learned from my experience to help others in their time of need and their time of crisis. One of the important components of ACCESS is providing emotional support to the families and loved ones because they have a long road ahead of them. I am grateful to Heidi for starting ACCESS because before ACCESS, there were no organizations dedicated to this vital aspect of surviving a tragedy.

When TWA Flight 800 crashed in 1996, I was living in the city with Jeremy. We were engaged and were going to be married in August. I remember seeing Heidi's story on TV and relating to her because she was just becoming engaged. Jeremy asked, "Why are you watching this?" I thought, "This person was just getting engaged and that is where I am." At that time, I could not imagine ever losing Jeremy. Then fast forward five years, and Heidi and I are sitting across from each other discussing our losses.

CHAPTER 7

Loss of my family in a private plane crash
by Elizabeth Spooner Norton

I lost my dad, my mom and my eighteen-year-old brother Jeffrey in a small private plane crash on March 22, 1990. Jeffrey had a scholarship offer at the South Dakota School of Mines, so a friend took him and my parents in his plane to research the school. When a spring storm iced the wings of the plane, they were in contact with the air traffic controllers for ten minutes before their plane went off the chart. The plane exploded and burned on impact.

Elizabeth with her parents and brother Jeffrey.

The Spooner family at Elizabeth's college graduation.

My dad was vivacious and full of energy and life. He had his doctorate in educational research and was a professor at the University of Colorado. He instilled educational and moral values in us. He was always there for every event we had. Just a couple of weeks before the accident, one of my friends was getting married and we talked about my dad walking me down the aisle in a few years.

My mom was so sweet! She had recently discovered a passion for helping women with unwanted pregnancies because she knew it was such a difficult thing for them. I saw her the day before she died. She told me she was the happiest she had ever been. I remember that she was wearing a pink shirt and she had those beautiful rosy cheeks and bright eyes. We hugged and said that we loved each other. She stood at the curb and waved to me as I drove off. It is a beautiful memory now. I did not know she was going on the plane.

My brother was a very athletic straight-A high school student. He was never afraid to stand up for the underdog. After he died, students wrote letters with many stories about Jeffrey. What caught my attention were all the students who had felt they somehow did not fit in, but had always been treated so kindly by Jeffrey. One day the football players were making fun of some band members at a football game, so Jeffrey took off his football equipment, put on a band jacket, and sat in the middle of the group of band members. It made the football players stop their taunting. Jeff and I were so close that whenever he needed help, he would ask me for advice.

When I saw a coroner and a policeman coming up the driveway, I already knew that their plane had crashed. I said, "The plane crashed?" They had me go into the house. I asked again, "The plane crashed?" They said, "Yes, it did." They shook their heads when I asked if anyone had survived. Because the coroner said they had burned to death, that whole night was torture because all I could think about was them burning. I could actually hear flames in my mind. Later I learned that they died instantly on impact before the fire.

When they came to inform me, I was by myself. The police officer went next door to get my neighbor. She sat with me until my boyfriend came to my side for the duration. My dad's family also came to stay with me. I was never alone.

As the only survivor of my immediate family, it was important for me to keep going on with life to represent them. It was easier said than done, but it was my goal. I got through the rest of the day, but I do not really remember it. There were a lot of people around. Within thirty minutes of my being notified, friends began calling me because they had seen it on the news. Even though the media did not yet have the names, everyone knew that my family had gone to South Dakota in a little plane. It was difficult to see photos of the wreckage on the front page the next day. It felt intrusive because their deaths were so personal to me.

For the first week, the house was filled with friends, family and church members. My family died on a Thursday and we had a memorial service the following Tuesday. It was hard for me because they were not officially dead until the remains were identified through dental records, which took about two weeks. All they could tell me was that there were three males and a female aboard the plane that crashed. They could not say that it was my family. In the back of my mind, I was thinking, "This could be somebody else's plane and the bodies not theirs. Maybe they were just lost and would be home later." I still watched the door even though they had not come home when they should have, but they never returned.

The memorial service was a big one for everybody in the community. Though the room held 1,200 people, they had to turn people away. There were so many people and I didn't know a lot of them. It was just me and my boyfriend hosting them because I had lost my whole family structure. At

Chapter 7 Loss of my family in a private plane crash

the memorial service and in newspaper articles, people said, "The Spooner family was so great. We are going to miss the Spooner family." But I was still alive. At the dinner after the memorial service, I overheard somebody saying, "It would have been better if they had all gone down together." I know they all meant that this was so painful for me that maybe it would have been better if I had died with them. That comment was very hurtful to me because I had survived for a reason.

The coroner was a wonderful man who came over about two weeks later with a box containing the only personal things found, which were my dad's wedding band and my mom's ring, watch and necklace. My mom's necklace had been cut from her coat. Neither of the rings looked like rings and the watch was melted. They were corroded, charred, and smelled of airplane fuel. Through these items, I could see the devastation that my family went through. That is when I knew they had died and were really gone. I cried and cried.

They found the plane almost immediately in a mountain range in a remote area in the Black Hills of South Dakota. There was no access to the site without hiking, so I have never been there. It took us two months to get my family back. Those were a hard two months because I did not yet have that last tangible part of them. It was important for me to get the remains. When I got their ashes, my aunt and I buried them at a memorial site. The first time I went there I remember feeling, "This is the first time our family has been together since they died." That was a healing thing for me and I can still go there if I feel the need. I cannot imagine what it must be like for those who never get remains.

When this first happened, I could not get out of bed. It seems that I was in bed for the first year. I obviously got up and went to work and all that, but I slept a lot. I was depressed a lot. I had colds all the time from the stress. I remember thinking that I felt I had been in the accident and hit my head on something because I could not remember anything. My memory has come back somewhat, but there are still memories that are permanently gone.

In the first months, the most essential thing was to take care of myself physically, mentally, and emotionally. I was only 22, so everyone wanted to make decisions for me. I wish I had followed my heart on everything because even if I were wrong, it would have been my mistake to make, not someone else's. I learned that it was important for me to believe in myself and to follow my intuition.

At the time of my family's accident, I was in graduate school studying special education and working full-time as a teacher's aide. I went back to work about a week after the accident. I really needed to give myself time to grieve. I finished out the semester, but then quit school for a while. I married my boyfriend about nine months after the accident and had a daughter about eighteen months after the accident. My daughter and my son have been healing for me. It has been wonderful to be a mom and to share experiences with them and to watch them grow. I finished my master's degree about two or three years after the accident and worked for a year. Even three years afterward, it was difficult to function in a normal way in a work environment, so I stayed home with my children.

I did not understand that the loss was always going to be a part of my life. I tried to ignore it and to keep going. The problem was that it eventually came back to haunt me and surfaced in the form of depression and isolation. When I finally realized this, I went through all my family's things so I could open up and cry. That made it better. After that, I could function again. I realized that I needed to embrace the tragedy and to recognize that it would always be a part of me.

It is very important to me that my children know their grandparents and their uncle because they were such an important part of my own life. I told my children about them from the beginning. Even when they were babies, I would say things like, "Your grandfather would have done this. Your grandma would have held you like this. This is a song my mom sang to me." That incorporated my family into their lives. Even now I can look at my son and say, "Your smile is just like Uncle Jeffrey's." I incorporate things that were a part of my childhood into their childhood. My family always listened to classical music in the evenings, so I always play classical music for my children.

I especially remember my family every year on the anniversary of the crash. A week before, I get out the box with the items from the crash, letters that people wrote to me, and my brother's teddy bear. I look them over and I hold them. I think about my family and I cry. On the day of the anniversary I may not do anything special, but I have to prepare for it because if I don't, I will be too depressed to get out of bed. Every year on Mother's Day, I plant purple flowers because my mom loved the color purple. I honored my brother by setting up a physics scholarship in his name. My dad was a veteran, so I set out a flag for him every year.

I have met many wonderful people since the accident. Right after the accident, one woman came up to me and said, "You have a lot of tenacity and strength within you. I know you are going to continue to do well." She called me every March 22 to tell me that she was thinking of me. Some people responded, "I am so sorry. I am so sorry you lost them. That must have been very difficult." Those types of comments make me feel better. They acknowledge that it happened and that it is sad. After that, we can talk about anything else. We can talk about the weather or we can talk about deeper issues. Once it is validated that it happened and that it is sad, it is okay.

It helped to hear and read good things about my family and the ways they touched others, such as stories of what my mom did for someone, and letters that the students sent to me about Jeffrey and what he meant to them. It was healing for me to know that their lives had been very productive and that others cared about them and about their deaths.

I turned to family a lot and my boyfriend was there for me, but I did most of it on my own. It was mostly just trial and error that got me through. It would have been so much easier to have someone who had been through it to talk to. At the time of the accident, there was no ACCESS, which is really unfortunate because I did not have a place like that to turn. ACCESS would have connected me with someone who understood and someone with whom I could go back and forth and say, "Did you feel this way? I am feeling this way right now. What did you do?" That would have been nice.

I did go to a grief support group for a little while, but it was mostly women who had lost their husbands. They were wonderful, but they did not understand the enormity of what I had been through. One woman who read about the crash in the newspaper or saw it on the news had a grandson who had lost his entire immediate family in a small aircraft when he was sixteen. When she got us together, it was the first time I had ever been with someone else who had lost his whole family in an airplane crash. We sat and talked for hours. He had been through a tragedy with the same emotional turmoil and was living a good life. It gave me huge hope that I would one day be able to see things clearly, and not be just a bundle of swirling emotional gray clouds of pain and hurt. I felt hopeless until I talked to him. Although I saw him only once, that was very healing for me because he had already been through it. It was the closest thing to ACCESS that I was able to experience.

One of the most difficult things for me is telling people the story of my loss. I have to explain it when people ask the usual questions, "Does your family live here? Do you have any siblings?" Sometimes when I tell the story, they cannot take in the whole thing. Often they try to trivialize, "Oh, well! I know somebody who lost somebody." Sometimes it is so overwhelming for them that I never hear from them again because they do not want to deal with my loss or do not know what to say. I cannot hide it inside because it is part of who I am. When they are ready to embrace that, they will come back. I have to avoid the urge to stuff my grief under the rug. In the short term, it is easier to just forget that this ever happened and keep going on with my life. But if I do that, I always pay for it later and it takes a while for me to realize why I am depressed or anxious. Even so many years later, I have to face how much I still miss them.

There are always ramifications of the accident that surface over and over again. I am in a position that most people my age are not. My mom was an only child, so I took on responsibilities that would normally be my mom's. I take care of her parents because there is no one else. I took care of my grandpa before he died. I take care of my grandma who has Alzheimer's.

The ACCESS volunteer grief mentor training program is among the top life-changing events for me because it allowed me to look at myself, the airplane accident, and my feelings with a whole group of other people who have been through the same thing. It was so easy to tell my own story and describe my own experience as I heard theirs. When I did that, I was finally really able to accept myself and say, "It is okay that I feel like this, and it is okay that I feel crazy sometimes, and it is okay that my life is entwined with an air tragedy. It is okay."

Until I met with all of the people at ACCESS, I was almost embarrassed about how much the crash still affected me. I do not know how to put it into words exactly, but it gave me a chance to let who I was on the inside be who I am on the outside. I realize that my experience is invaluable to other people. To speak about it is helpful to others because I represent someone who has a good joyful life despite sometimes feeling bad. People like me are able to tell a story, and our stories of survival are gifts that we have to offer others beginning the same journey. When we talk about our experiences, they might say, "Oh, yes! I am struggling with that too."

I know that life is bitter sometimes, but it is also very sweet sometimes. I bring the two together. For example, when I had my first child, it was beautiful to hold her and to know that I had survived for a reason. On the other hand, I was sad that Mom was not there. I knew how happy she would have been. It is okay to have both feelings at once. In the end, it makes me richer and more compassionate towards other people in pain going through difficult times. There is good within the bad.

The accident made me grow and change my life in several ways. My compassion and empathy increased. A person's story of loss and pain can make me cry very easily. I can help others at a deeper level because my own story of loss gives me credibility that I really do understand how much they hurt. Because of my loss, I live my life in the present to enjoy the little things. Some say, "Stop and smell the roses." This is so true. We should enjoy what God has created for us and that He has allowed us to live and to survive to see beautiful things in this world. We should stop to see the sunset or to really look at a flower. I am a special education teacher working with children between the ages of three and six. They live in the present and admire small things such as a little bug or flower. I appreciate their perspective. I have been given all these years that my brother was never given, and pretty soon I will be older than my mom and dad were when they died. I need to use these years to really appreciate and love life.

CHAPTER 8

Loss of my fiancé in a construction accident
by Julie Rudd

I lost my 28-year-old fiancé on June 11, 1992. That morning he left for a job site to represent his construction company in a housing project on 110th Street. They turned on the gas, and there was a gas leak that nobody knew about. At about 1 p.m., the building and the boiler exploded. He was standing in the part of the building that collapsed. Everybody else made it out. A man working on the elevators had just spoken with him and told the fire department and the police that there was another man that he did not see get out of the building. They went back in to look for him, but they did not find him until about 2:30 p.m. in the basement covered in rubble.

I had just come back to work from lunch. There were several urgent messages to call his company. Before I could even sit down to call, those people were already calling me again. Someone told me, "You have to go to Metropolitan Hospital. You have to leave right now. Eddie's been in an accident. You've gotta get in a cab and come up here." I kept asking, "What happened? How is he?" Nobody would tell me. All kinds of thoughts were running through my mind. I thought, "He obviously must be pretty badly hurt because no one will tell me anything. Maybe I am going to have to stop working to take care of him. There is going to be so much to figure out." When I walked into the emergency room, someone told me to come right through. A nurse led me down a hallway. I do not know why I even thought to ask, but I remember asking her, "Is he alive?" She did not say anything, but just looked at me like she was not supposed to be the one to tell me. She took me to a family room where Eddie's father and uncle were already waiting because he worked with them and they were the first to be notified. Then my mother and father came. I do not remember much about the next hour except feeling really nauseous. I remember falling to the ground. The realization was much worse than I ever could have anticipated, but at the same time, there was just utter disbelief of the facts and a complete inability to grasp the situation. That day is a blur, and I have it locked away so I cannot readily think about it.

Eddie and I had a really good friend Mark, who had known Eddie long before we were together. It was really important for me to walk outside to the pay phone to call Mark. He was the first one I told and he came up immediately. I did not want to leave the hospital because I knew Eddie was there. There was a finality I had to accept in order to leave without him. At some point in the evening, it was time for us to leave. I found that really difficult. By the time we got back to my house, there were a lot of people arriving. Mark had called his wife, so the calls had started going around and more and more people came over.

I put a lot on hold in those first few days. I was just in shock, and I could not really deal with it. I was distracted by all the people coming in to visit. The clamor of people around and the familiar faces were really necessary. I had to remember who was coming and where they were going to sleep. It was very therapeutic to have those details to focus on and to feel that I was responsible for them. I was also aware of the unwritten schedule of who was going to spend the night with me so I was not alone. The idea of being alone was unthinkable, so one of my parents, friends or my sister always spent the night with me for at least a month. I had people with me constantly.

I remembered exactly what he was wearing when he left for work. The day after Eddie died, *The New York Times* had an article about the explosion and a picture of his body on the stretcher. He was wearing the shirt that he wore to work that morning and looked like he was sleeping. It brought such incredible comfort because I never saw his body. Before that, I was thinking horrible things about what he might have looked like or what damage might have been done to him in the explosion.

In the beginning, I was very consumed with how he died, seeking justice and directing my anger at who was responsible for the gas leak and for the accident. I was also consumed with being validated as part of his family, but after Eddie died, they had no relationship with me. I found that extremely surprising and really hurtful. I also realized that, as a fiancée, I did not have any claim or any rights. That was another reason to feel terrible. After two or three months, I decided it was unproductive to be angry and that all that mattered was my relationship with Eddie and getting through this. Once I let the anger go, I was able to focus on my grief, which I needed to do. To analyze why it happened and why others treated me the way they did was only a waste of time.

There were friends and family all around me. Most helpful was their just letting me not be afraid to talk about Eddie. Some people thought that they should not bring up his name. They did not understand that I was thinking about him anyway. Most people are ill equipped to deal with a person who has just lost somebody. Some tried to help by saying, "You are young. You are going to get over this. You will meet someone else." They thought they were helping, but they were devaluing what I had with Eddie. They were not acknowledging the love I had for him. It was insulting to me and to Eddie. People did not really understand. Eddie was dead, but my love for him was not and he was still my fiancé. I was continuing my relationship with a person who happened to not be here. Eddie and I were friends with a lot of couples that we hung out with on weekends, but now I was not coupled up and they did not know how to deal with me as a single entity. They felt awkward with me and did not know what to say or how to include me in their lives.

My sister and my parents were crucial. They spent a lot of time with me and were really there for me. It redefined our relationship. A closeness grew between me and my sister that was born from her being there for me after my loss in every way. It brought our relationship to a new level which is still very much alive. Mark and his wife knew Eddie even longer than I did and were more instrumental in my grief process than any other friends. They did not shy away from the task, which is a hard one that many could not handle. They were fearless in that regard. I spent pretty much every weekend with them. They never danced around the topic and I always felt very free to cry and to talk about him. He was not a taboo subject for them. They have always made it very comfortable for me to talk about him and they talk about him too.

I was 23 and beginning my career as an assistant at a Columbia Pictures studio. I called everyone at work from the hospital to let them know that Eddie, whom they all knew, had died. The people in my office and the company sent limousines for the funeral. They made sure I had food in my house for weeks. My boss was so amazing. About three weeks after Eddie died, I thought it was time to go back to work. I realized after an hour at work that it was just completely ridiculous. I could not even type up memos because my perspective was so out of whack. My boss said, "Why are you even trying to come into work?" He allowed me to keep receiving paychecks for months, even though he had a temp doing my job.

I loved the influx of mail that came in. I got letters from people I knew and from others who we both knew. Eddie's friends wrote me letters about how sorry they were, and they told stories about him before I knew him that I had not heard before. Those memories made Eddie somehow come alive in my mind. It was like getting a part of him back. I felt comforted by being in our apartment and being amongst his things. Because I was only a fiancée with no rights to anything, I was glad we had lived together and that all of his things were in our apartment. It was important that I was the keeper of his things. When he was buried, I asked his family to let me pay the monthly bill for the upkeep of his plot. It was so important to me to be responsible for keeping up his grave.

Initially the most painful feeling was just dread. There was such a fear that I could not handle the concept of never ever seeing him again. I thought, "There is no way I am going to survive this. There is no way that I am going to make it." At 23 years of age, I had thought I knew what my whole life was going to be like. Suddenly it was gone. It was terrifying. To never see him again was like having the slate of my entire life wiped clean. That was scary. Alongside the pain and the ache were the fear and terror of having no idea what my life was going to be like. After a month or so, there were no longer sixty messages on the answering machine or a ton of cards in the mailbox. People had to get back to work and their lives. They thought that I must be doing all right at that point, but that is when his loss was actually just hitting me. It was just incredibly hard.

After a few months, I realized, "Okay, I am obviously not going to die from this." After about a year, I was not in shock anymore. I had a full grasp of the fact that he was gone. I was over those fantasies and hopes that he was just walking around somewhere with amnesia and that he was going to return and knock on the door at any minute. Once that hope went away, I had the harsh realization that I was still not ready to move on. Eddie was gone and the love of my life was gone. That was a very lonely time for me. Living a life without him was depressing and scary.

I learned that the grief process is a tough job. It is really a job and a lot of work. I had to break my daily life down into tiny increments that I could handle because it was just about getting through each day. I did whatever I needed to do to get through the day. Tomorrow was another day and I would start all over again. After a few weeks, I took pride in the simple achievement of surviving. For me it was crucial, but incredibly difficult, to just make it through one day. I was amazed that a day would turn into a week and a week into a month. I somehow found the strength within myself to survive.

I had to move about four months after Eddie died. It was hard to leave the place where Eddie and I had lived together. I kept Eddie's clothes, all of them, for a very long time. When I moved, I took them to my new apartment and unpacked them all right back into the new closet. Some of my friends and family said, "It is not really healthy." I thought, "But why? Just because I happen to be moving does not mean that I am ready. If it makes me feel good that the clothes are hanging in the closet, then the clothes are going to stay hanging in the closet." There are no specific set time frames that can apply to these things for everyone. Today I would advise, "If you get rid of the clothes prematurely and regret it, you cannot get them back. Why do something that you may regret?" Besides, who defines "too long"? I said to myself, "I will know when the time is right. It is going to be on my own time." I was working and dealing with my grief and could not be told how to do it. Whatever felt right was the right way. It is really unique and different for everybody.

I was adamant that Eddie be remembered. We went to the same high school and Eddie loved baseball, so I set up the Edward Kauf Memorial Scholarship for a baseball or softball player with a GPA of at least 3.0. I had trees planted and books donated to libraries in his name. That was productive and positive because I was doing something that involved him. It gave me a reason to get up in the morning and a way to deflect the pain.

Losing Eddie so early in my life made me cut to the chase about what is important in life and in a relationship. What is important is not your job, but that vacation with your family and other things that resonate later on in life. I had lost somebody and I knew what I missed about him. When I was sitting on the couch and heard the key in the door, I knew he was home. What a comforting feeling that gave me. I missed seeing him walk through the door after work dressed in his suit. I missed him cooking breakfast and running out for coffee. I missed the road trips that we took. I missed just ordering Chinese food and watching a movie together.

I had a fear of making plans because I was afraid I would just need to go off and cry. I went to a barbecue with our friends and suddenly the reality of Eddie being missing was so huge to me. I snuck off into their garage to cry. I thought, "What are other people going to think if I need to cry? Are people going to think I am a downer? Are they not going to want someone around who goes off and cries every couple of hours?" I needed to cry when I was grieving because crying let out the built-up emotion and cleansed me so I could deal again. That fear of people thinking I was a big downer made me uncomfortable and made me limit what I did.

For the first couple of years I spent a lot of time alone, which was not unhealthy for me. I did not want to meet new people because I was not ready to accept the idea of a whole new life without Eddie. I stayed very close to people who were already in my life such as my family and old friends. I really just dealt with my grief. I did not put it off because there was no getting away from it. At about two years, I began to feel comfortable with seeking out new friendships. It was slow. There was no replacement of the love for Eddie. It was just different.

I met my husband Paul through work about three years after Eddie died. I made a decision early on that I had to be forthcoming about my past because it will always be something I am dealing with. To this day I marvel that he was willing to get involved in my first real relationship since Eddie. He accepted that dimension of my life and says it is one of the reasons he loves me. One day I came home from work to find him sitting on the couch looking at scrapbooks with pictures of Eddie. I walked in and asked, "What are you doing?" He said, "I just wanted to get to know what Eddie was like." Eddie was still a huge part of my life and my thinking process. I thought, "This is unbelievable. This is beyond anything I could ever ask of anyone!" It was really good to know that there were people like that out there.

Grief has such a solitude to it because it is a unique path for each person. In the first few months, I had to be reborn from the old life. Because I had experienced a loss that others had not, I knew things that most 23-year-olds did not. I felt different and I was different. I was separated from everybody else, although my friends and family did nothing to make me feel isolated. It emanated from me. Compared to everybody else on the street, I felt like an alien because I was walking around feeling so different from them. Nobody could tell, but I was not the same after losing this significant other in my life. I wondered who was going to understand what I was going through. I craved to be with other people who had lost someone. The Jewish Board of Family and Children had a support group for grieving spouses. It was a group of people like me, and we were there for one another. To be in a room with other people who knew loss and knew what those long lonely nights were like was like being in a room full of wisdom. The ultimate wisdom was finally realizing that I was not alone because there were people who knew what I was feeling. I drew comfort from sitting even silently in a room with someone who had already been where I was now. Since it is such an isolating journey, it is important to be among people who have experienced it. They give you a knowing look that you are not crazy for your reactions. They validate your feelings and expressions. They may comment, "Oh, I did that. I did something like that." That is really helpful.

That is what ACCESS is for air crash survivors. It is built on the foundation that someone who has been down that road and is further along has so much light to shed. Everyone there knows how it feels and what it is going to feel like. It helps to know it is possible to get better. From the loss of my Eddie, I acquired wisdom that I did not ask for and did not want, but I can turn around and use it to help somebody who is in that incredible pain. Eddie would be proud of me for using his loss to give others even the smallest ray of hope. Without question, helping other people who are grieving has been the most rewarding thing I have ever done in my career or in other aspects of my life. It goes both ways. If I read about a young girl who lost her fiancé, I would always try to contact her because nobody did it for me. I found it helpful to help others.

Not a day goes by when I do not think about Eddie. He changed my outlook on life and shifted my perspective about what is important. I understand that every day could be our last. All those clichés about not wasting time become important. My ambition for work changed because

Chapter 8 Loss of my fiancé in a construction accident

I placed more importance on personal things. For instance, my husband travels a lot, so I adjusted my work so that we can travel together more. This never would have happened before. I see that side of my life as really important and the part I am going to remember. It is a change of perspective in how I balance my life.

A negative way it impacted me is that my fears are a little irrational. A lot of people go through life thinking that what happened to Eddie happens to other people. I too had always thought that nothing like this could happen to us. When he died, the thought that nothing bad could ever happen to me was over. I no longer have that cushion, and it makes me a little bit more fearful. For example, I worry when my loved ones fly that something might happen to them.

Today Eddie brings a smile to my face. I have decided that I was not supposed to have my whole life with him. Our time together had a beginning, a middle and an end. That makes me switch from feeling cheated out of life with him to feeling that the time with him was a gift. I was lucky to have been with him for those years. I am blessed that Eddie loved me and for our time together. The irony is that I am a better person for having experienced my loss. All those people who are newly grieving are on the same road. At the beginning, they can't see months or years ahead. I know where they are going because I am there. It makes me realize how far I have come. I do not feel the pain they are experiencing as intensely anymore, but I remember it. I know they can survive and by telling them my story, I hope they look at me and realize I am no stronger than they are. And since I survived, they can say, "If she could do it, maybe I can too."

CHAPTER 9

Loss of my daughter in 9/11 on United Flight 93
by Catherine Stefani

Cathy Stefani with her three children, Wayne, Tiffney and Nicole.

Nicole was a champion swimmer and all-around athlete.

I lost my daughter Nicole on United Flight 93. She was 21 years old and was a very loving daughter, sister and friend. When she walked into a room, her beautiful smile and laughter would brighten everyone's day. She was very kind and nonjudgmental towards everybody. Whenever she met people, they were immediately drawn to her.

She was always on the go. She was a full-time college student and earning her tuition by holding down three jobs. She would get up early for school, teach exercise classes, run five miles and work out. Then she would go to her night job at a restaurant. I told her many times that she needed to slow down. Now I am thankful that she did so many things that she wanted to do. She loved to travel and was returning home to California on 9/11 after visiting New York.

I woke up that morning with the alarm clock just before 6 a.m. Pacific Time as a newsman announced that a plane had hit the Towers in New York. I just lay there thinking, "Am I hearing this right? This cannot be possible." Since Nicole was flying home that morning, I turned on the TV just as a second plane hit the other Tower. I immediately thought, "Okay, she should be in the air already." I pictured her on the plane and I just had this bad feeling even though I knew nothing. For some reason, I didn't want to be by myself. My husband was already at work, so I woke up my fourteen-year-old son and called my older daughter Tiffney. I told her to turn on the TV. She said, "Mom, do you know what flight she is on?" I said, "Yes, I spoke to her last night." She was supposed to fly home on September 10, but her flight was canceled. I remember telling her, "Nicole, it will probably be safer for you to fly out in the morning." Her flight was changed to United 93 out of Newark. The news reported that the planes were from Chicago and Boston, so we assumed her plane was not involved. I thought, "Okay, I am going to get ready and go to work." At that very moment, we heard that another plane had crashed into the Pentagon and that there were other planes unaccounted for. They grounded all flights and were immediately landing all planes in the air. I just froze again and thought this whole thing could not be happening.

The friend that Nicole had met in New York called and told me that his plane had been forced to land in Toronto. He asked if I had heard from Nicole. I said, "No, did she leave?" He said, "Yes, she left a few minutes before me. I saw her plane take off." He thought she had probably landed safely too. When I got off the phone with him, I called Nicole's cell phone and left her a message. Tiffney and I were back and forth on the phone together when we heard of a fourth plane crashing in Pennsylvania. That was when my heart sank. My daughter said soberly, "Mom, they said it was a United plane. They haven't said the flight number yet." I said, "Well, Pennsylvania was a change-over stop for one of Nicole's friends, but Nicole was on a nonstop flight." But as soon as I got those words out, Tiffney came across the phone, "Mom, it was United Flight 93!" That was it! I remember yelling, "No! Not my baby! Not my baby girl!" My son took the phone away from me to talk to Tiffney and he started hugging me and holding me. We hung up, and from that moment on, everything was a blur. When I try to remember what happened that day, it is still just a blur. My mind and my body had a way of putting myself into a shock mode so I couldn't feel anything. I remember just saying, "Why can't I cry?" I cried, but I didn't cry the way that I wanted to cry. I wanted to picture her, but I couldn't even picture her face. I remember saying, "It can't be real. It can't be happening. How could this be happening?"

I called my husband's family, and they called United Airlines to confirm that she was aboard. I didn't need to call because I already knew the worst had happened. Initially United said they had no record that she was on the flight. I think my family tried to believe it to give me hope. Each time the door opened or the phone rang, the rest of the family thought it might be Nicole. It was helpful for them to believe she was okay, but I knew she was not going to make that phone call because she would have already done that. Then the news said there were survivors, but I saw only smoke remaining of the plane that crashed going over 500 miles an hour on impact.

I am not sure why it took United two or three hours after we heard about the crash on TV before I was notified that she was on the flight. I know that over 3,000 people died that day, but somebody should have come to my home personally to notify me or to offer their condolences. This was especially important since they had first told us she was not on the flight and were responsible for that initial false hope.

I remember switching into overdrive. I have many sisters, nieces and nephews, and I called every family member and everyone else I knew. I wonder how I ever did that. When I told them, most dropped to their knees and screamed. I was still wondering if this was real. It was like I was on the outside looking in and this was not my life. I answered the door every time somebody came, and I answered the phone every time it rang. Everyone offered to do it for me, but I wanted to be the one. I remember having so much family and so many people around me coming to my home. From early morning until after midnight, I remember just sitting on the couch. There are many things I am told that I did that I can't remember. One of the girls that Nicole worked with knew she was flying home and called to ask Nicole to cover her shift. When I told her that Nicole had died in one of the planes, she screamed and I heard the phone drop. She managed to call her work to let everyone know because Nicole was that special person who would always brighten up their day. One of her managers came over and they brought food to us every day. Everybody knew about it from me, my family and from Nicole's friends. For the next few weeks, we had a lot of people constantly coming and going from our home. It left me no time to focus on what was really happening. That was a good thing. The support of everyone there kept me going and helped me not have to just think about what had happened. My mind was preoccupied with the shock, denial and disbelief. When I saw Nicole's name and pictures on TV, I would say, "That's not my daughter. That's not her and that's not a part of me. That has to be somebody else's daughter." I was numb to feeling that she was a part of this. I couldn't feel anything. The shock of finding out that this happened and believing it were just not the same.

Sisters Tiffney and Nicole Miller.

I didn't want to go to bed, so I stayed up as long as I could. Nighttime was the worst because it was dark and quiet. I did sleep off and on, but then I had to wake up and realize it was not just a bad dream. Tiffney arrived the next day. As she pulled into the driveway, I remember thinking, "How is she going to be? This was her sister and they were under two years apart and were very close." My son was always next to me. He followed me everywhere to make sure I was okay.

The airline had a woman call to see how I was doing. She was there to listen and remained in contact with me for some time. I don't know why it was helpful to me, but it was at the time. There wasn't any other contact with United except they sent me a check to help with expenses. I didn't want it because it would be like agreeing to accept the money in exchange for my daughter. I just wanted my daughter back.

I watched TV constantly. I had it on from the moment I woke up until I went to bed at night. People would tell me I shouldn't be watching the news so much, but everything that was going on involved Nicole. I wanted everyone to know about Nicole. Yet when the media asked me to describe her, I just couldn't do it.

During that first week, it didn't seem real, yet I knew it was real. I had to face it for Tiffney and me to plan Nicole's memorial service. Nicole had so many family and friends that there were over 1,400 people at her memorial. It was very beautiful and everyone walked away feeling very peaceful. We had to go through her memorial with just a picture of her. With everyone else I had lost, such as my mother and father, we had a body.

Once the memorial service was over, I felt alone. It got very hard as it became quiet with no one around. There were times when I felt I was by myself and others were going on with their lives, even though I knew they were still hurting down deep. One sister said, "I am afraid to love my children now because I am afraid I am going to lose one of them." Whenever Nicole's friends and my sisters came around, all we did was cry. Sometimes they were trying not to cry because they didn't want to upset me, and I tried not to call or see them sometimes because I didn't want to upset them.

It helped me to be constantly on the go with things concerning her loss. That is what I needed to do. With her dying in a national tragedy, it was easy to find ways to continue to have her as part of my life. It wasn't like a car accident that people don't want to talk about any more after a week or two. People still want to talk about it, and I place a priority on doing that for Nicole.

I did not spend as much time with my other kids as I probably should have. I am still Nicole's mother and her loss is now a part of me. I had dreams of a future with all my children and now part of that is gone. Because of that, my children have not only lost a sister, they have lost a part of me too. Deep down in my heart, the only way I can deal with so much grief and pain is keeping her with me by doing everything for her and thinking about her even though she is not here. Nothing will ever keep me from missing her and nothing can ever replace her. I had to get it into my mind that I didn't have to give up my relationship with my other children to continue on with the one I lost. Sometimes as I go through so much pain and grief in all of this, I don't want to show it to my children because I don't want them to hurt anymore.

I remember my son sitting next to me on the bed while I was crying the evening after Nicole died. He said, "I don't think I ever told Nicole that I loved her and I have to tell her that." I tried to be strong for him. I told him, "She can hear you now, but I think you already did." I reminded him that there was always an "I love you" at the end of their phone calls. We talked about the day she left for her trip on September 6 when he was just starting high school. We were trying to help each other as we sat there with those memories.

The emotions really began to hit me about six weeks after she died. I would just cry. I would get this overwhelming feeling that it was going to happen and it just took over as I tried to swallow back the tears. It would happen anywhere at any time. My son would say, "Mom, you're having a bad day aren't you." I would say, "Yes, but I am going to get through it." It was very important to let my other children know I was going to have bad days, but that I was going to make it. They needed to know that because they were hurting too. Sometimes when my children were under a lot of stress, I tried to hold back and to not let them know I was upset too. I would go into the bathroom to cry by myself.

I thought I was not going to need any counseling. I was going to handle this by myself because no one could understand my pain or how I felt. After about six weeks, the emotions would just come out and I would break down and cry wherever I was. I wondered if this was going to be my life forever and if I would ever be happy again. I had never been to counseling, but I went. I remember sitting there crying as I told the first counselor my story. We weren't really connecting since she didn't have any children and she had never lost anyone. Then I found a counselor whose whole family was wiped out and who now had children. She didn't try to get answers from me and just let me talk about how I felt and what was going on. She was very helpful to me.

Immediately after Nicole died, we were invited to the crash site in Pennsylvania. I had a lifelong fear of flying and always said I would never get on an airplane because I would see planes crashing in my dreams. Besides, I didn't want to leave. It was where Nicole lived, so her room was there and her car was in the driveway. I just couldn't see myself leaving all that.

Finally in April, I managed to fly to New York to listen to the cockpit voice recorder. I struggled with it for two weeks. My aunt said, "Cathy, get yourself to the airport and then you can decide from there." I felt Nicole pushing me, "You've got to go. You've got to get over your fear of flying and get on a plane." I no longer feared dying in a crash. Nicole had gone through so much in her last forty minutes of life that I could certainly go through it and die that way too. The only fear I had was leaving my children to deal with someone else dying in an air crash. I gathered the strength to get on that airplane from Nicole. It was the best way for me to see what she went through. I cried all the way through security, getting on the plane, going through the aisles and seeing the cockpit. I tried to picture what she went through, but I couldn't do it. Something stopped me from dwelling on what had happened to her.

I retraced Nicole's steps from her last trip so I could see what she saw. She had been excited about seeing and doing all those things, so it was important to me to do them too. I flew into the same airport and went to the same restaurants. We took a train into New York and visited Times Square which she had visited. I have a picture of her standing in front of the Towers a few days before 9/11, so I went to Ground Zero. I never thought I would be able to do it, but I could hear her saying, "Mom, you need to go. This is something you need to do." I was on a high and so happy.

Nicole was known for her beautiful smile.

I thought I was not going to get anything back of Nicole's. That was something I had accepted after seeing coverage of the crash site. Then two weeks after Nicole died and the day after her memorial service, the coroner called. He said, "We have identified Nicole. She was one of the first eleven identified." Well, that was just horrible to me after having been resigned to not receiving any remains. I remember crying. They told me they had identified her by her teeth. She was known for her smile and she had beautiful teeth. She took such good care of her health and her body. Now she had died with literally no body. Her father said, "Cathy, it's not her anymore. She has a spirit and a soul and she is in heaven."

Nearly six months later, I got the call that the FBI was ready to release her remains. The coroner asked, "Do you want her sent back in a metal casket or do you want us to cremate her?" I had initially wanted her cremated, but I didn't know if that was right anymore. I asked the coroner what he thought. He told me, "We found more remains of Nicole than the others. If she were my daughter, I would bury her." At that moment, it just clicked with me and I said, "Okay, just send her back in a metal casket." It was so hard to comprehend that her remains were finally coming back the day after her 22nd birthday. We celebrated her birthday with a cake and showed videos of her and released balloons. There were a lot of people there, and it felt good to be able to do that for her. The next day I knew I had to go to the mortuary and face her remains. Nicole never made it home safely, but now she was finally coming home in a casket. It brought me back to the first few weeks after her death, which is usually the time when people deal with this.

They called when they picked up her casket to bring it to the mortuary and again when they had it set up in a room. I remember walking in and finding the people who worked there crying because they knew who Nicole was. I just broke down when I saw the casket. I had thought I would never get Nicole's remains back. Now I cried knowing that part of my child was here after all this time. A lot of my family came later. One by one as they came, I went through the whole thing of crying all over again.

They kept her remains at the mortuary for a week before we buried her. I thought, "I wish I could have her stay in that nice quiet room." The thought of burying her in the ground was really hard for me. I wanted to bury her with my mother, but if I did that, we couldn't have a tall stone. I just couldn't make that choice. I remember going to my mom's grave when it was raining and cold and finally making the decision to have her own stone and gravesite about 300 yards from my mother's. Once I made that decision, I felt horrible and came back home crying. I would sometimes wonder how many more of these emotionally pivotal decisions I could handle.

We buried her the morning of March 11 exactly six months after she died. It was a private burial with just her friends and my family. We released butterflies and they all flew right back. I had a peacefulness in knowing that what I did was right.

I flew to the crash site in Pennsylvania for the first anniversary of Nicole's death. We arrived several days before the other families, so I was able to go out to the site alone at first. The night before the anniversary, there was a private service for the families with singing and naming the photos of our loved ones on a large screen. The morning of the first anniversary was eerie. After many hot days, it was suddenly cloudy and windy. We were so cold that the military brought blankets for us during the public service. Governor Ridge and others spoke and there was a choir and an announcement of each of our loved ones with the ring of a bell. A dove was released for each of the lost passengers and crew. The doves flew back to land right behind us. A bus took us to the crash site where the President and a soldier laid a wreathe. We all met him and he shook our hands, but the attention on him took away from our personal reflections and our focus on the crash site. There were butterflies, wild turkeys and chirping crickets out there, and a lot of the greenery had grown back. Now I can picture where her plane went down. I found the overall experience very peaceful. I had not expected that. I thought I would just break down and cry and not be able to handle any of it.

I was supposed to get back some of her belongings, but all I got initially was one of her burned credit cards. It was from a store we had gone to just before she left, so it meant something. A few months later, they identified her jeans. I said. "Well, how do you know they are hers?" They said her license was in the pocket. Much later, they sent us pictures of belongings they had found for us to claim. That was very hard because the catalogue came the day we were leaving for Hawaii. My husband said, "You're not going to look at that now." Well, I was not going to wait after getting something like that. So I started looking at it and found 33 items of hers. I got Nicole's belongings back just before Christmas. Tiffney asked me to open the box when she was with me. She has been here many times, but I didn't want to upset her by having her go through the box. I cannot open it yet, but the right time will come when I want to see everything in it.

I think the word that is most difficult to hear is "closure". For me, that would be closing everything up about Nicole and forgetting about her. Some people used it after the memorial service or when I got back her remains or her belongings or when I visited the crash site. There is no such thing as closure to any of it because we are going to live with it the rest our lives.

Nicole was on my mind from the moment I woke up to when I went to bed and throughout the night. Sleep wasn't peaceful. For about a year after Nicole's death, my eating patterns were not good and I lost fifteen pounds. Everybody was telling me that I needed to eat, but it was very hard because I was always on the go. Nicole and I would go to the gym together, so it was very hard to go there because I would picture her running next to me on the treadmill. It took over a year to get back to the exercise that I had done all my life.

When I went back to work, it was so hard to see other people laughing and happy and having a good time. There are more important things than working fifty hours a week. I do not work as much. I try to focus a little more on myself because I put that aside for a long while after Nicole died.

I never was on medication, although many suggested it. Medications only delay the inevitable pain and make it more difficult to deal with. Once you are off medication and in your right mind, you still have to go through it. I had to go through the normal process of grieving. I didn't want anything to stop me from dealing with Nicole's loss. I know a lot of people turn to alcohol and drugs to cope with loss. I have not done that because I would never try to wash away my grief or her memory. Everybody eventually has to go through it.

I have not yet been able to go through her room. Some people told me I should do it, but those people obviously haven't lost a child or they would never impose that kind of advice upon me. I feel comfort in being able to go in there and see it the way she left it. At one point it helped to open up her shades and say good morning to her. In a way it's hard to have her things here, yet it's comforting and I am glad to have them. When the time comes, I will give her things to Tiffney and her cousins. I have given some of her stuffed animals to the little kids she knew and to children of people who have been really sensitive. Some of her stuffed animals have special meaning to me because I gave them to her on Easter and at other times, so I probably won't ever get rid of those.

To get me through the increasing pain as the shock wore off, I found it helpful to write my thoughts and feelings to Nicole. During that week when I faced her in the mortuary, I went there every day to write her about my feelings. I wrote how I felt sitting next to my daughter's casket. I told her it was a scene I didn't think would ever happen and how terrible it was. Writing her is the last thing I do at night. I always tell her how much I wish she were here with me again.

Sometimes when I feel especially alone and isolated, reading helps. I don't ever know what tomorrow might be like for me. Through reading, I know what others feel even years down the line. When I read about other losses, I know I am not crazy for feeling the way I feel. There are times when I cannot concentrate, but from my reading, I know that it is normal.

I know my life will never be the same as it was before 9/11. My heart has an emptiness that nobody can ever fill. It is not something that is going to go away. I remember hearing that grief is like fog. Some days it is so thick you can't see through it, some days you can partially see through it and other days it is clear. There are days when I don't know if I am going to make it. Other days I ask myself why I am feeling good because I thought I shouldn't be happy after losing Nicole. I have to laugh again once in a while because she would want that for me.

I am surprised at how I have been able to go through it because I had to make so many decisions and do so much planning on my own because I needed to do that myself. When I was putting videos of Nicole together, I remember someone asking me why I didn't have someone else do it. I wanted to do it even though it was very hard looking at all those videos of her life and seeing her happy and alive. It was painful, but it was something I had to do myself.

I don't think it was meant that I let go of something this horrible. There is a reason I had to go through it and I want to make sure that something important comes from her loss. I am a stronger person and a better person because of it. I can feel what other people are going through. Although I hurt so much inside and sometimes the pain is horrible, I remind myself that there are many others who are hurting too. It has changed me and I am not like I was before. I am more compassionate and caring.

I have met a lot of people who have lost their children and we have helped one another. Others don't really know what to say. It helps when they say, "I can't imagine what you are going through. I don't think I would be able to survive the loss of one of my children." That is the best thing they could say. I tell them that I thought I never would survive either. I had the choice to sink or swim and I chose to go on, not only for my other children and my family, but also because Nicole would want me to go on.

I will talk to people wherever I am. If someone asks me whose picture is on my necklace or if I am Nicole's mother, I can just come out and talk about her. If they ask how many children I have, I tell them I have three children, but I lost one on 9/11. I find they are open to hearing about my loss and want to feel that connection. I feel it even more when I talk to someone who has lost a child or someone else in their family. I understand. I can feel for them and it's very helpful to them to know I am getting through it. I remember seeing the news after another air disaster. As I saw people crying in disbelief that their children were gone, I had chills because I knew what they were facing and what their life was going to be like now.

We have had bench dedications and a lot of ceremonies to remember Nicole. We're continuing her memory and I think that is very important. It is helpful that they are still talking about 9/11 and Nicole because I know her memory is staying alive. Sometimes it can be painful to turn on the TV when they are showing her crash site and it is in front of me again. Tiffney and I have necklaces with Nicole's picture showing her beautiful smile and her personality. I wear mine every day.

I still buy Nicole cards on her birthday, Christmas, Easter and Valentine's Day because I always get my kids a card and a little gift for all the special occasions. Sometimes I get her a little teddy bear too. She has a lot of purple teddy bears sitting in her room from our family because her favorite color was purple. At Christmas there were always five, but now there are four. I light a candle in front of her last Christmas picture. The first year when we were putting up the stockings, my son asked me what to do with Nicole's. I said, "Well, you can put it up if you want." So we put up her stocking every year.

I celebrate her birthdays. We had the first one at the restaurant where she worked. On the second one, her friends wrote in her memory book and brought something for her memorial garden such as a butterfly or plant. Her garden began from the potted flowers that so many people left for her in the cemetery. I brought them home and planted them. They gave us flags saying, "Our nation will eternally honor the heroes of Flight 93." I have Nicole's in her garden. It is very peaceful to sit or work among the sound of the birds and the beauty of the flowers. There is a rose tree that the people from my work gave me. Everything there has life and beauty. I go there sometimes instead of the cemetery when I need to be with her. I know she is there all around me. I have a connection with it because the flowers grow and die and they come back to grow again. I feel Nicole has gone on to another life just as the beauty of everything that is in her garden will eventually go on.

CHAPTER 10

Loss of my son in a motor vehicle accident
by Sharon Leighton

It was raining awfully hard as we sat down to supper that night. Bobby was a college freshman who had just flown home for Christmas. He looked so much taller and grown up than I remembered him just months earlier when we had helped him move into his tiny dorm room over a thousand miles away. It had been hard for Danny and me to leave him there as we flew back. When we met him at the airport, I realized that to the outside world, he now looked like a grown man, but to me he would always be my little boy.

It seemed so right to have Bobby back home sitting there talking with his father about computers and politics. Although it would be for only three weeks, I enjoyed taking in the entire spectacle and looked forward to having our daughter Jennifer home from graduate school to join us in a few more days.

I loved the enterprising and independent young man that Bobby was becoming, but I missed seeing him daily and being involved in the day-to-day nuances of his life. We sat at supper so long sharing in his plans for his career and catching up on the news of his friends and our family, that it had grown dark around us almost imperceptibly. Danny retired to his computer in the study while Bobby and I turned the lights on and cleared the table. I was picking up the last spoon from the table when one of Bobby's closest friends called to say that three of them were getting together at John's house. John, Bobby and Shawn were inseparable in high school. They had known one another since sixth grade and had always been involved in the same activities. Everyone recognized them as a trio because they were always together. They had brought accolades to their school as great soccer players, as well as for their work on the debate team. If they were not studying or involved with school activities, the three of them were always together shooting baskets or watching TV at one of their houses.

The rain was sweeping the driveway in sheets and the thermometer seemed stuck at 32 degrees. Bobby said, "I'll be back by eleven." As I watched him back out, frosty wet leaves blew into the garage before the door closed. I thought of the next day when we could go over some books and papers in his room to weed out what he no longer wanted. Only he could decide what was important to him. Danny was just turning on the ten o'clock news when the phone rang. He turned the TV down and said, "Okay, we'll be right there." As I heard him, I glanced over and saw him look at the receiver. I said, "What?" Then I thought, "Right! Just as I'm about to step into the shower, you accept an impromptu invitation for us to go to my uncle's house to watch a game!" But it wasn't that. Continuing to look down at the phone, he said quietly, "Bobby is at the medical center and we have to go there now." I asked, "What's wrong?" As he put down the phone, he said, "They didn't say. They just said to come."

It was so rainy and dark that we could barely see the road. Danny drove as fast as he could, but I still pleaded with him a little irritably, "Please, let's get there and find out what is going on." My cell phone was not charged, so all I could do was urge the car forward from the passenger seat and wish that the hospital were not so far away.

There were three ambulances next to the emergency department as we drove up. I don't remember what we did with our car. Someone must have parked it. We ran in quickly and told a woman at the desk who we were. I had stopped at the same desk two years ago when Bobby broke his leg, so I knew where the patient bays were. It was confusing to me that she did not direct us through the doors of the emergency department to one of those rooms. He was not in the waiting room. I asked her, "Can you tell us what happened? Where is he?" She said that someone would be right out.

A nurse with a green notebook under her arm emerged when the doors to the patient care area opened. We asked her about Bobby as she led us through the emergency department into a back room with stained-glass windows and a white linen-covered table. It was a chapel. She began, "Your son was in an accident, a very bad accident. He was brought here in full cardiac arrest. He never responded to all of our attempts at resuscitation, so..." She hadn't finished the words when I just gasped a deep ragged breath in. I knew what she would say next. I needed to stop her and to somehow change what she was about to say. They had given up and let him die. I broke in, "Do everything you can to keep him alive. Don't give up! Where is he? I need to see him!" She said they had already done everything. I thought, "What have they done to our Bobby?" I needed to find him. A doctor with a long white coat came in and introduced himself and somberly explained that Bobby had suffered fatal head and chest injuries, and had essentially died immediately on impact. His car was hit head-on when another car crossed into his lane.

They had to leave the tubes and IV's in place until someone could authorize their removal. Our Bobby, our life, was lying flat on the stretcher with a tube in his mouth and other tubes coming out from under the sheets from his chest. The room was quiet, but there were wastebaskets overflowing with gloves and packages from disposable medical equipment from the earlier frantic moments of trying to save his life. Although his face was bruised, he was there. His arms, full of puncture wounds, looked so small now. I put my head on his chest and half-expected him to reach up to comfort me. I think Danny stared away at the wall, but I'm not sure because I couldn't see through the water in my eyes. My ear was gently resting on Bobby's chest now. He was suddenly so vulnerable and helpless that I felt I had to somehow protect him. We were told there was an army of people gathered in the waiting room wanting to know about Bobby. Danny went out and simply shook his head. Then they all knew. For a minute, I felt that I was somehow observing myself and the stretcher. I was looking down from the ceiling above the doorway. From that perspective, I was hoping that the scene of me with my head on Bobby's quiet form would switch back to the dining room table earlier in the evening or to the airport where we had greeted Bobby that afternoon. At that point, I could descend and warn him not to go out.

Someone brought up a chair for me. I sat down and took Bobby's hand and opened it so I could bury my face in him somehow. As people came in, I stayed sheltered within Bobby's left hand. I just wanted to keep that one-on-one contact I had so missed for the past three months. He had just been so strong, alive and full of confidence with hopes for the future. I pushed my face further and further into the hand which I so well remembered first inspecting eighteen years earlier. I had never expected it would grow big enough to cup my whole face. Danny exhaled with a haunting moan that gave way to a cautious gasp. I ordered him, "Tell me this is just a dream, an awful dream!" I thought, "Please! This can't be. How can he be so full of life one minute and then….? We should have told him it was too cold or too wet or too dangerous. Why did that car cross into his lane? Why did he have to be there at that exact time? I can't take this." I put my cheek firmly against Bobby's forehead and, for a second, I thought I could feel him telling me that he didn't want it like this. It was not his time. He should be going on with his life. It was all just wrong and upside down. We spent hours there. I don't know how long. People came and left, but I never left his side or let go of his hand. I embraced him as best I could and thought, "How could this be? No!" There was nothing outside that boy on that stretcher. He had been our life and the embodiment of our own futures. When he smiled and when he felt good, we did too. When he was sad or disappointed, we were too. And now he was gone, and we felt like we were gone too.

A minister came into the room. I was buried in my son's hand. I was crushing it over my eyes as hard as I could to protect me from seeing any of this. He asked if he could say a prayer and I nodded my head. I don't remember what he said because it was not going to help. Bobby was so still and unresponsive. I told him how much I loved him and that I could not go on without him. He was my life, and there was no sense in anything anymore. I don't remember if I said it out loud, but I was screaming all those thoughts. Danny whispered, "It's time to go now." He embraced Bobby's sheeted waist and my shoulders and he shook in little gasps. He then went back over to the wall and I heard him sit in a chair. I lifted my head and looked into Bobby's face. He was asleep. I hesitantly decided that I had to let him sleep, and knew that he would not be coming home to do that anymore.

I don't remember coming home, but I was there. There were so many people at our house. I was in my bed. I dreamed but I never slept. I tried lying in the fetal position and tried lying facedown, but mostly I lay still on my back clutching my face and eyes. I was hoping to sleep so that I could wake up from this nightmare. It hurt to move and it hurt to breathe. Danny was off doing the things that had to be done. He was making funeral arrangements and notifying people. I knew that because they were all getting done without me. The next thing I knew, Jennifer was crawling next to me in bed. We hugged and cried. It felt so good to hold her. We stared at the ceiling together. We did not talk. She never even took off her jacket that first night. There were people in the living room, but I made no pretense of being a hostess and neither did Jennifer. I knew that one day turned into another because the dreary room would become more dreary, and then dark, and then just dreary again. I wanted none of this funeral stuff. I wanted none of the outside world. Jennifer and I touched foreheads and wet cheeks. I could sense that my pain was intermixing with hers. We didn't talk. Someone, I think it was my aunt, whispered that there was some macaroni and cheese on the bed stand. Neither Jennifer nor I touched it.

Danny came in and gently whispered that he had to go to the funeral home to pick out a casket, and asked if I wanted to go. I knew he needed someone with him, so Jennifer and I went with him. Jenny gathered up Bobby's suit, dress shoes and shirt. I do not remember much of that day. I walked around a showroom and shook my head affirmatively with each question that Danny posed. He was being an adult, but I was not. He was grieving and Jennifer was too, but I was just self-involved with my own hurt. I felt guilty. My aunt, bless her soul, took care of the catering for the funeral and must have been responsible for the miraculous appearance of food for house guests and cleaning up afterward.

I vaguely remember sitting in the front pew at church. There was an open casket. I could not look at Bobby. I just kept my eyes on the white tile floor. I heard sobbing from Jennifer and a lot of muffled sobbing in back

Chapter 10 Loss of my son in a motor vehicle accident

of me. Hundreds of young people filed past his casket in the front of the church. They stared at him, and then they just turned away. He had been their teammate, their classmate and their friend for years. Now they just walked away leaving him behind. They bowed their heads, but never looked back. I turned and watched them exit the church.

I would not turn away from him. I approached him. I touched his hand and was surprised that it was so cool. That coolness hit me because, except for that, I could still imagine I was going to wake him from a deep sleep. My husband and my daughter came up behind me, and we all stood arm-in-arm around our Bobby. He was so still and uncharacteristically unresponsive to us. We motioned for the funeral director and asked to close the casket ourselves. I wanted to be the last person to see his face. As we closed it, I bent down, kissed him one last time and kept my eyes on him until the lid was shut. The last eyes to gaze upon him were mine rather than some stranger's. We walked to the back of the church, but I waited and then followed as they carried him out. I made sure he was ever so gently and safely placed into the back of the hearse. I really wanted him to sit with us on this last journey together. My nephew drove our car. Danny said that for the first time in his life, he could not drive. Jennifer and I were in the back seat and he rode in front.

It was December 14, yet there were still leaves falling, and I could smell the musty odor of death in the air. We drove into the ancient town cemetery, where I had so long ago purchased eight plots just before they were about to double in cost. Danny had gently chastised me for it at the time. I wondered now if I had somehow jinxed our lives. Were those empty lots beckoning to our family? I had been to so many burials! They all looked the same with the canvas stretching over the hole and the casket hovering over them both. I got out and many people stood by and spoke to me before the burial service began. Then somehow we were back at the church with sandwiches and food all around. Danny rose to the occasion to act as a gracious host, and my aunt rushed around to be sure the photos and flowers were in place.

I should have done all those things. My daughter should have learned from me how to act sociably, and then to grieve quietly later. I could not play that game. I was dead inside. I sat there and stared away when people engaged me. I nodded. I may have even commented, but I don't remember any content. Jennifer followed my lead.

I had retired just two months earlier, and was not yet sure what I was going to do with my free time. I had planned on visiting Bobby the next summer and seeing Jenny every few months. Danny went back to work after two weeks. Jenny decided to take the next semester off. She and I went into Bobby's room after about two weeks. Neither of us could do it alone. We picked up a trophy he had won in baseball when he was about eight. Then there were the stacks of notebooks from every course he had taken in high school. He and I had planned to go through all these things over his break. I had washed all his bedding the day before he came. It was so wrong that everything was there ready for him, yet he never came back that first night, or the next night, or the next.

The first Christmas right after Bobby died passed without a celebration of any sort. The tree disappeared and I am not sure what happened to most of the presents. At 3 a.m. that Christmas morning, I turned on the TV to some carols and wondered why anyone was singing. For several years, we had no tree and just a few little gifts. I remember the second muted Christmas. Jenny gave me a heart-shaped locket necklace with two pictures inside. One was of all four of us in front of the tree the year before he died and the other was of Jenny, Danny and me. She said it was so Bobby would see it and realize that there was someone missing and that he was that someone. He would know he needed to come back.

Jenny says she never wakes up without thinking about him. I don't have to tell her that I think of Bobby every day. In the moments that he is not directly on my mind, there is a sadness that pervades everything good because I miss him so. I go about my life. We go out to eat, we shop, we pay bills, we visit, and we have birthday parties.

I want nothing to do with his birthday. It is a sad time in which he should be celebrating another year of life. Now his birthdays are but another year of his absence. I remember his birth and the birthdays in which we had cake and he unwrapped his gifts, but those without him are empty. As for his death date, I really do not want to remember that either. I cannot commemorate that. I do not visit the cemetery because I don't want to read the inscription nor see the cold, hard stone and the earth which are supposed to represent him. I do not want him to be there and he is not there. Some people say they go there to remember him. Why would I go there to remember him when I think about him all the time? I don't need to go to any special place to do that. I just wish there were some place I could go to be with Bobby and forget about his death.

I have never changed my morning habit of sitting in front of my computer at the same table where Bobby, Danny and I ate together that stormy night that he died. He headed out the door to meet his friends and has not yet come back. I watch the door that should open to bring him back. I sit ready. His bedroom has two beds now, one for each grandson. A few of his clothes are folded and tucked carefully into a plastic bin in the attic with his class ring, some of his most treasured mementoes and a photo of the whole family at his high school graduation. I added photos of Jennifer's wedding and his

Chapter 10 Loss of my son in a motor vehicle accident

nephews. I bought him a new camera for Christmas the year he died. It is still wrapped in Christmas paper and folded into the remains of his favorite high school shirt, the one he was wearing that night. They are all ready for him.

I wait, and I will wait until I am physically no longer able to wait. Although I function and everyone sees me smile and interact, inside I am that loyal dog who never strays from the hope that the beloved person lost will return to the same place where I last saw him. Since he went out that door, I am but a façade of the person who had a living son named Bobby. I have to believe he is coming back. That's the only thing that will make it right again and take away the pain that sometimes still takes away my breath and makes me numb to all other things. As I set the table, place the food on the table, eat, pick up, set up birthday cakes and parties and Thanksgiving and Christmas dinners, I watch that door. I may travel away from the house and all over the house, but I eventually always come back to that place to wait.

I don't feel guilty about missing Bobby every day. Danny misses him too. I am so grateful that I have a husband who will not talk nervously to fill the silence. We just quietly sit sometimes until both of us finally admit we are thinking of Bobby. Sometimes Jenny calls to say she is thinking about him, and sometimes I call her to do the same. We leave the phone on speaker mode and may not say anything as we putter around just knowing that we are together in our thoughts.

I am not crazy or dysfunctional. I have satisfied the societal requirement to move on, but only superficially. If you were to talk with me on the phone, visit me or interact with me in the store, you would not know. But I'm different. I have pain and sorrow just beneath the physical surface and sitting right on the emotional surface. It is always front and center in my heart. Once in a while, Bobby's absence weighs so heavily that it stops me short and I am distracted. I can be in the middle of a transaction or a discussion and need to pause. Danny was showing me how to use a computer application just a few days ago, and I remembered how Bobby used to help me so often in that way. Danny's words were suddenly lost to me as I gazed out the window and then stood up. He asked, "Are you paying attention?" Then he looked up at me and knew. We came back to it later.

The most permanent effect upon me is a feeling of inadequacy from feeling broken at some level. My daughter always tells me that she depends on me every day for advice and just knowing I am here. I am not deserving of so much love, trust and expectation, because I can never live up to her vision of me. Another permanent change is that I can see beyond the meaningless distractions of life. I have only a few close friends now and can count them on one hand. The others have long since drifted away. It was too hard to listen to senseless banter about things I could not control or little things that did not matter.

It has been over twelve years since Bobby died. As I write this, my eyes are blurring and my hands tremble as I sob. We had a wonderful wedding for Jenny and David in the local park overlooking the ocean. They have two beautiful little boys, a seven-year-old named Bobby after his uncle, and a two-year-old. I was there at the births of both of my grandsons and helped Jenny nurse each one. We smiled and laughed happy tears as they first opened their eyes. Jenny lives in Utah, but she and her family visit us often and we go out to visit them several times a year. We have big Christmas celebrations at our house with lots of smiles and joy.

I think about Bobby all the time and we talk about him often. I have not yet gotten to the point of being comfortable with thinking about what Bobby would be like now in his thirties. Bobby is forever that strong young man of eighteen with unlimited potential. It would not matter what he did because whatever it was, he would do it well and with his characteristic optimism. He always saw the bright side of everything. He was unshaken by a disappointing grade or a rebuff. He knew who he was and no one else controlled his happiness.

Through all the good that befalls our family, I cannot help but wish Bobby were still an active part of it. I devote myself to appreciating and enjoying my family and those few close friends who can understand that I will always miss him.

CHAPTER 11

Loss of my husband in a private plane crash
by Mary Conklin

Mary and John Conklin.

John and Mary Conklin with their two sons.

I lost my husband in a private airplane crash in July 2000. He was an airline pilot and absolutely loved to fly. Since I am also a pilot, the initial attraction was that we both loved to fly. We just started talking when we met at an airport, and we were together from then on. Within two or three months after our meeting, he moved out to my area and found a job flying for a law firm in Washington DC. We built our own house because he was also a contractor. We lived on our farm with our own private runway and two planes because flying was just part of our routine.

We had a nice family reunion a few weeks before John died. His parents decided to celebrate their fiftieth wedding anniversary by taking the whole family to Club Med in Mexico. We had never been all together before, so we were fortunate that everyone spent time with John. We rented a big sailboat and took a sailing trip. We have lots of pictures of John sailing with his brother and his dad. All of us had a fabulous time.

We had been married for nineteen years and our lives were really good with our sons who were twelve and thirteen years old. I was working on my master's in counseling. John was an absolutely great dad and was always busy with the boys. The night before he died, he had gone directly from his last trip for the airlines to spend the night in a tent at a Boy Scout camp with my older son. When he got back, he told me he needed to put the airplane into the hangar. I was upstairs after a pretty long day of working outside and taking my master's comprehensive exam. When I heard the airplane engine start up, I thought, "Oh, he is just going to taxi it over to the hangar." He loved to fly so much that if he turned on an airplane, he could not just taxi it. The engine went into full throttle. The next thing I knew, he took off and flew north. Some friends were having a get together just three miles north and he decided to fly around up there.

Ten or fifteen minutes later, the phone rang. John had just crashed the airplane. I ran out of the room immediately and told my sons to just stay put. I jumped into our suburban and drove straight up to where they said he had crashed. During that drive, it was almost like I was watching myself drive. I was hoping that he had just done some damage to the airplane, but not to himself. I did not know what was going on.

When I arrived, somebody I knew came walking across the field before I saw the airplane. He said, "Mary, he's dead." I could not comprehend that. All I knew was that I needed to start running to him. As I ran across the field, I saw that the accident was pretty bad. There was no fire, but one wing was about 25 feet from the airplane. The whole top was gone and the other wing was crumpled underneath the airplane. John was strapped into the pilot's seat in front. He was slumped forward with a lot of trauma to his head and his entire body. As soon as I saw him I knew he was dead because he was not bleeding. As I touched him, I felt like I was in a vacuum with just me and him and the airplane in this field. I was looking down upon myself in this whole scene.

I got there before any of the rescue crews or officials arrived. Everyone stayed away from me until policemen started arriving on the scene. One of the police tried to get me to move away from my husband's body. I just told him, "Absolutely not!" The emergency rescue squad people came up to make sure that I was okay. I sat there and stayed with him. I just felt that I had to be there with him. I stayed there for probably a good hour and a half. I am not sure if it was something said to me or not, but I heard, "It is time for you to go home and talk to your sons about what is going on." All of a sudden, it just felt right to leave.

When I came home, the boys knew something was going on because they had heard the rescue vehicles. I said, "Boys, we have to go upstairs and let's go into my bedroom. I need to tell you something." I took them upstairs and the three of us sat on the bed. I said, "Your dad just crashed the airplane and he died. I am sorry he died." My older son got very angry and started picking up things and throwing them. I tried to hold him, but he ran down to his room. I knew he had to do what he was doing. My younger son just sat there and cried with me. Neighbors heard about the crash pretty quickly because it was on the news. The reporters had already begun flying over and taking videos while I was at the scene. People started visiting within an hour after I came back.

When we returned to the accident scene later, John was in a body bag. They let me be alone with him while I talked to him. It was dark, but there

Chapter 11 Loss of my husband in a private plane crash

John Conklin was a devoted husband and father as well as a professional pilot.

were lights on the scene and there was tape all around it. At that moment I felt in control. I just thought, "Okay, I have to do what I need to do right now to handle this." My friend drove me back to the house when they put him in an ambulance to take him to the morgue. I started calling people including his parents, the rest of his family and my family. I do not know how many people I called. I could not reach his parents right away, so I called his brother to tell him what had happened and that I could not get in touch with their parents. He told me they were in Chicago and that he would call them. He would be at our house as soon as he could.

When somebody got me to lie down for a while, I went up to our bedroom with both of my boys. We slept together in that queen-sized bed and were just inseparable for the next few nights.

I got a phone call at about 6 a.m. the next morning. I do not know if I had slept or not, but someone said that I had to immediately get the airplane logbooks to the crash site for the FAA to inspect. That was a scary thing for me because I could not imagine why I had to get them up to the scene right away. I immediately got up and drove the logbooks up there and handed them over to the FAA. They just took them and no one said they were sorry. There were no condolences or anything. No one talked to me.

John had worked for the airline for sixteen years, but within twelve hours after the accident, I no longer had Internet access to any of the information that we had had all those years. I no longer got any magazines or mail from the airline at all. It was like his job had never even existed. It was just obliterated. The accident happened on a Saturday evening and the chief pilot told me to have his keys and everything for access to the jet bridges and the jets to him by Wednesday. I was pretty numb. I was busy organizing a memorial service, handling people coming to the house and taking care of my sons. It was a lot for them to expect of me to drive 63 miles each way to O'Hare to hand in his personal things. There were quite a few things that I had to gather up, and it was emotionally wrenching. Usually I had gone to the airport for a trip to have fun. Now it was really hard as I walked down the concourse. I had to see other pilots in their uniforms and be reminded that I would never see my husband there again. It was hard for me to access the employees' operations area at the airport because I did not have an ID. A support person should have met me to take me through security, but ideally a care support person should have come to our house instead of making me travel to the airport at such a difficult time.

At the memorial service, the church was overflowing with pilots and flight attendants who had known my husband and me. After the service, they did not call anymore and it seemed like all of our airline friends were just gone. The airline let us fly for two years after his death, but when I went to the airport to fly, I was treated so differently than before by the ticket agents and everyone I dealt with to get on the flights. I felt ostracized and like an alien to everyone there. They had always treated us very well, but after John died, it was like he had never existed and they had never known us.

The initial support I had was from my own personal friends. The only real lasting friends were those I had before I was married. Some came out and stayed with me for a week here and a week there. After three months, they went on with their own lives. My friends in the area were not the same. I was left out of everything that we used to do as a couple. I felt ostracized. My being widowed was treated like a very contagious disease that kept people away. I think they feared that they would be widowed too. Then I felt really bad for my sons. They were left out of all the things that they used to do with their dad and other families.

I was not sure what was happening. The loss was bad enough. In addition, now I felt I was losing everything and everybody. I started to wonder if I was going crazy because I was still grieving and everybody thought I could just move on. I was supposed to be happy and be over it. It was not like that. My grief was immense. I kept looking at my sons and seeing my husband. I realized that everything was totally different and that my life was never going to be the same again.

Very early on, one of the most hurtful things for me was when a man said, "Well, I am getting to shuttle the Widow Conklin around." I had a first name. I was 45 years old and my sons were not yet teenagers. Widowhood should not come for a long time. When he referred to me in that way, he may just as well have punched me in the stomach. The other hurtful comment was, "You are only 45 and there are a lot of good guys out there. You'll get married again." I did not want to be married again. I wanted John back. I could not imagine spending the rest of my life without him. I was wondering, "Who do they think could come in and be my husband? What are they thinking?" I was not yet a widow. I was married for a long time after he died, a long, long time. Others made me feel guilty for not bringing in someone to become a dad and a male figure in my sons' lives, but nobody else could come in and be John. When people said things like that, I would go home and just cry.

I did whatever I had to do to take care of my sons. Just existing from day to day was a big deal. I had to drive them to school every day and come home to think about what I should be doing. I had this urgency to be home for something. I had to remind myself that there was no one at home because John was not there and the boys were at school.

Chapter 11 Loss of my husband in a private plane crash

If I was a few minutes late getting home from grocery shopping or something else, my sons would panic. They would absolutely panic because they thought that something bad had happened to me. I would walk in and find them crying or just crazed with fear. Eventually we got cell phones and that was helpful. I wanted to be both parents to them, but I just could not do it because their dad was not there anymore. I was doing the best I could just going through the motions. I went where I was supposed to go at any particular time and did what I had to do. The rest of the time I was just sitting and not knowing what to do.

For about three months, I did everything really well. It was summertime and we lived on a farm, so there was a lot of work to do. I decided to be supermom and took over everything that John had been doing. That whole time is a real blur because I was robotic, but I felt pretty proud of myself. Then I was exhausted and just broke down and could not do anything anymore. That is when I went into a real black hole. Having him die like that was the worst thing that could have happened to me and my sons. I knew I needed to do something to get out of the hole. I had to get my mind out of the house. I really needed to have a schedule. That need to get moving again came from John because he was always such a busy person. I did not want to let him down. I had just completed my master's degree, so I decided to go back to work on my doctorate. My husband died in July, and by January I was back in school. My younger son did not like it at all when I started school. With most of my classes in the evenings, he was home alone more than he should have been. After that first semester, I made sure to take just day classes. In general, I started coming out of the hole when I went back to school. It was the best thing for me because it was the only thing that I had going in my life that was the same. I had been in school for two years when he died, and I just wanted one thing to be normal when nothing else was.

Our church had a great pastor and the church members were very supportive of the boys. There were a lot of activities through the youth group that they both joined. The youth organizers made sure my boys were notified of the meetings and encouraged them to come. That was really helpful and I am grateful to them.

It took me a long time to do anything with my husband's things. For five or six months, nothing could be moved. Then I decided to get rid of the clothes. As I got rid of certain things, more and more stuff could go, but I could not do it all at once. It just evolved. After all these years, I have a box with everything I want to keep. I mainly kept only the pictures because the memories are really all that matter. I gave everything else to people I thought would appreciate them the most.

Even though my in-laws lived only three hours away, they had trouble coming to our house because it reminded them too much of their son. The first Christmas after John died, we went to their house and it felt like John was a four-letter word. It was not to be said. It was the big elephant in the room. For over a week, his name was brought up maybe once or twice and then dismissed. It was strange to be there without any presence of John. My boys felt they could not say anything about their dad. It got worse and worse. By the end of that visit there was a big explosion. I told my mother-in-law, "I just cannot believe that you cannot talk about your son." We had to leave. After that first year, we traveled at Christmas.

There have been a lot of ups and downs in the years since John died. I had to manage my sons' grief and sometimes they managed mine. There were times when the memories of that phone call notifying me of the crash took me back to that day. Sirens would startle me and bring me back even though I do not remember hearing the sirens at the accident scene.

Our lives have changed completely in most ways, except that we are still involved in aviation. Now my perspective on life is quite different. Oprah said that real friends are not the ones that will go in the limousine with you. They are the ones willing to take the bus when the chips are down. When something terrible like this happens, you learn who those real friends are. There are very few of them. I had thought I had a wealth of friends, but they did not stick around long when this happened. I learned that there were other people out there to meet me in the shape I was in at the time. They accepted me for who I was at that moment and did not expect me to be any other way. Things were better when I concentrated only on people who were totally accepting of me.

When I was at the accident site and John was in the body bag, I had promised him that I would raise the boys just like we had planned. After his death, he still had a great influence on them. Since we all loved aviation, we did not stop flying. Both of my boys took flying lessons. My older son was motivated by my desire for more education and was valedictorian of his class. I was so proud, but I missed his dad during that graduation. My son has been flying for Delta Airlines since he graduated from college. When he is flying, John is there. My younger son took solo lessons and wants to get his pilot's license. There are times when I am flying by myself and I feel John sitting there right next to me. That always feels good. He is my guardian angel up there.

One of the most significant things that happened since John died was my connecting with ACCESS. I did not get a whole lot of help and not too many people said things that were helpful until then. I was on the Internet a lot at night because I could not sleep for a long time. ACCESS popped up in one of my searches. I am not one to type in my name and other contact information on a website to have people contact me, but I did. On the website, Heidi was there with all these famous people. I thought she would hardly talk to me and would refer me right out to someone else. Instead, Heidi was available to me immediately and was pretty incredible. She talked to me and gave me enough information to make me feel like I was really okay and that, "Yes, life was going to be quite different, but this stuff happened to other people too." At least it was not just me. Before talking to her, I just kept feeling like I was really going downhill and that there was not any getting out of it. Our conversations were really quite helpful. I felt connected to her pretty quickly. She told me that she would have someone else contact me as well.

I had an ACCESS volunteer grief mentor who is one of the most wonderful people in the world. She just related to me really well. Her situation is somewhat similar to mine. She has two sons and her husband died in a light airplane crash. Our communication was only by email at first because she lives in England. She is very bright and articulate and always wrote back to me right away. Her responses were a big pick-up for me. I would write her about everything that had happened to me during the day and things that were upsetting. She would write back and tell me that she had felt that way too. Then she would tell me about some little incident that had happened to her that related very well to what I had experienced. It just worked. She seemed so normal to me. It had been four or five years since her husband had died, but she just seemed like she was together. I learned that I am not the only one who lost friends and whose neighbors treated me and my kids differently. It was good knowing it was not just me. That meant a lot. I had started wondering if something was terribly wrong with me and if I had become some sort of a crazy person in the eyes of my friends when they did not want to be around me anymore. It helped to know that it had happened to her too.

The last flight I took under my husband's family airline program was to meet Madeline, my ACCESS volunteer grief mentor. What a great person she is! There were a few times after a couple of years when I was even able to help her. For example, it really bothered her that she had not been allowed to go to her husband's accident site. I answered her questions about my experiences with that. She began researching her husband's accident. Finally, she was allowed to go to the accident site to honor her husband there. That was important for her.

Several years later, I learned about an ACCESS volunteer grief mentor training. I met a lot of people there who were already mentors. The fact that ACCESS never quits is the big thing for me because dealing with John's death is an ongoing journey.

I do not know why I wrote my name on the Internet that night and wrote to Heidi, but that was one of the best things I ever did. Connecting with my mentor helped because of her similar situation of raising two sons on her own. The death of my husband, and all of the events that have occurred as a result, have given me life experience and wisdom. I learned more from my loss than I have in any graduate school class. It has helped me become a better person and it certainly has made me look at life quite differently. I appreciate things a lot more than I ever did. I do not take things for granted like I used to. I make sure that I do not leave words unsaid to my sons. They know how very much I love them no matter how tough things are.

Now I reach out to others, especially people having a crisis in their lives. I always want to listen and talk to them. It helps them to have someone ask about what happened. It is good for them to talk because the more they talk about it, the more they can normalize it within themselves. It is cathartic to talk with someone who is sincerely listening.

My sons and I always talk about John and include him in a lot of our conversations. He is not going to be forgotten and we are going to continue to talk about him. It is in a different context than when he was living, but we can imagine what he would be thinking and what he would be doing at particular times. I try to tell my sons all the stories about him that they have not heard.

I donate money in John's name to certain events, the church and anyone who has done a lot for our family. The boys and I try to go out to dinner on his birthday. His birthday is a good day. I make sure they know that their dad is still around someplace and that he is extremely proud of them. The crash date is just not a good day. I try to avoid that memory even though it is right there. Even the weeks leading up to it get pretty hard. I feel it for a week or two ahead of time. I just know it is coming. Though we try to ignore it, we know it is there and spend it together.

My sons are not always in the same place that I am. A few days ago, I got a text message from my younger son that he really missed his dad right then. I asked him, "What's going on?" He said he had no particular reason, but just really missed his dad. My older son remembers going to the airport with his dad in his uniform, and now he is wearing the uniform. I wonder if he is thinking, "This is what my dad was doing not too long ago. Just a few years ago, he was the one walking through the terminal with his uniform on."

Early on, I was doing the right things robotically and just going through the motions. Now I do things more because I really want to. At times, it is still painful and comes on as strong as if it were just yesterday. Every once in a while, I break down and spend hours crying or writing to John in my journal about what is going on. Through my experiences with ACCESS, I know it is okay to grieve and it is my way of being with him. I let myself go with the flow of my emotions now. I don't care if anyone else thinks that it is not okay to occasionally spend an afternoon with my head under the covers. When I get out from under those covers, I feel a whole lot better.

CHAPTER 12

Loss of my brother and his family on Northwest Flight 255
by Joan Pontante

Bill and Kathryn Best died with their three young children on Flight 255.

On the day of the crash, Billy Jr. was climbing a tree and his grandfather worried that he might fall and be hurt. Later he wished that Billy had fallen because he and his family might not have been on the flight that crashed.

Bill and Kathryn's children, Billy Jr., Katelyn and Hillary.

I lost my brother Bill, his wife Kathryn, my five-year-old nephew and my three-year-old and four-month-old nieces on Northwest Flight 255 on August 16, 1987. Bill was like my son because our mother died when he was really young, so I became his mother as well as his sister. When he died, it was like losing my son and grandchildren, as well as my brother and his family.

Bill's whole family had flown home to visit us for a week. We had a family picnic at my dad's. When five-year-old Billy climbed a tree, my father shouted for him to come down because he was afraid he would fall and break a leg. My dad said afterward that he wished Billy had broken his leg because he and the rest of the family might not have been on that flight. When we were saying our goodbyes, my three-year-old niece Hillary wanted to kiss my son goodbye. I can still remember him letting her kiss him. He hugged her. Those are my last memories of that day.

After they left, I went to bed and my daughter was watching TV with my sister-in-law Tessa. Her husband called to say there had been a plane crash. Tessa came into my bedroom and said, "Joan, there has been a plane crash. What flight was Bill on?" When I asked where the crash had happened and she answered Detroit, I said, "Oh, my God!" because Bill had told me they were going through Detroit. I began calling Northwest, but I could not get through. When I called the airport in

Syracuse, they said they would call me back, but they never did. At about 1 a.m., Tessa's father called to say they had confirmed that it was Bill's plane.

That started our nightmare. One of the hardest things I had to do right away was to tell my father. I called my other brother to go with me, and we woke him up to tell him. Bill's work involved flying every week for business, so my father always worried that he would get a phone call one day that Bill's plane went down. He never dreamed it could be the entire family.

Infant Katelyn and three-year-old Hillary.

Billy Jr. and Hillary on the day of the crash.

There were not many other young babies on board besides my nieces, so they identified them by elimination. The only survivor was a little girl the same age as our Hillary. At first we kept getting calls from the hospital hoping we could identify the little girl. She had purple nail polish, so we tried to remember if Hillary had purple nail polish. I can remember my father saying, "It doesn't matter. We'll take her even if she is not ours!" Eventually the little girl's grandfather identified her as his little Cecilia.

Our crash happened back before airlines had any family support, so we waited not knowing any more about the crash. We assumed the bodies would arrive the next day, but their remains did not come until five days after the crash. Identifying them was a process of elimination because they were sitting over the fuel tank. To this day, I do not really know what we received of their remains. Not being able to see anything has always left a void in my heart.

Three weeks after the crash, we flew out to Arizona to close up my brother's house. One of the most heartbreaking things was walking into that house left with toys on the floor and the children's artwork on the refrigerator. We gave all the toys to my nephew's daycare center. My father cried so hard that he shook as he watched those things being taken away.

My brother suggested, "Don't keep talking to Dad about all this because it is too hard for him." But my father wanted to talk about them every day, so we talked about happy memories and the good times. Finally my brother realized that we had to talk about it because we could not just write them off and forget about them. Even this morning, my son and I were joking about all the things that Uncle Bill used to do. He would come home from college and get all of his nieces and nephews together to go bowling. He loved doing things with the kids.

After the crash, I cried every day. I was a hairdresser and would tell my

Chapter 12 Loss of my brother and his family on Northwest Flight 255

clients, "If you see me crying, just keep talking." They would let me cry. Eventually I could talk with them again. I remember our first Christmas. My father and everybody else in our family were sitting at my table, but I was in the kitchen sobbing about not having Bill's family there. I could not say my brother's name, I could not say the kids' names, and I could not say any of their names without crying. Sometimes I would think I saw my brother when I saw somebody about the same height and build. When I realized it was not Bill, I would remember he was gone and miss him all over again.

It took me a year to go out to the cemetery. My father would say, "Did you go out and see it?" I would say, "No, I cannot go out and see their names on a headstone." I could not face seeing their names there because it would make it final. Finally, after a year, I went to the cemetery for the first time to face the fact that they were there. At the first anniversary at the crash site, we met the doctors and nurses who had called us for help to identify the one survivor from the crash. Meeting them was important because in our initial conversations with them, we imagined that it was our Hillary who had survived and it provided us a tiny ray of hope that we desperately needed. When they informed us that Hillary did not survive, it was like losing her all over again.

I always think of my brother and his family on their birthdays. It is a very rough time for me. I try to visualize what they might look like now, how Bill would look in his fifties and how the children would look all grown up. It still affects me although it has been over twenty years. I still have days when I get emotional and cry.

Bill said that people would forget him if he died, but we did not forget him. We built a plaza named after him. I am the custodian of a scholarship in Bill's name. When my granddaughter was the class valedictorian, she won her Great Uncle Bill's scholarship. The night of the graduation, my father and I surprised her as we went on stage to present it to her.

About four years after the accident, my brother came to me in a dream and told me that he was fine. I was still crying every day, but that was the turning point of knowing that maybe everything would be okay. When the crash happened, some of the victims' families saw rainbows. Quite a few years later when I was in the cemetery, I said, "Show me a sign that you are all fine. Show me something." That same afternoon when my sister-in-law came over, I told her I had asked for a sign. As we sat there a rainbow appeared behind my house out of the blue. I just asked for a sign, and this was the same sign that all the family members in our Northwest group saw after the crash. So in my heart, I really feel that they are up there having a good time.

I did not fly for years except when I had to close up my brother's house early on. Many years later, there was a dedication for them in Mesa. My father said that I had to start flying again. My husband and I took separate flights so that my kids would not be left without parents because we knew it could happen. You may not believe it could happen to you, but it can. The day that I started flying, I asked to speak to the pilots and I have continued to do that ever since. I always introduce myself and I say, "I lost five family members on Northwest 255 because the pilot did not do his checklist, so he took everybody down with him." Some of the older pilots told me that the Northwest 255 crash is used in their training films. On one flight after we had leveled off, I heard "We've done our checklist" over the intercom. No one else on the plane knew that he was talking to me, but that made me feel I had done something worthwhile to assure that it does not happen again.

A group in the Detroit area contacted everybody to form a support group, which was the first support group of family members from a large aviation accident. I handled my grief by getting involved. I was invited to an international meeting of survivors in Washington and began attending each year to connect with other family members. I did not want others going through what our family went through without the help of someone else who had been through this type of loss.

I have been working with ACCESS for many years. When I talk about what happened to our family, I feel that I am helping others. I was matched with a woman who lost seven family members, and another who lost her entire family in a helicopter crash. I can connect with those who lost multiple family members because I went through the same thing. I let them know I am here for them in any way I can help. I am here to listen.

Cecilia and Joan met for the first time at an ACCESS grief mentor training event. When she was only four, Cecilia was the sole survivor of the crash in which Joan lost five family members.

A recent ACCESS meeting unexpectedly filled an important void for me. The one survivor from the Northwest 255 crash was there. Her mother, father and brother were all killed in the crash, so her aunt raised her in California and I had never met her. I had always wondered what she looked like, what she was doing, and who she became. As I was registering for the ACCESS grief mentor training session, I saw her name on the list of attendees. My heart stopped. This was the little girl with the purple nail polish whom we initially thought might be Hillary. As I looked at her as a grown woman with a full life, it was like finding my niece. I could not believe it. I was thinking, "What do I do? What do I say?" I tried to visualize my niece because they were the same age. Meeting and hugging her closed up a void in my heart. It was like finding a missing piece of my life because we had talked about her so much and we had wondered about her. It was even more remarkable because we both went there with the same mission to reach out to others in need. I still cannot believe the coincidence of going to an ACCESS meeting in New York and meeting someone so important to me.

I honor my brother, his wife and their three kids by speaking about them. I feel closest to them and find the most comfort on the hill where the crash happened because that is the last place they were alive. I feel them there. Each year at the anniversary, we bring fresh flowers to the memorial and we talk about all of them. That is our way of memorializing them while we go on with our lives.

CHAPTER 13

Loss of my baby to sudden infant death syndrome
by Lisa Brooks

Before Nathan was born, my husband Jamie and I were busy at our jobs. I was the manager of a bookstore and Jamie was an investment banker. During the week, at least one of us sometimes worked so late that we hardly saw one another. We shared few meals except on weekends. That all changed after Nathan was born. I left my job to stay home with Nathan. I could not believe how fulfilling it was to hold him or even to just watch him sleep. I planned shopping, errands and phone calls around his naps. After just a few weeks, it seemed as if Nathan had always been a part of our lives. Jamie usually managed to be home in the evenings for dinner. On weekends, we sent out for food to just sit back and enjoy our little one.

My mother lived forty minutes away and came over a few mornings during the week. She would take him for a walk so I could nap if we had been up all night. On weekends, Jamie would often do the night feedings. Nathan had been gaining weight steadily since we had started the new formula. The pediatrician was pleased with his progress and announced that Nathan was in the middle of the growth curves for height, weight and head size.

Several times since we had brought Nathan home, I had called my mother in tears when he continued to scream after we had already tried everything we could think of to calm him down. My mother said to just close the door and let him cry himself to sleep. After a seemingly interminable period of fewer than five minutes by the clock, he was usually sound asleep.

Our Nathan was turning four months old in two days. He hardly cried all that day. I think he smiled several times. I took pictures of him in his little velour yellow suit from my aunt who sent it to me before we knew his gender. It was the first baby gift I received and it was still brand-new because he had just grown into it. He protested when I put it on him, but after a little extra cuddling, I propped him up on the elbow of the couch and took a picture of him. He was transfixed with the flash from the camera.

He seemed fussier than normal that evening, but I knew that I had to let him cry himself to sleep. I always hated doing that. I wanted to hold him, but that didn't help, and neither did trying all the usual things to comfort him. I had already fed, burped, and changed him. I had tried singing, rocking, and walking him. Jamie had walked him around the apartment holding Nathan's back against his waist. That usually made him happy and quiet, but not tonight. Jamie finally handed him back to me and said, "I guess he is just too tired." Nathan continued to cry, so Jamie tried rocking him in his arms the way we had successfully comforted him when he was first home from the hospital. I knew he was exhausted because he had not napped since morning.

After a good feeding, I again burped him, changed him into his blue gown and put him into the crib to go to sleep. He continued to cry. My husband assured me and my mother reminded me that in order for us to keep our sanity, we needed to accept that he would sometimes cry. I knew they were right, but still it ran against every fiber of my being to not scoop him up because his screams pierced my heart. It seemed like he cried longer than five minutes, but he eventually stopped. I had the little intercom monitor next to our bed and heard nothing that night. Usually he woke us up by 5 a.m. My mother called at 8 a.m. expecting that he was already up. We decided that at long last he was learning to sleep through one feeding in the night. A half hour later, she showed up with her best friend, Sandy, who had not yet met our little Nathan. I decided to wake him up to be sociable. I opened up a bottle and brought it in with me.

I gently turned the knob and opened the door slowly so I wouldn't startle him. I whispered, "You're a sweet little boy to let Mummy sleep." When I saw him, I knew something was wrong. I scooped him up and he was limp with dark liquid coming from the side of his mouth. I held him close to warm his face that felt cold against my chest while I bounced up and down and urged him like never before, "It's time to wake up now!" At first I said it gently, then louder and louder until I was no longer talking to him, but asking someone to help me with my pleas.

The next thing I remember is a crowd around me and someone asking me questions. Nathan was hidden from me by a sea of people crouched over him. And then he was a tiny spot on a huge stretcher. I was in a car riding beside my mother. When we got to the hospital, I was sitting someplace while I heard my mother just outside talking quietly to a man dressed in blue scrubs with a red name tag. When my husband got there, he just sat down next to me silently. We didn't talk. I didn't have anything to say out loud. And then a stocky man in a suit squatted down in front of us and said he was the hospital chaplain. I told him something like, "Our baby is here." He explained that that was why he was here. Just then I saw that he was followed by a tall boy-faced doctor who approached us and said softly, "I am very sorry. We did everything we could, but he didn't make it."

They brought me in to see my baby. I just wanted to hold him. He was not dressed. He was just wrapped up neatly in a hospital sheet when a nurse picked him up from the stretcher and gently handed him to me. I noticed from her hands that she must be my mother's age. I squeezed him tightly, but he didn't move. I believed that he just needed to get warmed up because he was so cold. I couldn't warm him through the bulk of the sheet, so I set him down and unwrapped him. I asked for a blanket and put him directly against my sweater and grabbed the blanket to put around us. My husband put his arms around the chair from the front and embraced us both. I reached under the blanket and managed to put my hand on the top of his head and then rubbed his back. He never cried, and it had been almost twelve hours since his last feeding. I just couldn't warm him up. I held him tighter and looked into his face. When he was first born, he had looked blue and they had suctioned him and rubbed his back briskly with a blanket until he woke up in protest. I rubbed his back now with my hand and then with the rough blanket. Nothing happened. I rubbed his back some more and held him even tighter and rocked back and forth with him almost violently. Then I loosened my hug so I wouldn't smother him. My husband came over and reached down and took him more tenderly than I had ever seen him hold anything. His big hands put our little one back into the nest of the rumpled stiff white blanket that dwarfed his little face. He looked so tiny and distant from us. He slept too soundly now. I said, "He cried last night," and to myself I said, "He was trying to tell us something. If only we could have known! I didn't listen to my heart. He called for help and I ignored him."

My mother did so much. I remember staring at the ceiling in our bedroom. There was a watermark that I tried to mentally morph into some pattern. I just needed to figure out what it was. Nothing took the burning in my stomach away. His room was empty now except for the bear that my mother-in-law had given me at my shower and the white rocking chair where we had fed, burped and rocked him. We had not been to our church since I had graduated from the high school. Now we were there in the front with a crowd of people. I cried a lot and I never tried to stop. My husband sobbed a few times, but he was mainly blank-faced. Some of the people who hugged me now had never hugged me before. As I gazed at Nathan, I thought, "I didn't know they made black velvet suits that small. It makes his face look so pale." I wanted to scoop him up, but knew it was the wrong time. After everyone had left, we did that one last time. I held our baby that one last time and my husband held us both. I saw my mother at the doorway, and she held me just before we left the room. We left him behind. We left our baby alone there with strangers to sleep.

After the funeral, I did not want to leave the apartment. My mother came over nearly every day. She did our grocery shopping and our laundry because I did not want to go out. She and I sat together and she talked about me when I was a baby. She talked about how wonderful Nathan was. She had no other grandchildren, so it must have been so hard for her, and yet she made it all about me. She offered to take me to the cemetery. She had taken care of getting a little stone next to her grandparents' grave. I didn't want to see it. I told her that while I enjoyed her remembering Nathan, I could not go there.

My husband was wonderful although he was grieving too. About a month after Nathan died, he brought over some of our closest friends one Saturday night. They brought casseroles and told me they were thinking about us both. One asked me if we were going to have any more children. He didn't mean it to be cruel, but that was totally irrelevant to my grief. I thought, "That would not bring Nathan back." I never wanted to risk doing that to another sweet baby. If I had followed my heart and sat up with him through the night, at least I would have known what happened and when it happened. I was in another room sleeping and relied on hearing his cries for help when he needed me. But that night after he fell asleep, something happened and he could not cry out loud enough to wake me. I may have slept through some hushed urgent whimpering. I was not with him when he died. He died alone in his crib in another room. I slept soundly ignoring his pleas. He had cried harder and longer than ever that night before he fell asleep. It was a warning. He knew things were not right and I just didn't get it. Having another baby would not only remind me of Nathan, but remind me of how irresponsible I was with this tiny bundle who reached out to warn me in the only way he could that things were just not right.

I know all about crib death now, but that does not take away my regrets. It only taught me that it happens to other people too. After two months, Jamie wanted us to join a support group. I offered that he could go, but I was not ready to talk about Nathan. I put Nathan's photos away. We had quiet dinners at home. I felt guilty for being so uncommunicative, but Jamie never complained. Jamie and I were watching TV one night. Suddenly out of the blue, Jamie abruptly shut it off. He stood up and began to tell me all his thoughts and reactions that he had pent up inside. He commented, "I was watching TV, but not seeing any of it because I am thinking about Nathan and worrying about whether he is okay now. I have not been able to concentrate on anything since Nathan died. It is unfair that Nathan never had the opportunity to grow up. I miss him every minute. I know just by watching you and sitting with you that you are feeling the same way." He went on to say he was angry, but didn't know whom to be angry with, so he was just sad. I talked about my feelings that night too. Before that, we

Chapter 13 Loss of my baby to sudden infant death syndrome

had just gone about our household activities of getting meals, opening mail, and working on our computers in silence. We agreed that we could now talk about it together. He agreed with me that it was too soon to discuss it beyond ourselves and our parents. Still we usually just sat together and knew we were both thinking the same thoughts without saying anything.

Finally, about three months later, I went to a McDonald's with my mother. That was a big step for me. There were children of all ages playing in the little jumping area. It was so cruel because they were all older than Nathan when he died. I saw toddlers, but Nathan never walked. He would have done that around his first birthday. I knew all the stages because I had studied them. Each time I recognized another month birthday, I knew what Nathan would be doing. He was born on November 6, so every sixth of the month, I reluctantly calculated his would-be age and matched it with what he would be doing. I knew when he would be saying "Momma" and when he would be crawling. Now all these little children were taunting me by reminding me of what would never be for my baby. I had to leave.

When we returned home, I hugged myself tightly as I rocked alone in the chair where I used to hold Nathan for so many hours. I thought, "If only I had held him through that night, he might be cooing in my arms now." It took time, and I now think of it as an accident. It just happened, but somehow I will always feel that I might have helped him in some way.

On the sixth of March, when Nathan would have been sixteen months old and just a little more than a year after he died, I learned I was pregnant. When I felt the nausea, I decided that was good because I could somehow make up for what I felt I had done wrong with Nathan by taking better care of his brother or sister. When our little son was born on the fifteenth of November, I cried because the entire process echoed that of Nathan's birth two years earlier. It was the same hospital and the same nursery. I wanted to name him Nathan to erase the pain, but it would never work. Our baby boy was David Nathan, and I would do everything to be sure that he would grow strong and know about his brother Nathan.

Our family and friends threw us a baby shower two months before David was born. One of the gifts was a beautiful bassinet. I had not mentioned that I was never again going to let my baby out of my sight at night. On his own, and without my having to say anything about it, my husband put the bassinet next to our bed before we went to the hospital. I know it is not PC, but now I follow my heart rather than the current or in vogue recommendations by others. I don't care what people say. We kept David in our bedroom until he was six months old.

The greatest lesson I learned from Nathan is that every moment with a child is precious and not guaranteed. I already knew that before Nathan died, but now I think about it and talk about it. I do not ignore my instincts. When David was four months old, he had a really bad evening. It reminded me of that fateful night with Nathan. After I called my pediatrician, a nurse practitioner called me back. She merely tried to reassure me that he was fine, but did not listen to my concerns about his screaming. I asked her what I could do to be sure he was really okay, and told her that I had lost a baby when he screamed like that before. She told me that if I was so concerned, I should go to the emergency room. She was sarcastic, but we did take him to the emergency room. They were very sweet and understanding when I explained what had happened to our Nathan at this age. The doctors and nurses showed me how to spot danger signs and symptoms such as dehydration, failure to eat, fever, rashes, inattention and high-pitched screams. This was reassuring because Nathan had none of those the night he died. David went right to sleep on the way home from the emergency room. I did stay up through the night with David in my arms in the same rocking chair where I wish I had rocked Nathan on the night he died. Now I was honoring his memory by rocking David to sleep, and then watching him in his crib next to our bed.

It has been six years since Nathan died. When I am asked how the experience changed me, I answer simply that it taught me to say to other mothers, "If you are worried about anything to do with your child's health, do not let anyone reassure you without demonstrating to your satisfaction that your child is okay." This may seem over-protective, but if you do not pursue it, you would never forgive yourself if your child got sicker or even worse. From all of my reading and conversations with other parents and professionals, I am assured that I could not have prevented Nathan's death that night, but at least I would have been there when it happened and he would not have been alone. It was an accident and it was not my fault, but I always wish I could go back and redo the evening before he died.

CHAPTER 14

Loss of my mother on TWA Flight 800
by Dr. Lawrence Gustin

Larry with his parents, Anne and Lawrence Gustin.

I lost my mother on TWA Flight 800 on July 17, 1996. My parents had just retired from Philadelphia to Florida and bought a home only a few miles away from me. The flight was planned for my parents and me to attend my niece and nephew's christenings in Paris. When my brother canceled the ceremonies, my father and I canceled our tickets because he was closing out his professional work and I was busy with my medical practice. My mother decided to go by herself to visit them anyway. My mom had never been on a transoceanic flight and had an inherent fear of flying. A year before the crash, my father made a practice run to Paris to see the first grandchild and to assure my mother that overseas flying was safe.

There was a connecting flight from Tampa to JFK. When my mom arrived at JFK and the plane was delayed, she called and said, "I'm not feeling well. I would rather just not make this trip." It had been a long day and she still had the ocean part of the flight left. He replied, "Oh, you've made it this far. Go ahead. See the grandkids. It's what you really want to do." She said, "Okay," and got on the plane. He felt some guilt for convincing her to overcome her last minute doubts because she had always told us to trust our intuitions.

I found out about the crash from the television. I was on call for my practice and had come home around 8:30 p.m. After a few phone calls and household errands, I turned on the television when the news of the crash was breaking. At that exact same time, my mother's sister called me screaming, "Your mother was on that plane!" I said, "There's no way!" because the plane was supposed to leave at 6 p.m. or earlier. As soon as I got off the phone with her, my father called and said, "It was her plane. It was delayed taking off." At that moment I called my associate and asked him to take over the call for our practice and rushed over to my dad's house.

We tried to get through to the airlines. We were on the phone constantly until about 3:30 a.m. When someone finally answered, I inquired if my mother was on the flight manifest. The woman said, "If you do not hear from her, I would assume she was." She promptly ended the call with, "Thank you for calling TWA and have a nice day." At that point, there was a total disconnect. There was not even an acknowledgment that the plane had crashed. About 8:30 the next morning, we got through again. They were planning to have everyone come to the Ramada in New York. After I got my dad settled down, I collected my mother's dental records because I knew we might need them for identification. My father would not fly, so we drove thirty hours nonstop from Florida to New York. When we first arrived, we were separately questioned by the FBI and the NYPD. There was still a possibility of a bomb causing the crash and we had stepped off the flight the last minute. It was traumatic for my father who had not yet recovered from the initial shock of the crash and the long car trip. I understand why they asked, "Why weren't you on the plane? Is there anything to be gained by her death? Who is the inheritor of the estate?"

At the Ramada, the families were sequestered into the main meeting room to watch announcements from the FBI, NTSB and the coroner's office. Some people were there for a few days, but we were there for a couple of weeks. TWA announced that the families had to leave about the time we were notified that my mother had been identified. We began making funeral arrangements and left. After the funeral and burial in Philadelphia, we had a full memorial service and reception in Florida because my parents had a lot of friends and family there who could not attend the Philadelphia service.

I viewed the remains of my mom. TWA, the coroner and the funeral home were against it, but I signed every waiver. Although she was my mother, I had some objective viewpoint because of my background in medicine. I do not recommend it to everyone, but I had to be sure it was my mother. When any questions arose from family members, I could set their minds at ease.

If Mom's body hadn't been recovered, it would have been harder. Some remains of a great majority of the victims from Flight 800, including those of my mother, were left in the ocean and never recovered or identified. For me, my mother has two graves, the site of the burial in Philadelphia and the crash site in the ocean represented by the TWA Flight 800 Memorial.

Some of my mother's possessions were found immediately floating on the water. Her wallet with her social security card and credit cards was found on the beach four months later. About a year later, we received her wallet, some clothing, gifts and boxes. Eventually we received her boarding pass and one piece of empty luggage. A lot of it was burned or gasoline-soaked. We received the first box two days before Christmas, which was not the best time. We stored it on the back patio until after Christmas. The next year they set up a warehouse with everything recovered for the families to claim. It took almost two years to get back the rest of those personal effects. In all, we received about 25% of what my mother took on the plane.

The plane was reconstructed in a hangar on Long Island. It was very strange to walk through the plane and actually go to the seats. It was on a desolate part of Long Island, so it was very quiet and very eerie like a ghost ship. Although my father was not able to go, I took pictures for him. He had an additional special tie to this plane because a year before the crash, he had flown the same flight on the same plane in the same seat that my mother died in.

My father was not able to go through my mom's personal effects for almost five years after the crash. After multiple sortings, my dad had it down to a few items, such as a special coat and sweater, her wedding gown, and certain photographs. The most meaningful things were reminiscent of the happiest occasions and memories. For me, they were her 65th birthday gifts and cards. It was good to share the rest of her possessions with not only friends and family, but also with strangers who could benefit from them.

When my father and I first returned home, we had no idea about how to deal with her loss. Not being pressured was most helpful for Dad. I encouraged him to act slowly in making decisions. There was no rush. He had so many adjustments to make. His generation had very specific assigned roles. Dad made the income and Mom did all the home detail. After returning from New York, I had to show my father how to turn on the washing machine and do other things to live on his own.

Tragedies can bring out the best and worst in families. The loss of my mother drove our family further apart. Generally, my relationship with my brother worsened. My father told me, "We need to let him know that even though she was flying over to see his family, he didn't cause the accident." We had made it very clear from the beginning that it was not his fault. Because my brother resided in Paris, he wasn't very supportive of my father. It was all left on my shoulders. My brother didn't come to Long Island until at least a week after the crash, and then he stayed only a day. When he came to Philadelphia for the funeral, he again stayed for only a day.

While I was away in New York, my associate was covering our practice in Florida. He called daily to tell me that he was tired and to ask when I was coming back. I had hoped for more understanding. When I returned to Florida, my associates and employees commented, "You're not yourself. You're depressed. You're making us depressed." Rather than any sort of bolstering, everybody was concerned with how they were affected. I was extremely tired and very wiped out.

We were disappointed when people who planned to attend the funeral and memorial service didn't show up or even call. They later commented, "Well, we didn't know how to deal with what happened." That extended the pain because we were somehow responsible not only for our own emotions, but for those of others as well. There was a very small core of friends and family who were there for us and did not judge us. How people related to me after the crash made a big difference in choosing who remained close. Some formerly casual friends became very dear, and some very close friends became totally distant and dropped out of my life. They later admitted that they couldn't deal with it themselves and did not know what to say.

After we returned to Florida from New York, our TWA representative contacted us once or twice. The Salvation Army, which was an integral part of emotional interaction with the families in Long Island, made a follow-up visit to ask how we were coping. After the first couple of months, my father and I felt very isolated. We were expected to be totally normal again, which was just not the case. TWA cut off all communication. All of a sudden, it just seemed like it didn't matter to them anymore. We heard, "Do not bother us. It happened. Go away!" Aside from the legalities and the investigations, there was a human component with 230 people lost, but they left us with no emotional resources.

Unfortunately, at the time of our crash, ACCESS did not exist, so we didn't have such a resource to fall back upon. One idea that we all have for making the post-crash life easier is to have groups such as ACCESS involved from the beginning to handle the emotional side of it because they have no time limits on their commitment and have firsthand experience with such a loss.

For the first two years after the crash, I was more nervous and anxious than usual. My work was quite demanding, so I immersed myself in it. I stayed later at night and found reasons to be at my office instead of home to finish up paperwork and do extra work. Work was therapeutic for me, but I went too far in that extreme. Later I cut back on my workload. I began doing things to simply make me happy, such as travel and activities with my dad.

Support is different both in quality and quantity over time. It is intense right after the incident. As time goes on, those who care and are really close don't talk about it as much. If it comes up, they listen. Support is having people there if I want to mention my mother or what happened. One of the hardest things that my father and I had to deal with was the fear of her being forgotten. We found the memorials and remembrances very helpful. Many people disagreed, but we celebrated her birthday, their wedding anniversary and holidays. For instance, on my mom's birthday and on their anniversary, I took my father out for dinner. I kept some of the important events alive.

Chapter 14 Loss of my mother on TWA Flight 800

The anniversary of the crash on July 17 is always an aware day. I go up to the TWA 800 Memorial on Long Island to remember her and to visit with the other families. For me, it is important to be near where my mom died even though she lived in Philadelphia and Florida. Attending the memorials on Long Island and participating in airline support groups preserve the memory of my mom. Losing family members or close friends means a part of you is gone, so keeping their memory alive makes you a little more whole.

Larry and his father with ACCESS founder Heidi Snow on the 10th Anniversary of TWA Flight 800 in front of the Memory Wall at the TWA Memorial on Long Island.

Once things finally settled back to a routine, I reevaluated my priorities and restructured my personal life and career. I gained a whole different outlook on life. I realized that we have no guaranteed number of years of life. I began doing things not only for my family, but for myself as well. Things that used to bother me no longer upset me, and I am more sensitive to the feelings of others. Five years after the crash, I realized it was the right time to switch my career to pediatric disability which I enjoyed. It was a change I would have never considered without the life-changing impact of the crash.

I have learned to accept that there are certain events and outcomes we cannot control. Before the crash, I thought I could control and had responsibility for outcomes, but now I realize that I can control only how I deal with what happens. I would tell those who still have their loved ones and family intact to not sweat the little stuff. There are too many more important things. In the long run, it is people that matter. Now after having lost my father, it has really hit home that we need to make the most of the time we have with them.

Looking back on my life since the crash, it took a long time to find my own way. No one could direct me. I had to forge my own way ahead and find what worked for me. I find that life is different, but still good. There is no getting over it, but I incorporate my loss into a new and different life. People said, "Why don't you get over it? What's taking you so long?" Rather than getting upset, I simply realize that people who have not been through it cannot understand.

I learned about ACCESS because its founder, Heidi Snow, lost her fiancé on TWA Flight 800, and I was fortunate enough to know her during our stays in New York and subsequent reunions. I have been involved since she was first putting it together. One of the main benefits of ACCESS is bringing in a nonjudgmental third party who has been through it years earlier. We who have been through an air tragedy can provide some benefit in listening to someone who is grieving. It relieves a lot of anxiety and tension for them to be able to say what they feel without being judged. It is what it is. No one can tell another how to feel or whether a feeling is right or wrong. ACCESS mentors know this and do not try to control feelings and actions. It is safe.

When I am with someone who has been through a tragedy or a loss, it is not what I say that is important. Even if I say nothing and am just there, that is okay. Sometimes I can simply honestly say, "I really don't know how you're feeling or what you're going through, but I want you to know I am here for you."

By mentoring another person through ACCESS, I gain new understanding of my own experience even after fifteen years. People do not get over it, forget about it or close it out of their lives. It is an integral part of them, and they learn and grow from it. When mentoring and talking with an individual who has called ACCESS, I receive additional insight on how I dealt with it and how grieving goes on as a continual learning process. As mentors, we are not the end-all experts. We are still learning, so it is a positive experience for the mentors as well as the callers who call ACCESS for help. We are obviously not going to relieve or eliminate their loss or grieving, but we can be that person who says, "I have been there. I am here. I care." That means an awful lot.

CHAPTER 15

Loss of my fiancé in 9/11
by Karen M. Carlucci, LCSW

Engagement of Peter Frank and Karen Carlucci.

I lost my fiancé Peter on September 11, 2001. We were living together in New York City and getting married the next month in October. Pete had his MBA and worked as a financial asset manager for a small firm in the North Tower of the World Trade Center. He was very motivated and driven towards his career goals. He thrived in competitive environments. As part of that, he loved to be active in hardcore sports with his many athletic friends.

We had met through a mutual friend six years earlier when we all went out to eat together. At the time, we did not hit it off. When I was ready to leave, he insisted on coming out with me to get a cab. It was really late, so I was just ready to go home. After he stopped the cab, he asked, "Will I see you again?" I just said, "Probably not," as the cab sped away. I realized that I might have been rude, so I called to apologize. We talked for a long time. I began, "I just want to apologize for fleeing the other night because I was just real tired and wanted to get home." He said, "Let's go out to dinner Saturday night." After that, we went out every weekend. I remember thinking how lucky I was that I called him back. We dated for three years before we moved in together.

Peter with his boxer, Chavez.

We had our own typical routine. He would get up very early, walk our boxer Chavez, put on his suit, and head off to work. We would talk a couple of times a day. For dinner, I would cook or we would go out to eat. We were in the midst of planning our wedding, so I was very focused on the details of that. The last weekend before 9/11, he had his bachelor party in Atlantic City with his buddies.

The morning of 9/11, he was in a rush to

leave and I was getting ready for a training session. He had a new suit and a haircut. I said, "You look good in your new suit." I remember him leaving and hearing the door shut. I went out into the hallway to ask him what he wanted for dinner, but he was already out of view. I just said, "Okay, I will talk to him later."

At work I was preparing for a training session. As people were arriving, they began chatting about the news that they had just read on the Internet about an airplane hitting a building in New York City. As the details emerged about the building and the size of the plane, I was naturally wondering what had happened, but I didn't want everyone attending the training to become preoccupied with it. As the story escalated, I realized I should call Pete because it sounded like the accident happened near his office. I was working on 34th Street, so I was not downtown. In fact, I had never been to his office in the Towers, so I did not have a visual of where he was. Everyone was hyping up the situation and becoming increasingly animated as the horror of the situation was growing more and more clear. I calmly went to my desk and called him. There was a busy signal. I knew that was not good. I immediately emailed him that I heard that a plane had hit the World Trade Center and to get back to me when he could. I knew those two attempts were sufficient to contact him and that I would hear from him soon.

As the minutes went by, I began to recognize that this was a serious situation because Pete was in the building and I had not heard from him. I told the people who were patiently waiting that I would not be continuing the training because my fiancé was in the Towers. Everyone looked so worried, scared and horrified even before anyone realized how devastating this was going to be. We didn't know what it was. We did not understand the magnitude. On the surface, I was calm and just taking things in stride. I said, "Okay, let's not jump to conclusions," and I went back to my desk. Pete and I had cell phones, but we didn't use them very much. Pete's cell phone was at home, so he didn't have it with him, but I called it once anyway. My phone at work rang nonstop as everyone called who knew my number at work. They asked, "Are you okay in the city? Where's Pete?" I said over and over again, "I don't know where he is. He was in the building and I need to hang up because he might try to call me." His parents and his older sister insisted he was fine and must be walking home. From the reaction of others, it began to hit me that this was a nightmare that was going to swallow me up.

I called the New York downtown hospital, "I am looking for my fiancé. He was working in the World Trade Center, and maybe he was brought there." I now realize how ridiculous it was to think they could tell me anything about Pete. The woman said, "Honey, do you know how crazy it is down here?" Then she hung up.

Chapter 15 Loss of my fiancé in 9/11

I had to make a decision, "Well, now what do I do? Do I go down there? Do I go home? What do you do in this situation? What?" There was no logical response for where to go or who to call next. Finally, I said, "I have to do something." Normally I would go home, walk the dog and get something to eat. Pete's sister had a friend walk our dog, so I did not have to do that. Now what was my plan? That was when the trauma really started. I was just stunned. I did not understand or know what steps to take. I was powerless over the situation and so was everyone else.

I ended up walking all the way home from 34th Street to Bleeker Street in the Village with one of my friends who was helping me plan our wedding. She was wonderful in her denial of the magnitude of the disaster. She kept repeating, "Don't worry. This is going to be fine. It's going to be fine." I said, "It is not necessarily going to be fine." I knew it wasn't going to be fine. I just knew because I was piecing together the little bits of information and I had not heard from him. I looked at my engagement ring and thought, "I am not getting married." I thought how ridiculous it was that I got dressed this morning thinking that it was going to be a normal day. The radio had even commented on the gorgeous weather. Then what a horrible day!

I was not prepared to walk thirty something blocks in my new shoes, so they were killing me by 6th Avenue. As I walked downtown, I had the full view of the orange and black smoke against the blue cloudless sky of the day. I thought, "I can't believe what has happened and that he is down there!" When I walked back into our apartment, I suddenly had the worst feeling ever. I knew, "This is a totally different world for me. This is not even our home anymore." Of course I was hopeful he could turn up as I thought, "This is not yet over." But as every minute went by, I just knew the chances that he had survived were diminishing.

There was a big misunderstanding. While our friend who walked our dog was in our apartment, he heard someone leave a message on our answering machine, "I am walking away from the building, and I am just calling to be sure you are okay." When he recounted the message to Pete's sister, she told everyone, "Pete just left a message that he is walking home." She called me before I left for our apartment to say he was just fine, while I was thinking, "He is not." I knew he would not have called the home number. He would have called my work. The message was from Pete's friend who escaped from Tower Two. He was trying to reach Pete. When I listened to the message, it was so garbled that I understood how it could have been mistaken for Pete's voice.

When my friend's husband came over, he said, "People won't be flying for months and months. You are going to have to cancel your honeymoon." That was just not helping. I said, "Thank you, but I will figure that out later."

I was not alone when they left. Pete's friend Glenn, who worked in the Village, came to relieve my friends and stay overnight. Glenn and I were just beside ourselves. It was so painful because we did not want to watch TV and we did not want to eat. I could not sleep. Outside the window, the smoke and the odor traveled up to 14th Street. It smelled like poison that no one should smell. I put on my shoes and told him, "I am going down there." After we talked to our friends in a firefighter group, he said firmly, "You are not going down there. It is too dangerous." When our friend Colin came over, I told them both, "I can't stay here." I called my parents and told them I was coming home to New Jersey. I packed up some things that were important to me that I might need, and I went to Penn Station with them.

The train ride took an hour. It was awkward because we were trying to be normal when this was one of the worst things that could have happened. Then my friends could no longer keep it together, and I knew I was finally about to totally fall apart as we got off the train. I didn't even know how I was going to get from the train to the car. My father was speechless, and then hugged me saying, "I am so sorry." Just walking into my parents' house was horrible. It was like a sick joke. There was a pile of wedding responses in front of me. One of them read, "Yes, we are coming and we are so excited." It was now just a harsh reality that none of this was going to happen.

I just went through the motions. I had to eat, but I wasn't hungry. I regressed to being like a toddler. It was as if I couldn't do anything by myself. I was scared to be alone for two seconds. If someone left the room, I started shaking. I took baby steps in getting dressed. My parents and my friends were there. If I needed to go outside, they would go with me.

I remember people coming over and looking horrified when they saw me. My loss was a real-life tragedy before their eyes. It made everything they were seeing on TV real. There were some people who were just too uncomfortable. They came to see me once and I never saw them again because it was just too much for them. Then there were those who came over and said, "Okay, we are going to get through this." They tended to me and they were very present. They were comforting. Some brought me books. I read about loss, bereavement and spiritual things. That helped me a lot.

A few days later, I had to go back to the city sooner than I wanted to get more belongings. I remember taking the train. No one was driving because they were afraid of another attack in the tunnel. Everyone was reading about 9/11 in the newspapers while I was on the train. Everyone was talking about it. When we got to the city, everything was partitioned off and they would not let us below 14th Street. I explained, "I have to get to my apartment. I have to get my things and my fiancé's things." Finally one of them said, "Okay". My family and I had to walk. It was exhausting and we were horrified by

Chapter 15 Loss of my fiancé in 9/11

the smell of the ongoing fires. When we got to our apartment, a part of me wanted to be there and a part of me did not want to be there. Everything was uncomfortable.

I could not do this alone. I had to talk to somebody. I knew I had to get into therapy and found a therapist quickly. I do not remember how I physically got there. I must have gotten a ride. I was crying as I tried to talk, but he was very calm and steady. I said, "How am I supposed to go through this? I can't do this." I will never forget what he said, "You should keep talking about it, but you are going to be very uncomfortable for a very long time." As painful as it was to hear, I was so glad he said it because it was the truth. I needed someone with the courage to just acknowledge that it would really hurt for a very long time. It meant I was not going crazy because it was supposed to be horrible.

A little at a time, I began to do little things that I liked. My friends took me shopping or out to lunch. I could only handle so much. Everybody around me was still buzzing about 9/11, but they were still proceeding with their lives. I thought, "Okay, this bad thing happened. It is sad. It is horrible. I cannot believe it, but I am still going to go to work, go shopping, and go to a movie." However, I could not do anything and I could not enjoy anything. I felt like an alien in public even though I knew I was one of so many people that were feeling this way. That others were in my same position was oddly comforting. I recognized that this was going to have long-term effects on many other people. That is when I started reaching out to others. I would read the newspapers and look for people who were about to be married or living with someone because I was in that bizarre gray area of not yet being married. I connected with them and would go to support groups to meet others.

Pete and I were set to be married on October 19, 2001. We were planning a big wedding with about 200 family members and friends. All the details were in place. Pete had arranged our honeymoon in the Caribbean. Since we had been together for nearly six years, there was no need for a long engagement. It was ironic that even our short engagement was not short enough. When I came home to my parent's house on September 12 and saw all those response cards in the mail, I told my mom we had to cancel everything. I wanted to just get it over with. I had to start taking it apart because taking action helped me. I said, "You're going to call this place and I'm going to call that place." It was very hard to do, but it helped to tell people it was canceled. The less I kept it to myself, the more tolerable it became. I would say, "Hi, I'm sorry to tell you this, but my fiancé died, so I have to cancel." There was something about saying that over and over again. I already knew it was real, but saying it helped me live with it.

I took on the things I could do, and my mom took on the things she could do. My gorgeous wedding dress had just arrived in a plastic bag which I never opened. It is still there unopened. My mother called to explain what had happened. It was very awkward. I remember her saying, "Do we return it?" They said, "No, just keep the dress unless you don't want it. We will refund your money either way." It was a strange situation. We were literally undoing everything. A friend of mine took on canceling the honeymoon and I had to cancel Pete's gym membership. It was surreal. There was something important about being active rather than just passive. It felt good to take action in little pieces and to not take on too much.

I had taken my engagement ring off right away because that was just what I needed to do. It was a symbol of "You're about to be married. You're going to be a bride". I had just ordered my wedding band, so I wondered, "Should I cancel the wedding band we ordered?" That was a hard decision, so I told one of his friends, "I guess I don't need the wedding band." His friend said, "What do you mean? That's your wedding band. You ordered it and you should just go get it! It's whatever you want it to be." Pete's friend and I went into Manhattan and down to the Diamond District. When I explained that I was picking up my wedding band, the clerk said, "Okay, congratulations and good luck!" I responded, "Well, actually my fiancé was killed in 9/11." He just stood there and didn't say a word. I have it on now and I always wear it. It has its own symbolic meaning to me. Some decisions are important. I have learned that I do not have to rush to make them, but I initially thought I did. Sometimes I needed to take my time to attack important issues.

One of my friends found an organization which was a hub of information about the different resources available to us. She offered, "I'll go with you." I said, "Absolutely, I have to go." As we went into the city and were walking there, I remember not understanding what to expect. I was at once overwhelmed and comforted to know, "Oh, this is where I have to be because this is where everyone goes who is like me. This is where I belong right now." I realized I was not alone. I didn't want to be one of those people that had to go, but it was the best place for me. It was like going to the land of misfits. I discovered that they did not know what to do with me because I was a fiancée. I remember being very upset about it. They said, "You just need to collect some information if you can manage to do that." I needed a lease and utility bills to show how long we had lived at our address, and documents showing an imminent marriage. I was so fortunate to have people to help me piece this information together. I felt very strongly about this fiancé issue and was eventually counted as a domestic partner.

Everyone said, "I am very sorry this has happened to you." That sentence was very important. In general, I felt cared for. That was just so important. Those who know people going through a tragedy should not be afraid to say, "I am here and I am going to help you. Do you want me to sit with you and say nothing, or would you like me to do more?" The most helpful thing was being with friends who were still comfortable to be with me. They would come over to my parents' house in New Jersey all the way from the city. Even though they had to go to work and had kids, they made me feel like I was a priority. They let me know it was okay with them to be in this with me. I could talk about Pete, and they knew, "If she can talk about it, we can talk about it. She's talking about Pete, so we can ask about him." If I felt angry, none of my close friends took offense. If I didn't want to talk, no one took offense. I might say, "I know you took me out to the mall, but now I have to get out of here." They would say, "Okay, let's go." They were there for me emotionally, and spent hours with me on the phone as I repeated the same things over and over again. I cannot express how much that meant to me. I just don't know how I can ever repay them except to be there for them if they ever suffer a loss like mine.

CHAPTER 16

Loss of my mother to cardiac arrest
by Dr. Susan R. Snow

My mother always beamed with an unbridled smile emanating from her love of those around her and of life itself. She smiled doing commonplace activities that most of us regard as drudgery. She brought that spirit into all the lives she touched, not only when she greeted her friends, but also when she ironed, set the table, put away dishes, or drove family to appointments and lessons. Her radiance transformed an otherwise boring or dreary moment into a bright and meaningful one.

My mother with her smile that warmed us all.

My mother was 65 and loved her grandchildren, her children, her husband and her brothers, sisters, nieces, nephews, and her community. She especially loved children, and never tired of tending to their needs for affection, food, clothing and play. It was not unusual for her to have ten or more grandchildren at once at the house. Rather than being fretful over the myriad of their simultaneous needs, she treasured the clothes and diapers to change, the faces and hands to wipe, the knees to bandage and hair to comb. She imbued such joy into the whole process that each ordinary day was a festive event.

My mother's flock of grandchildren were her pride and joy. She loved attending to their needs and turning each day into a festive event.

Her love of children stemmed from her early family life. She was one of nine children and was always there to change diapers for the youngest four. Her parents died when she was young, so whenever she earned money, she carefully allotted just enough to pay for her essential medical appointments for her severe asthma, but the rest was for the household, clothing and toys for her younger sisters and brothers. Before she was married, she taught eight grades in a one-room schoolhouse. Then, as far back as I can remember, she was superintendent for our local Sunday school. In those days, virtually everyone in the community attended and there were frequently 160 children enrolled. She ushered thousands of children through their preschool to high school years. She found good teachers, ordered teaching materials, and oversaw the Christmas, Easter and Children's Day recitals, as well as various fundraising activities. Looking back, I do not know how she managed to coordinate it all to be so seamless, organized and effective.

There were countless people in the community whom she transported, visited and helped in any way she could. Her older sister never drove, so my mother loved taking her places. When our next-door neighbor died suddenly, she drove his wife up to her daughter's college to inform her in person. When a neighbor had newborn twins in addition to four other children, my mother picked up her laundry every day. She liked to hang the clothes out in the sun and deliver them back all ironed and folded. There are many other instances of her helping others that I witnessed, and countless others I will never know about. In the years since she passed away, it always makes me happy when people recount the acts of kindness she did for them.

I was lucky to be her daughter. I always loved being around her and missed her whenever she was not there. When I was little, I remember being so sad when she had to go to Ladies' Guild meetings on Tuesday nights, and being so glad to hug her in welcome when she returned. Everything came so easily as she made our lives so smooth. The rough spots just didn't seem so rough, and the good times were all the more delightful. Because of her, I was able to pursue my interest in academics and medicine. Without her, I could not have done any of it. My son was born my freshman year of college and my daughter the first year of my master's degree. My mother sustained us all at every step of the way with physical and emotional support. Despite our living three hours away, she was always helping to mother my kids when my academic work was most intense. They enjoyed many weekends and all their vacations with her and my father.

My mother and my daughter spent all vacations and most weekends together.

They knew their grandmother had unconditional love for them and joy with their presence. She would patiently spend hours and hours playing board games with my son. I remember her doing the same for me. She always found the time to sit and play one game after another. She never seemed too busy or flustered despite being so asthmatic and having so many family and community responsibilities. My daughter always felt safe whenever she sat in her lap or stood next to her. She was their only reliable comfort while I was caught up in my academics and medical training.

I was in both the PhD and MD program at Dartmouth Medical School. At my graduation, my mother was uncharacteristically disappointed that my

Chapter 16 Loss of my mother to cardiac arrest

PhD in respiratory physiology was delayed for another year because of my thesis advisor's illness. She had never expressed impatience for an outcome. It meant only that after this graduation for my MD, there would be another medical school graduation next year for my PhD. She must have sensed that its delay meant that she would not be there to celebrate that second doctorate which would have been impossible without her.

It was the morning of my children's February vacation, and I had arranged for them to go directly to my parents in Maine after school. They were all going to Florida the next day. Since the arrangements were all set, I was absorbed in busywork at the hospital trying to just survive a grueling medical internship. As I was finishing up charts from morning rounds, I got the call. I do not remember the exact words, but this is what I remember in a man's voice, "Your mother has had an accident and you need to come." He said "intubated", so I knew it was very serious. I did not sign off my patients until I completed some paperwork. To even say that now is appalling because I should have left immediately. There was a lot of other house staff to do those routine last minutes of work. It was almost arrogant to think I was indispensable there when I was really indispensable to my children. How brainwashed I was to fear that responding appropriately to news like that would somehow adversely affect anyone. Not only did my family need me, but I needed them. Since this was way outside my repertoire of even remotely expected personal contingencies, there was no prepared response for such catastrophic news, so I never considered leaving abruptly.

We drove three hours to the hospital. I vaguely remember my family already seated on a couch overlooking the glass room with her ICU bed. I know I saw my mother intubated and unconscious, but it was so overwhelming that I have no memory of that image.

It was a welcomed respite to have objective discussion. A cardiologist friend from Massachusetts was there with us and commented that after my mother stabilized, she should be transferred to a better hospital where this would not have happened in the first place. The medical standard for the medication that caused her cardiac arrest was for it to be initially administered in the hospital with cardiac monitoring to check for adverse effects and to determine the optimal dosage. In her case, the doctor had dispensed with the safe and acceptable initial inpatient trial. Instead, he jumped to his own risky and ultimately fatal protocol. He began it orally without any monitoring. He had been doubling the dose based on blood levels without reevaluating her. When we asked him why he had not followed standard practice, he responded, "I didn't think she would want to take the time to be admitted." She had no idea of the dangerous path he had chosen for her. She always followed medical advice to the letter. As an intern, I was new into the medical system and I didn't yet realize that some physicians veer from the standard of care to the detriment of patients. The entire discussion had no impact except as a distraction from the rapidly encroaching formidable abyss of grief.

She was the very person to whom I would have turned at a time like this. She alone could always make it better. Now she just lay there. We were all stunned to see her intubated and unresponsive to us. We waited for her to awaken, but didn't consider the odds against it or for it. We were too bewildered to even weigh the possibilities for her recovery.

The next day or so, I remember the neurologist chasing us away from her bedside to examine her with a group of house staff. He proclaimed that she was brain dead and would never wake up. Before it even found any target in my own heart, my father's face went into his huge hands. Those hands had embraced his sweet Marjorie since they were teens, and had built a huge brick church and a massive canning company. They had planted huge gardens, and designed, constructed and fixed anything anyone could ever want. Now they could only hold his face. I wanted to bring her home to die in her own bed, but to my father, she was already gone.

When she was found unconscious in her car and resuscitated, she was stable and her heart was fine, but her brain had suffered from lack of oxygen. Now they extubated her and she breathed on her own, but she never woke up. I visited her a few days later as she breathed quietly in a room with no IV's or oxygen or airway support. With continued aggressive support for another few weeks, she might have reawakened because those were the days before CT scans and MRI's. The physical exam that declared her brain dead was often inaccurate because of the drugs used for sedation during intubation. I should have insisted on more time before giving up on her recovery. Instead, I just watched as my father complied with their request to declare her "Do Not Resuscitate" or DNR, which in this case was permission for "Do not treat". Because she received no IV's or oxygen or pulmonary support during her unconsciousness, her death in days was inevitable. She tried to survive because she continued despite dehydration and starvation for more than a week. I wish I had protested when my father succumbed to that authoritarian pronouncement. She was never given an adequate chance to reawaken.

The day she was found unconscious was her birthday, their anniversary and the day my father had retired. She was just going to get a routine blood test at the local hospital. My father had offered to go with her, but she knew he had much to do before their trip, so she declined the offer. She looked out the window and commented on the freezing wind and blowing snow. My father said, "She just walked out that door and never came back." She was found slumped in the car in cardiac arrest from an abnormal heart rhythm,

Chapter 16 Loss of my mother to cardiac arrest

ventricular fibrillation. I don't know if it would have made a difference, but if there had been someone with her, at least she would not have been alone waiting to be discovered by a stranger.

Their clothes were all packed in a suitcase waiting only to be closed. I supposed the suitcase should be unpacked, but there was no sense. Why put clothes back into her bureau drawers? Her clothes no longer belonged anywhere.

I vaguely remember someone informing me by phone that another intern had to delay his vacation because of my three-day absence. Maybe they did not know the seriousness of my mother's condition. All I heard was that I had to come back to work. My mother was the most important person in our world, and it was unbelievably irrational for me to abandon my father, my children, my mother and my own needs at this pivotal time.

I got the call that she had expired days later on March 7 as I was taking call from home in the middle of the night. I had just seen her at the end of my bed. My son, who was thirteen, came into my room and already knew. She was his rock and they talked by phone every day whenever they were not together. On the morning that she arrested, he had the feeling that he and his sister should not go to school, so they just stayed home. He didn't know how he knew.

Somehow we were back in Maine. There was a viewing, but I remember none of it except touching her hand and being startled that it was cold. Then I remember us all heading to the parking lot and realizing the kids were not with us. Someone remarked, "Where are the kids?" My father or one of my sisters quipped, "Around Grammie. They are always around her!" Sure enough, they were all gathered around their Grammie studying her intently with fixed gazes. They ranged in age between five and fifteen and were not capable of conceiving that it would be the last time they would gather around her, and that she would not ever again be amongst them. One minute she was mothering her precious collection of grandchildren, and then she lay there without acknowledging them as they flocked around her. They did not understand how this could be. They could be patient because she had been patient with them. She would get up and reach her arms towards them, or maybe this one time they would watch her sleep and she would be up later. They followed us silently to the car.

I remember nothing of the funeral or the casket, whether it was open or closed. I think the casket was silver and that I sat between my two children in the second row on the right. Beyond the funeral, the church held much of my mother. Even years later, I cannot sing or speak there because my voice will break. I usually wipe my eyes and hope no one notices.

My mother passed away the first week of March in the midst of my internship. Three months later was my PhD graduation and the beginning of my second year of residency without my mother. For that second medical school graduation, my father arrived at our house with chicken he had barbecued. My flute teacher, a very close friend of the family, came too. I remember this thin, enfeebled, 92-year-old nearly blind man coming through the door to honor my mother at her wake, and now he sweetly accompanied my father to my PhD graduation where my mother could not be.

Tear-stained letter from my nine-year-old daughter after her grandmother's death. We found it nearly thirty years later.

My daughter's birthday was two weeks after my mother died. My mother had always made every birthday a special event for every grandchild and others. My cousin just recently told me how much it meant to her when my mother gave her denim hot pants for her birthday. Months before every birthday or holiday, she would thoughtfully compile gifts she knew would make them happy. Sure enough, we found presents ready for my daughter's upcoming birthday on the shelves of my mother's closet. My daughter was only nine, but she wrote a heartfelt letter which we found just a few months ago tucked away into a long-forgotten suitcase. There are streaks on the ink that are wet spots from her tears. It reads, "February 26th my grandmother died of a heart attack and I miss her a lot… When we went to see her, she just layed there. She couldn't see. She couldn't hear. She didn't know anyone was near her. This happened the day of her birthday and her anniversary. March 22 was my birthday. I'm in Maine now with my Grandfather…"

Nothing mattered anymore because it was all just wrong. She was the matriarch and the glue of a huge family. She had many brothers and sisters, four children, fifteen grandchildren and an entire community that depended on her. The news was just the beginning because her loss was too big to conceive over those first moments, days, weeks, months and years after her death.

My father pleaded into the air, "I am only half a person now. If I could just take the years I have left and divide them with her, we could live them together." It all seemed reasonable, and in any negotiation would make sense and be accepted. He would do anything to just bring her back with him for even a minute. My father was always going and going. I never saw him relax except a few times on a Florida trip. At home, he was always designing machinery for the canning company with a yellow pencil on a white pad of paper. Although he held titles from vice president to president there, rather

Chapter 16 Loss of my mother to cardiac arrest

than being at his desk, he could usually be found around the machines deeply engrossed in fixing, building or designing equipment. Whether working in his huge garden, cooking for large church fundraisers, or at his duties as church organist and host of family activities, he was going all the time. After my mother died, my father could not fix it, but he had to do something. He sprang into action by cleaning out everything of hers. As remembrances went out the door, he probably hoped that the pain would go too.

The next few years were mechanical and reactive. I was in too much shock to even sense the pain. I was just stunned beyond belief into simply reflexive activity. I could not absorb my own loss, let alone those of my children and my father. I didn't know where to begin, so I didn't. The gravity of it was just too overwhelming to appreciate. I attended fairly well to the logistics of caring for my children, but I was as oblivious to their suffering as I was to my own. My son's performance in school declined. He was dealing with overwhelming loss and grief alone. I was buried in completing my residency, taking board exams, and beginning my medical practice.

Our huge family was united through her. A symbol of that one family was the annual Christmas photo card of her children and grandchildren that my mother sent out for over forty years. That stopped and our locus for cohesiveness was lost with her death. Each of us began to have separate activities and holidays. For years, I tried to maintain a semblance of unity amongst my mother's growing family, but now I accept that we are different. I pour my resources into my own children and grandchildren while spending as much time with my father as possible.

My father knew my mother since grade school and this photo is one of his favorites.

It has been about thirty years since my mother died, but she is with me always. She is that presence that accepts me unconditionally as I am. She says, "You are right," whenever I doubt myself, "You are good," when others seem to turn against me, and, "It will be okay," when the future seems bleak. She gives me a sense of self and that strength to forge ahead.

My father's favorite picture of my mother taken on a Florida vacation.

I still have an overwhelming desire to have her back as before. I want to see her acknowledge all the new people and events in our lives. I need to know that she knows that my father is still cooking for us all on Thanksgiving and that when he walks past her schoolgirl and Florida photos, he says, "You were a wonderful woman." That is his way of saying, "Marge, I still love you and miss you."

They talk about unbridled joy. We all knew it, but since my mother died, the big events and the small are tinged with restraint and incompleteness. My younger daughter was valedictorian of her high school exactly forty years after I was valedictorian there. My father went to both graduations, but my mother missed my daughter's. As my daughter gave her speech that mentioned her grandfather, my mother should have been there. My father and I really needed her joyous reflection of the event. I need to see her acknowledge her four new grandchildren and 26 great-grandchildren born since she passed. Without our lives being seen through her eyes, they are less bright and less focused. Before she died, we lived charmed and magical lives. Now we live normally.

When I talk about my mother or try to read anything she wrote, the tears well up because the pain is always hovering. My son still feels the loss, but it makes him too sad to talk about it. As I broach the topic, I see him staring beyond me to a place still too painful to enter or to share.

No one should have to hear me talk about how much I miss my mother. My support is open communication with a very close girlfriend who lost her mother suddenly many years ago. We talk whenever one of us is feeling down and we take turns mentoring one another. We welcome one another's insights as motherless daughters. When one of us manages to put an emotion or perspective into words, the other has often had the same feeling without being able to express it.

In retrospect, my mother demonstrated to all of us how to survive grief. By the time I was born, she had lost enough loved ones to spend her whole life grieving. I saw her tears at funerals and her concern and rapid response to illness or death of loved ones and people in the community. At the same time, she had to struggle to breathe from her severe asthma and its complications. She had a lot to be bitter about and many reasons to be a victim. She was unwavering in embracing her pain and accepting it as part of her, so she was content with herself and happy with her interactions with the loved ones still in her life. She smiled and saw the bright side of each moment of our lives. I still miss her very much, but my grief is very private and invisible to most of those around me.

CHAPTER 17

Loss of my husband on TWA Flight 800
by Martha Rhein

Kirk and Martha Rhein were high school sweethearts.

Kirk and Martha Rhein with their four children.

I lost my husband Kirk in the TWA Flight 800 crash on July 17, 1996. He was 43 years old and we had four children ages four, six, thirteen, and sixteen.

Kirk and I grew up together and were high school sweethearts in Ohio. Kirk went to New York City for graduate school, and we moved there and married in 1975. When he died, he was on a business trip to Paris with three others. They were supposed to fly from Springfield to Washington and then to Paris. They missed their flight, so they drove to JFK for Flight 800.

The children and I were in Ohio at Kirk's parents' house with his brothers and sisters and their children. We vacationed there every year because both of our parents had summer homes there. We would bring our families together. It was very much a priority for both of us. Kirk had left to go back to New York a week earlier. Since he was busy working and traveling, we stayed in Ohio.

It was very much surreal when I learned about Flight 800 that night. We were staying in a cottage with no TV and no radio. We got a call from one of Kirk's brothers who knew that Kirk was flying to Paris. I did not know the airline or the flight number, but I knew they had missed their flight from DC and were taking a flight at about 7 p.m. from JFK.

When my brother-in-law told me about the crash, I called the wife of one of the men traveling with Kirk. When she listened to her answering machine, her husband said they were flying on TWA. While I did not have any official confirmation until the next morning, I knew in my heart that Kirk was on that plane. I called a close personal friend in his company. He called the travel agent who had booked the flight and confirmed that they were re-booked aboard TWA Flight 800. That is all I needed to know he was on the plane.

For a number of hours, I thought it was possible that Kirk had survived. I had not seen the TV and had none of details of the crash. A couple of friends in my hometown drove to the Ramada Inn to view the manifest. They learned that he was on the plane and that there were no survivors. They called me at about five in the morning, so I had a little bit of hope for six or seven hours after the first phone calls. I felt an overwhelming numbness in trying to comprehend it.

I flipped back and forth between thinking, "This couldn't have happened," and, "Oh, my God, this has happened!" It was too shocking. It was not real. It couldn't have happened. I was trying to grasp the reality of it because this kind of thing is impossible. This couldn't have happened to him, to me, our four children, or to everyone who knew him.

Kirk's sister and her daughter were vacationing in New York City. When she heard about the crash, she immediately went to the Ramada Inn for us. I was in Ohio surrounded by family, so I had immediate family support that was very comforting. Both sets of parents, siblings, children and a few close college friends came to our cottage. While my pain was deeper, we were all suffering from this horrific tragedy. I had to get a little bit of my strength together. After four days, we went back to New York. I decided to leave the two younger children at home because they were not able to comprehend the permanency of his death. My two older children preferred to stay home with their younger brother and sister.

I immediately went out to the Ramada Inn at JFK. My sister-in-law, who had been there around the clock since the morning of the 18th, was able to help me through that very painful time. The first evening at the Ramada Inn, I was greeted and comforted by a woman left with three small children after losing her husband in the Pan Am 103 air disaster eight years earlier. I was taken with her ability to sit with me and to listen and respond to my questions. She told me that she and her children were okay. Although there were certainly bumps and ups and downs in the road, she and her children had come out on the other side. Just seeing that she had come through it was a huge help and source of strength for me. She gave me hope that I too would come through it okay. Through the rough days ahead, I was able to draw strength from reflecting back on that special evening with her.

I started planning the memorial service on the Tuesday after the air crash. The airline assigned us escorts who kept us informed as we anxiously awaited news on the recovery process. They helped schedule the transportation for my family coming in for Kirk's memorial service. Many acquaintances and business associates wanted to come to terms with Kirk's death. It was very unsettling for me that they had not yet found Kirk's remains. Although I knew he had died, there was always that little element of "Did he survive?" The service was very much how I wanted to celebrate Kirk's life. Many, including our eldest daughter Rachel, spoke and represented the early years, the mid years and the later years of his life. Rudy Giuliani spoke because Kirk had been his partner in a Manhattan law firm and he was instrumental in handling the TWA tragedy. It was very moving as he expressed his sorrow and grief over our loss. Friends and family came back to our house and reminisced about all the wonderful things that Kirk had done.

The night before the service, I was informed that Kirk's remains had been found. They were able to get him to my hometown by Saturday morning for a burial service after the memorial service. I was advised by the coroner's office that I should not look at Kirk's body. I took their word on that and have no regrets. My mother-in-law wanted to see his remains, but I made the decision to let nobody view them. I have been at peace with that because I know that he wouldn't look anything like the Kirk we knew and loved. We were all instrumental in designing his headstone, which was very important for the healing process.

I wanted to know how he died and what he felt and thought at the time of his death. When we received the autopsy report, we were comforted to learn that Kirk did not feel pain and probably did not know he was dying. It happened very quickly, so he did not suffer.

Sleeping and eating in the very beginning were hard. I had bad dreams. Thankfully there was a lot of food brought to the house. That was a godsend because mealtime did not come at any set time, and I could not think about what the children were eating. I started smoking again for about six months until I realized it was not a good thing to run the risk of shortening my life and having my children deal with yet another tragedy. When I look back on it, I wonder what I was thinking. The reality is that I was not thinking or caring about these things. I was so overwhelmed and consumed with my grief that I was numb to the outside world. It was okay for a time, but I knew I should not get stuck there. I could be there while I was embraced by that numbness and most intense level of pain, but I could not stay there. I knew Kirk would want me to find happiness and stay healthy. He would want me to raise our children in the best possible way I could. That meant that I had to take care of myself because I was now their only parent. There were times when I had an overwhelming feeling that I could not do it all on my own. It was often two steps forward and one back. Going for a run or to an exercise class was an exhausting idea. I had no physical energy. After a few months, a fellow jogger insisted, "Let's go. Let's go for a walk." She got me back outdoors. I always felt better after a walk.

I asked the woman I had met from Pan Am 103 how she got through the days and how she was able to just breathe and to take care of her children. She told me a few things that I took to heart and practiced. She told me that the best thing she did was to get psychological help for herself and for her children. That was something new for me. After the first couple of weeks, I called a psychologist. It was extraordinarily helpful to have someone who could validate my feelings as being okay and who was not judgmental. She allowed me to feel okay with the mourning process and with my grief. It was very helpful because people are on different timelines. As time went by, some in my family could not understand and wanted me to be okay and to get over my pain and to move on. It did not happen as quickly as my friends wished. Grief is a road that I had to travel alone.

Birthdays, anniversaries and holidays triggered different emotions for each of us in the family. When it was very painful for me and I was saddest, my close friends and even my children did not necessarily understand. My two younger children did not like to see me sad or in pain because that made them sad. All four of my children had counseling at different times. For example, my son went to a group with other children who had lost a parent. It was comforting for all four children to know that they were not the only children who had lost a parent.

Initially my thoughts were, "How will I ever get through this tragedy as a single parent of these four children?" I was not sure how I would do it, but day by day and step by step, I found the strength with the help of therapists, friends, family, clergy and the teachers at my children's school. There are still hills and valleys in our lives because of this tragedy. Sometimes the pain hits as severely as it was that first day, but it does not last as long. I remember thinking, "When will I stop thinking about Kirk every waking second? When will that happen?" I cannot remember when I could think about other things besides Kirk. That was when I knew I was moving ahead through the grieving process. I still think of him every day, but it is no longer every second.

Kirk and I were at a place where we wanted to be personally and professionally. All of a sudden that chapter was closed. I became the single parent, the plumber, fix-it person, chef and shopper without any backup. Parenting coupled with running a household in the very beginning was overwhelming. There were days when I would just shut down and say, "I can't do all this! I can't do it all. I can't do it all by myself." Now I know it is okay and normal. By admitting it, I can ask for the help I need when I cannot do it all alone. There are still days when it is overwhelming.

The words that were the most helpful were, "Life will be different, but it will go on. It is not an easy road and there is no set timeline." In some ways, it is a life-long road. Even though life will never be the same, there are still

Chapter 17 Loss of my husband on TWA Flight 800

moments of joy and peace. The joy gets more frequent, and I become more receptive of the love and support that is out there for me. Because of my experience, I am more compassionate to others who are experiencing any kind of tragedy.

The most hurtful comment was, "Kirk is in a better place." I knew he would have preferred to still be with his friends and family raising his children and working in his profession. I was also hurt when people said, "This was God's way. He was such a good person that he was needed in heaven." It hurt when people told me to find someone else, to move on, and that life would be the same again. At that time, I did not know that life would go on. It has gone on, but there will be no replacing Kirk. Life is different. If I find love and marry again, it will not be the same. There was nothing better at those raw moments in the beginning than to hear simply that others were very sorry for my loss.

Martha and her four children after the loss of her husband Kirk.

I have taken care of our children, and together we have moved on. We have embraced the changes and learned to appreciate our extended family during those most difficult holiday times. We have all found peace with the tragedy, and we have hope and empathy and compassion for all those who suffer any kind of a tragedy similar to ours. We have been able to get through those dark days and come out on the other side.

CHAPTER 18

Loss of my husband in 9/11
by Monica Iken

Michael and Monica Iken.

I lost my husband Michael on September 11, 2001. He worked for Euro Brokers on the 84th floor of Tower Two. We were planning a baby and looking forward to starting a family.

September 11 started out like any other day. Michael got up before 6. He showered, got dressed and then came in to say goodbye. He kissed me and said, "I love you. Have a good day." Then he left for work. I could sleep until 9 a.m. because I was looking for a teaching job. Having a little more time to sleep in the mornings was very nice.

The phone woke me up. Michael said, "I am fine. I am okay. Everything is fine and I am..." I interrupted, "Excuse me?" And he said, "Are you watching TV? Turn on the TV. A commuter plane hit Tower One." Nothing was registering at this point because I was just waking up. I put on the TV and saw a massive fireball in Tower One. I could not believe what I was seeing, but he was so calm. He repeated, "Everything is fine and everything is under control. It is okay. I gotta go." He called back a few minutes later, "Call the family and friends. Tell them I am okay. They told us to stay put. The building is secure." He was still very calm, so I thought, "He knows better than I do." I was watching this big fireball on TV and thinking, "Why are they still in the building? Well, they say they are safe and it is just a commuter plane." He said, "I gotta go." So I said, "Okay." I got up to find the phonebook to start calling family and friends because they would worry if they saw what was on TV.

The moment I came back to sit down in front of the TV, I saw a jumbo jet heading straight for Tower Two, which was his building. I thought, "Nah, this cannot be what I am seeing. Nah! No way! Not! How can this be possible?" It was just a surreal experience. I felt, "I am not actually watching this on TV. This is just a figment of my imagination. This is really not happening." And then it hit the Tower. I screamed, "Oh, my God!" I thought, "Where did it hit? What floor did it hit? Where was Michael? Did he get out?" The phone rang every few seconds. Each time it rang, my heart was in my throat hoping and needing it to be Michael. I kept anticipating hearing Michael's voice and telling myself, "He is going to call. I talked to his friend's wife and her husband got out. His friend is his buddy and they do everything together." But it was never Michael. All day long I was saying, "Oh! Not a problem. He got out. He just cannot get through on the phone. The cell phones are not working. He probably did not take it with him. He probably just ran out of the building. He would have to walk home from the Towers, which would take a long time." Then I thought, "Anything could have happened. He could have been injured. He could have been hit in the head. He could have gone to the hospital." For the whole day, I thought he was coming back and said, "He is fine. There is nothing wrong. He got out."

I did not know how much time elapsed from one phone call to the next. As night drew on, reality started setting in. I started thinking, "Well, where is he? Oh, my God! He is not coming home. He just cannot get to a phone." I knew something was not right. We had never spent a night apart. I had to sleep without him. That first night he came to me in a dream and said, "Everything is fine. Everything is under control. I am okay. I am safe." I thought, "This is not a good sign."

The next day everything was closed including all the roads and all transportation. As soon as my friends and I could go into the city, we jumped onto the Metro North and went down to 42nd Street. When we got out of the train, it was a war zone. There were no people and no cars. We could not believe there was not a soul out there. It was as if the end of the world had come and we were alone in a twilight zone. We made phone calls and separated to look for him by going to hospitals, family and friends. We filled out a missing person's report. He was number 46. We used the media to show pictures of him and asked if anybody recognized him. I was so desperate because I wanted to know where he was last seen. I asked, "Has anybody seen Michael? Did he run out with someone? Was he helping someone?" The worst thoughts ran through my head, "Did he know that he was in trouble? Did he suffer?" It was the nightmare of all nightmares to not know where he was and what happened to him. It was just so hard to go through those first days as I began to realize he was not coming home. I thought, "Eventually he is going to come home. He got hit on the head. He just has amnesia. He is not coherent. He's in a hospital somewhere. He's a John Doe." As time went on, I realized this was not looking good. I was glued to the TV all day long to see if I could find him. I held onto every ounce of hope I possibly could. Then, as the number of days grew and the weeks grew, I began to think, "No one is going to survive that long in the rubble. He is not here. He is not coming home."

My life was changed in a minute. One minute I was talking to my husband on the phone, and the next minute he was gone. I just could not deal with the realization that he was not coming home and that he died that way. It was very painful to believe that he was gone. I didn't know what to do. I went into a really bad state. I was totally outside myself living a surreal experience. I was going about life, but not there. It is hard to explain that feeling of "Is this really happening to me?" Then I felt anger. Why didn't he leave the building? How dare he not leave the building! His friend got out, so why didn't he get out? I felt selfish for blaming him even though I knew it was not his fault. He would have helped everyone along the way. He was trying to do something good for someone else. He was just that way. That is why I fell in love with him in the first place. I could not be angry with him for that.

His family felt that we needed to have a memorial for Michael, so we had a service on September 26 with pictures, flowers and bagpipes in Mineola for his family and his friends from Long Island. On the 27th, I had a beautiful ceremony at St. Patrick's Church.

In the beginning, I needed a lot of people around me. My best friend had to sleep with me in our bed because I could not sleep by myself. The best and most helpful thing was people who simply listened. They would just listen to my stories over and over again. Once in a while they would join in with me to tell stories. I felt his energy there with us when we talked about his life. It helped his memory live on in my heart and among his friends and family, and even among people who had not known him.

I just could not move. I did not want to leave the apartment. I could not think straight. I was not eating or sleeping. I wanted to be wherever he was. I thought, "What am I going to do with myself?" Then I started to realize he would not want that for me. He would want me to get up and get moving. One of the things he loved about me was that I did not get depressed. I was happy all the time and he never saw me crying. I had to say, "What would he want for me? The terrorists took my husband and my soul mate. Was I now going to give them myself too?" I could not do that.

I had to force myself to get it together and begin to see therapists, talk to people and get out. I kept very, very busy. From that point on, I did not spend any time in our apartment because every room had a reminder of what we did there and who we were. I began devoting myself to working on the 9/11 Memorial. I went out all day, ate out late, and came back only to sleep. When I was back at the apartment, every time the doorbell rang, I thought he was coming home. It was so hard being there without him. We were going to buy a place, so I knew Michael wanted me to do that. It was a big thing to move because it was closing the chapter on that place where we had lived together. I moved alone. I never anticipated something like that happening to me. It was so difficult.

I gave some of his things to his friends and family that I thought they would like. The rest came with me when I moved so I could memorialize his things and keep them with me. Since I would not have the 9/11 Memorial for a while, I needed something in my own space to reflect upon and to acknowledge him. It is a chest with clothes in it, personal effects and pictures on top, and the flag that they gave us draped over it.

My daily routine changed. I couldn't do anything I normally would do prior to 9/11. I just avoided doing things that Michael and I had done together. I couldn't eat the same foods I used to eat with Michael. I couldn't go to the same places I used to go with Michael. I couldn't walk in the same places we used to walk. I couldn't play cards. I found new things to do away from my home. I went to different places and traveled a lot because I had to get away. I didn't watch TV because I didn't have time for unimportant things in my life. I realized, "Life is really shorter than I thought. Life can be over in a split second." I needed to do whatever I needed to do to enjoy it.

It was important to connect with people who had suffered and survived the same kind of loss. It helped to speak to people from air disasters and Oklahoma City who had experienced tragic unexpected loss. I could feel a connection with those people. Only people who had gone through it could honestly relate to me and understand that pain. I also relied upon friends I met through this tragedy. We worked together by talking, crying and comforting one another. I did not lean so much on people who had never suffered a loss like mine because they could not comprehend the pain I was experiencing. They could not understand why they couldn't just take the pain away. Many people said, "Oh, you are out in public. You are starting a 9/11 Memorial foundation. You are moving on with your life." They did not know that I was sad every day, but I had to live to do all those things because Michael would want me to do that.

Another comment that did not help was, "Well, you are attractive. You just lost your husband. He would not want you to wait. It is time to move on with your life." I found that very painful because I had already met someone to spend my life with and have children with. He was taken away from me, but our relationship did not just go away. That was the last thing I wanted to hear. I thought, "Our love was unconditional and that is a rare gift. Do they expect me to just go out and replace him? Do they think I can just substitute one for another and forget about losing him and my pain?" It did not work that way. Over time, it actually got worse as I came to realize that he was not here and would never be here again. The hardest part was accepting that

I had to function without him. I would never again see him walking through the door and smiling at me with those big blue eyes.

Never in my life could I ever have imagined this happening. I struggled to understand why it happened. I was living in it and trying to do the best I could. His time here was very limited, but I was blessed to have him in my life. I believe that Michael and the others were angels hand-selected for another mission and a higher calling. I believe that we go to a more peaceful future. I am less afraid to take risks now because I have the best angel waiting for me. I feel that Michael is with me every day. Every day I say, "He is in a better place. I am the one who is suffering. He is not suffering anymore. The way I can make him happy is to survive."

I did not get any remains, so I had to say goodbye to a picture. I have only memories and pictures. People do not realize how painful that is. We are always hoping to receive remains, but that likelihood is now pretty slim. If I had even a bone fragment, I would not feel that he just went poof into the air. The closest connection I have to his actual remains is the site where he died, but for now it was just a big hole in the middle of downtown Manhattan. I did not choose this to be his cemetery, but it is his final resting place. It is where he went to work and where he died, so it is the right place to acknowledge anniversaries, birthdays and anything else important. I feel he is there because when I go there, I feel his energy. For now, I have nothing. I have no urn, no coffin, and no cemetery. I have nowhere to have any peace.

For me, it was not acceptable to hibernate and allow the world to go on without knowing and honoring Michael, so I work to be sure that everyone will know Michael Patrick Iken. They will know who he was, what he was and what he stood for. That effort is the key for me to survive his loss. He would be very proud and honored to know what I am doing for his memory. His family had difficulty relating to my work on the Memorial. We are still separated in some ways by our different beliefs about how to grieve. That is okay because I realize that each of us grieves in our own way. There is no consensus on grieving and people have to do it the way they need to do it. I have to remind myself all the time, "It is okay, Monica, to do whatever you need to do." I will do whatever will help me to get through this tragedy in my life. I would tell another in my position, "Whatever you need to do, you should do. Do not listen to others if you know you are doing something good that is helping you survive." Rather than caring what anyone said to me, I learned to look deep within myself to find whatever it took for me to heal. No one should judge me on that call.

It is difficult to see a bright side, but that is why I founded the September's Mission, an organization to help best memorialize all the lives lost in 9/11. That keeps me going everyday as I am busy making sure I can honor Michael in his final resting place at Ground Zero. I am doing something positive for everyone who was lost by helping to create the most beautiful memorial the world will ever see. I know that I am here to make sure that Michael is remembered along with all those who suffered such horrific deaths. That is my gift of hope for all the families. That is my hope for the future and how I get through another day without him.

CHAPTER 19

Loss of my mother to sudden cardiac death
by Jane Begala

I had just gone through a terrible breakup with a boyfriend after discovering his infidelities. My mother fortified me with her dismissal of him and her belief in me. As always, she was there for me when I needed her. Now my plans centered around rising from the ashes of that relationship, and again believing in myself as a woman and as a public health professional. As I was transitioning to life in California, I was in daily phone contact with my mother in New Hampshire. She was my intimate confidante and knew about the man dating me and my application to the UC Irvine Executive MBA program.

    I was in my new boyfriend's apartment in southern California when the phone rang. I will never forget that phone call. It came very early one Sunday morning in August out of nowhere. It was so difficult to attribute the voice on the phone to my father because it wailed at me. He was in such intense agony that I could barely understand much beyond his wish that I come home immediately. He begged me to quickly fly across the country to be by his side. My mother had woken up that morning in good spirits. Within thirty minutes and without warning and without complaint, she suffered a massive heart attack and died of adult sudden death syndrome.

    I screamed against the universe as much as I cried. I descended to very primal emotions and an internal and even external wailing. Because my mother had never been sick in my entire life, the shock of her sudden death was unnerving to my very inner fiber. I could think of nothing but seeing for myself that my mother had really died. This was very much mixed with an urgency to correct the situation, as if I had the power and control to do so. With help from my boyfriend, I immediately got a flight home. I do not remember even one moment of going to the airport, boarding the plane, or landing. I can't even remember who picked me up at the airport.

    I kept thinking that someone had made a mistake. I even thought that maybe something had happened to my father mentally because this wasn't making any sense. I expected that when I saw my mother, I would detect a breath and know that this was just a mistake. First seeing my mother in the hospital, where they had pronounced her dead on arrival, was so poignant and bittersweet that I will remember it for the rest of my life. Hovering over her with a final kiss, I was just stopped in my tracks when she did not move or beckon to me. She did not respond to my hugs and tears. I was immediately confronted with the fact that she was dead because there is no way my mother would not respond to me. In a way, I was as dumbstruck by her natural beauty as I was that she was no longer alive. Even in her 70's, my mother did not have gray hair and had a beautiful complexion. I will never forget how exquisitely beautiful she was in her pajamas without makeup, and now without a heartbeat.

There was not any opportunity or any forewarning that I was going to have to say goodbye to my mother that day in August. She could run circles around me all day, and then come home to cook while I collapsed on the couch. I never thought about her death. Because my father was seven years older than my mother, it was assumed that he would die first.

Some of the most tender memories are of my mother's wake. I went to the funeral home for hours to just sit on the little prayer kneeler to talk with her. I told her all the things I wished I had done with her such as traveling to England. I tried to express how much I love her, how multi-layered that love is, and how it will always persist. I am very happy to have not one iota of doubt that my mother knew how very much I love her. Our relationship was so close, so open and so receptive, that I will always be grateful that she knew how I just adored her.

The funeral and burial services included some of her favorite hymns and prayers. They were in the local church I had attended since childhood. What was especially important to me is that the Veterans' Cemetery allowed us to bring picnic baskets with my mother's best china cups and thermoses of coffee. We all shared a last cup of coffee with my mother. It was a fitting memorial because my mother always had coffee for anyone who visited. Many important conversations occurred around that coffee at her dining room table.

A lot of family attending my mother's funeral and burial came back to my father's house for sandwiches and conversation. I was responsible for making sure everything was served properly and that people were introduced to one another. I was relieved when they left so I could use my energy for my father who definitely needed me.

My entire life changed pivotally at the moment my mother died. My father got down on his knees and begged me to stay with him. He had faith that I could get into an MBA program in New England. I decided to come back and just open my life to total change. I moved all my belongings back to New Hampshire. This included shipping my car back after it had just been shipped to California. I walked into the provost's office at UC Irvine to withdraw from my coveted place in the upcoming class of the Executive MBA program.

I began spending very long hours learning my father's medical history and getting his financial affairs in order that my mother had kept solo all the years of their marriage. My daughter role with my father morphed into what my mother used to do for him. Because of his physical frailty, I became his advocate, his power of attorney, financial planner, and health care proxy. I spent a lot of time at doctors' offices and at the Veterans' Administration.

My brother lived in Arizona and had always been distant emotionally from us. Even after my mother died, he hardly ever called either my father or me to see how we were doing. For him, life resumed as before. My mother's funeral had given him an excuse to take a break from work and to show his children the New Hampshire coastline. I set up educational trusts for his children. I tell them my mother's history and about her contributions to the community because my brother never mentions my mother to them.

My father needed to remove my mother's clothing from sight and insisted that I clear doorknobs and closets of her belongings. I gave most of her clothes to charity. I kept some of her nurse uniforms and coats that I remembered from my childhood.

I operated from many different channels after my mother died. A huge part of my psyche became focused on helping my father process his grief. He was so distraught and so inconsolable that he was unable to attend her burial. Much of my grief path at first was shared with my father. We sat silently around the house with full knowledge and comfort that we were there for one another and were feeling the same loss. We would hardly eat. When we did eat, we often went out. We would start to tell stories about my mother during these dinners together. Frequently the waitress would come over to ask if there was something wrong with the food because one or both of us would start to cry at the tiniest thing. I found that his circle of elderly friends was especially helpful. They took the time and patience to be with us in our grief. They could pull on past losses that resonated with the acuity of our recent loss. The full extent of my own grief became very private and expressed as screams or sobs in the car while driving alone. I started grief counseling and attended a support group at my church. I read about death and dying.

My father and I were emotional train wrecks for years. We continued to stumble, pick ourselves back up, lean on one another, and occasionally walk through what we called our "valley of death". We both believed that there

My father and I shared our grief in the wake of my mother's death.

was a sure-footed way out of the valley and that it was not a permanent state of entrapment. I knew that my father would one day join my mother. He just died a year ago. Now one death somehow resonates to another. When I start feeling despondent about my father, it inevitably morphs into even deeper feelings of loss specific to my mother. Since my father's death, I revisit that valley again, but this time I go alone.

Others meant well when they commented, "This too will pass," regarding my pain and grief. My grief does not have a short life. Even though it brings pain, I do not wish to forget my mother or my loss. They greatly dishonor my grief when they are impatient for me to be over my mother's death. I often felt very pressured to move on and to stop mentioning my mother and my loss, even though it is the most profound event of my entire life and still influences me every day at some level.

Once an avid gym devotee, I so languished from the emotional burden of the loss that I was unable to run or swim or jump in any kind of vigorous physical manifestation for years. The breathing exercises of yoga were sometimes comforting and at least reminded me that I was still alive. Finally, after years of paralysis, my dog nudged me wet-nosed with loving eyes to start walking with her. Movement was mine again.

Every holiday and every birthday are painful reminders of her absence. When each date that was special to my mother arrives on the calendar, it cuts like a knife reopening the horrible knowledge that she is gone. I get particularly blue at the beginning of August, which is the month she died. Most often I do not initially remember why I am becoming blue.

There are huge blurs of memory that streak through these years without my mother. The loss is so profound that even the memory blackout periods provide very little comfort over fifteen years later. Emotions that bubble up to the surface are emblematic of the geyser that still lies within me. When I reflexively reach for the phone to share some infinitesimal detail of my day with my mother, I freeze in the knowledge that she cannot be on the other end of the line. I could never have anticipated the extent of the utter loss from her death. My mother enabled me to feel fulfilled, applauded and accompanied. She was the May Pole in the center of my life, so I still feel her absence in all events.

My heart pounds in my ears remembering my father retell the incredibly intimate stories of how he fell in love with my mother, what tender signs she gave that the feelings were reciprocated, and what it meant for him to have her in his life. He recounted precious stories of their first Thanksgiving together, and how she passed me around to her circle of nurse friends when I was born. These stories are treasures. I lean into them like a new branch seeking the sun. I stretch to embrace every detail of "what was" for the complete inability to accept "what now is".

I seek out family and friends who knew my mother. From their knowledge of her and their willingness to talk about her, two of my mother's best friends are now my close friends. In fact, my only dear friends are those who have lost one or both parents because I seek that fundamental shared experience so central to my life as a basis for communication. The moments in which I have been held and understood by another have always been with those who have gone through a similarly impactful personal loss and who made major decisions that changed the course of their own lives as a result of that loss. It is not that they had the right words or touch, but rather that they acknowledged the shared experience and how painful it still was for them. It is a rare subset of people actively grieving and remembering a person more than a year after death because there is no sacred space in which to hold that memory in our society. When I pull these conscious knowing friends and family to me and discuss my mother with them, it helps make the loss seem at least tolerable.

I look for signs of my mother in the world at large. Sometimes it is a kindness that someone shows that is characteristic and reminiscent of my mother. Sometimes it is looking into the mirror and seeing more likeness to my mother in my own face as I age. Whenever I have difficult decisions to make, I think about how my mother would have advised me. I have started to apply what I learned from how she mothered me into mothering myself.

From these years of grieving, I learned that my father was right. I could get into any school or find any source of employment, but that matters less than I ever imagined. All that is really non-negotiable in life is even one more hour with my mother. I have found that coping is a two-track concept. One track is accepting that my mother is not part of my ongoing reality and soothing my heart that aches for her. The other track is having moments of courage to pick up my life and live it even though it is a life now uninhabited by her.

My loss has taught me about my own survival skills, about very deep pools of pain that are so private and profound that they sometimes take my breath away, about the salvation available only through prayer, and about compassion for myself and others. My advice to those who still have their mothers is to practice loving kindness and the awareness that life is unpredictable and fleeting. There are precious treasures to be unearthed from the memories and from creating rituals of remembrance. For instance, something as small as my mother's habit of always sighting and picking up pennies has become a precious everyday ritual of mine. I have found pennies, or rather they appear as if dropped from heaven, at the strangest times when I need support and when I need a reminder that I was loved and raised by a wonderful woman, and that I am hers forever.

CHAPTER 20

Loss of my father to suicide
by Seth O'Connor

Although I am a chemical engineer, I know medical lingo from my father who was an obstetrician in New York City. I was raised on family kitchen table conversations about his experiences from hospital rounds, hard days in the office, and being on call.

One of his most passionate topics was the trend to revert to the natural good old days of home childbirth. Unfortunately, that carries with it the mortality of those days. At least once a year, my father saw a case when things went wrong and a perfectly healthy infant died only because the delivery happened away from the advantages of modern medicine. I mention this because I always told him he could save lives by writing to counter the hundreds of books touting the advantages of home delivery.

Now Dad was off call indefinitely though he was not quite 54. He had been diagnosed with metastatic colon cancer several months earlier and had helped his group find his replacement. I knew he was upset at the loss of his practice because he often remarked how he missed his work and his patients. My sisters and I were planning to take turns staying with my parents while Dad was going through chemotherapy and radiation treatments after tomorrow's colostomy.

I had just arrived at my parents' home. Dinner with them tonight was different than it had been years earlier. When I was growing up, the table had always been so animated. The frantic energy of my two younger sisters, who now both lived in California, was absent. The house was quiet and the cold drab early darkness of November enveloped everything including our feelings.

Even when he was exhausted, Dad had always expressed interest in our lives. Tonight he did not ask about my family, my job or my trip. For a while, the silence was unbroken except for the clinking of silverware and a comment that the salmon was good. My father avoided my glance. I knew he was worried about tomorrow's surgery and the prospect of being progressively less active.

My mother and I desperately groped to fill the silence. We talked about my wife, the new rug and something about taxes. I have often regretted that my mother and I were so uncomfortable with Dad's infirmity that we avoided talking about it. Rather than asking how he felt about it and sharing our feelings, we talked about things that paled in significance. If only I had told him how valuable he was in my life and that it did not matter that he might not feel up to his usual activities. In avoiding discussion of his disease, which was the big white elephant in the room, we ignored our concerns and minimized his. We left him alone in his emotional turmoil.

Because I had arrived in the evening, we had supper late and finished after 10 p.m. Dad and Mom retired to their bedroom. We left the dishes for our beloved housekeeper, Mrs. Farley, who was like one of the family. Mrs. Farley didn't really need the income anymore, and my mother didn't need a housekeeper, but they seemed to need one another at some level.

I can't really say what woke me at 3:10 a.m. from a sound sleep. I heard nothing, but stared at the clock wondering why I was suddenly wide-awake. The light in my bathroom across the hall shone from under the door. Odd, they had their own bathroom off their bedroom and I had left the door open and the light off. I knocked quietly, "Mom? Dad?" No answer. I tried the door which was not locked, but there was resistance. I pushed hard and something dragged on the floor as I slowly forced the door open. Puddles and steaks of red were on the floor, and my father was slumped behind the door in a heap. I stooped down and pushed his head back to see him pale and his eyes half-closed. He did not answer to his name when I said, "Dad, can you hear me?" He fell against me as I rose to get help. I saw a knife on the floor and ran with sticky feet to the phone in the hall entry to call 911. As I dialed, I yelled to my mother, "Come quick! Dad cut himself in the bathroom. I am calling for help." They began giving me instructions. They said, "Is he conscious?" I knew that he was not. Then they said, "Is he breathing?" I had not checked, but I didn't think so. My mother was now in the bathroom. I asked her if he was breathing, but she never answered.

I ran down the stairs to open the door for the paramedics and realized my hands were covered in blood. It seemed there was more blood around than could possibly be from just one person. I could hear the sirens now and ran up to find my mother pressing a towel on his neck. Her eyes were clenched shut and her face hardened into a fixed grimace. The paramedics quickly rolled him onto a sheet and pulled him into the hallway. They began chest compressions and put him on a monitor. They put in IV's and an airway and quickly lifted him onto their stretcher which disappeared down the stairs and out the door.

I ran to my parents' bathroom and rinsed off my hands and arms. I covered my blood-soaked shirt with one of Dad's sweatshirts. I snatched

Chapter 20 Loss of my father to suicide

a clean blouse and skirt from my mother's closet and I wet a facecloth for my mother to use on the way. We rode silently. We were told to wait in the emergency department after they handed us a thick pile of papers to fill out on a clipboard and asked my mother for insurance cards. She had not brought her purse. I had never seen her go anywhere without her purse. It was always on her shoulder to provide everything from money and credit cards to combs, pens, Band-Aids and Kleenex.

Through glass slits in the door from the waiting room, we saw the upper half of the trauma room. There was a bevy of doctors and nurses calling out orders. We could see over their heads as blood packets were put high on hangers. A radiology technician with a portable x-ray machine waited outside the room. The secretary ordered someone to repage vascular. I felt hopeful. A nurse broke away and spoke to a man dressed in green scrubs. Suddenly everyone stopped and stood back. They looked at one another and then down. More people left the room than it should have been able to hold. Others began putting needles into plastic bins on the wall. The secretary said, "Page housekeeping."

The doctor who seemed to be in charge talked with a woman in pink scrubs while she looked at the clock and then wrote on her clipboard. I stood up when the doctor came out, but he went over to a man sitting on a couch behind us. He escorted him into a little side room. As he closed the door, I heard him say, "I am so sorry." We went to the desk again and were told that another emergency had arrived at the same time as my father. A gray-haired doctor and a younger assistant took us aside and commented that we should follow them. They walked into a small room opposite the soda machine. The older one moved a chair in front of us and explained that they never restored a pulse in my father. He had exsanguinated to such a degree at home that he was already gone before I had called 911. He had known my father for years and commented, "Paul knew exactly what he was doing when he severed his left carotid lengthwise." Then he got technical and talked to us as if he were discussing a case with his colleague about any patient he had just pronounced dead. He talked about a trial of transfusions, Doppler pulse checks and other things. I could understand the terms, but found no sense to process it. It no longer mattered. After a few sentences, all I heard was "blah, blah, blah" beyond the din of worrying about the impact of all this on my mother.

I offered to talk to my sisters. They took us into another little room with a white wall phone. My mother sat down and gazed at her hands folded in her lap. She readjusted them several times. I had never had to tell anyone something like this before. I had to be the man. I could not be the boy. I called Dawn first. She was the youngest. I told her in a professional tone,

"Dad was discouraged about the cancer and he took his own life tonight. He is gone. We need to take care of our mother now." At once, I realized how cold that sounded. She made me repeat it three times and then she was silent for a while. She began asking details. I said, "Mom is sitting with me right here and she and I will talk to you when you get here. Let us know as soon as you know when you will be coming." She asked if I had told Emily yet. She said she would call her. I was mad at myself. My mother needed to hear my version of what had happened and it would have been perfectly appropriate to tell Dawn everything we knew. Then I thought, "What kind of father would put his son in this position? How could he do this to me and to Mom and his daughters? Sure it was painful for him to think of being impaired and dependent, but what about us?" I realized I should be mad at the cancer for triggering this entire event, but it was easier to blame my father.

My mother and I went in to see him. He was covered in sheets up to his chin and his eyes were closed. My mother stood there looking at him for what seemed like an hour. I glanced at Dad, but then stared at my mother. She had a blank expression, but her eyes were red and watery. She kissed his cheek, stood up straight, turned away and walked towards the door. Then she came back to look at him again. She said, "Why?" and then her voice broke and she began to cry. She hugged him firmly around his shoulders and kissed his cheek and forehead gently. She drew in a deep breath as if she had a lot to say. She said, "I love you," in a cracked voice. Again she began sobbing and could not finish. She turned to me and said, "We talked about this. I don't mean we talked about THIS, but we talked about what would happen if his cancer took him." Then her voice trailed away and she had that blank expression again. She was staring at me, but somehow not seeing me. She turned slowly back to Dad and said, "I need you right now." She spoke in the tone that one might use to command a child to come to dinner from behind a closed bedroom door, but there was more than a closed door between them now. He just lay there and ignored her plea. When she turned back to me, I went over to her and hugged her. I had not hugged my mother since I was a little kid. Sometimes when we parted, she would stand on her tiptoes and kiss me on the cheek, but we never embraced one another like this. She wept into my chest and I stared at my father silently wondering, "Why?"

A chaplain came in. She told my mother she was very sorry and asked to pray with her. As she put her hand on my mother's shoulder, she offered, "Sometimes it is hard to figure out why things happen like this, but they do. That does not make it any easier for you. God knows, and somehow if you can trust Him, you will be able to accept it one day."

I could see my mother shaking and hear her gasping as she held back her sobs. I suggested, "Mom, why don't we leave now?" She turned back and wrapped her arms around his chest and lifted him against her in a final hug. She then gently laid him back down and kissed him again on his forehead and cheek. The chaplain put her arm around my mother's waist and they walked out past me through the door. There were several nurses hovering around the doorway. They beckoned to me and asked me some questions, but I don't remember what they were. Then they handed me a big plastic bag of his personal effects.

As I finished with the nurses, one of the pastors from our church arrived. My mother knew the minister and suddenly seemed animated and engaged for a few minutes. It was 7 a.m. and she had not slept since finding Dad. On the drive home, she was quiet again and stared straight ahead. When we got back, she sat down in the sunny living room in her chair that was next to Dad's easy chair. After dinner they would sit there beside one another watching the news and reading the newspaper until they went to bed. Now she sat there alone in the daytime. He had already gone to his rest.

I went up to clean the bathroom and put the bloody clothes into the wash, but the bathroom was immaculate and I heard the dryer running in the little kitchenette down the hall from my parents' room. Emily had called Mrs. Farley about Dad, and she had taken it upon herself to rush over and clean everything up. The dishes were done and there was a note that there were sandwiches in the refrigerator.

My mother fell asleep in her chair. At least her eyes were closed. All at once I needed to purge the house of my father's things to spare my mother any sad memories. As I barged into their bedroom, I immediately recognized that their lives were so merged that tampering with any of his things would tamper with hers. She would have to decide what to do with everything and when to do it.

I did not sleep at all that day and my mother never went to bed. When my sisters arrived late that night, my mother and I picked them up at the airport. They hugged me, which was uncharacteristic of our family. Now it was not awkward and it felt right to hug them. All three of us concentrated on Mom. As we dealt with arrangements and concern for our mother, we deferred our own grief.

My sisters assumed a hyperactive response. Within two days and without my mother's input, they cleaned out his things even before the funeral. They emptied his medicine cabinet and his bureau and closets. I heard them nervously laughing about some 70's shirts that they had always worried he would embarrass them by wearing. They saved out clothes that they took to the funeral home. They had me fill the trunk and backseat with at least a dozen huge overfilled bags for a downtown shelter. They had me box up all his periodicals and files for recycling. All the books in the study, except for some children's books, went to Goodwill.

My father killed himself on Thursday, and his service was the next Monday. We had four hours of public visitation and there was a steady throng of people passing by and pausing at his casket. My mother sat in the front, and everyone stopped and bent over to talk with her. I did not recognize one woman approaching me until she said, "You were such an imp! I always worried that you would hurt yourself trying to climb up on those bookcases!" Then I recognized her as the daughter of one of my father's nurses. She had taken care of us for a week when my parents went to the Cape for some medical conference when I was about five. I had wanted to get out of the house and was literally climbing the walls. The conversation seemed inappropriate, but it was a nice distraction.

My mother's only truly executive decision had been that the grandchildren not be a part of this unstable period in her life. For the funeral, we decided that there would be no eulogies because he was young enough that everyone knew what a great person he was both personally and professionally. The attendance at the service was massive with standing room only because Dad very well-known in the medical community.

We came back to the church from the cemetery in the late afternoon for a reception that my sisters had planned. I stood beside my mother and brought her sandwiches and punch as she accepted the condolences of hundreds of guests. I was awed by the sheer number of people who were teary-eyed from losing their friend and colleague.

The house seemed so drab. My mother never again went into the hallway with that bathroom in which he took his life. She went up to her bedroom using the back stairs to avoid passing it. My mother said that she did not want to stay there and needed a fresh start. My sisters stayed with her for several weeks. Before I left, I went over the financials and summarized them for my mother.

The Christmas holidays were only weeks away when Dad died. Christmases had always been my mother's glorious presentation to everyone. She would impeccably decorate the house and fill the tree with an abundance of gifts and special stockings for everyone. The whole family would gather and the celebration awed everyone. Over this first Christmas season without Dad, my sisters went back home with their families briefly until Christmas night. My wife and I arrived Christmas Eve and found my mother sitting in the dark in her favorite chair. She said she had not realized that daylight was gone. The scene was a stark contrast to the brightly lit tree and anticipation of Christmas morning from past years.

We brought her a little toy poodle puppy which hopped onto her lap, licked her face and then jumped down and began running from one end of the grand living room to the other. The puppy skidded on the floor and collided with the wall. My mother smiled for the first time since Dad's death. She gathered up towels for bedding and cuddled him as he fell asleep. Meanwhile, she protested that we had to take him back. By Christmas morning, her attention was focused on preventing the tiny ball of fur from being stepped on. She carried him around and smiled when he protested as she tried to set him in the large plastic bin she was using as his bed.

My sisters had moved to California within months of one another about seven years earlier and Mom had taken her long separations from them very hard. Within a few months of Dad's death, she and her little poodle moved next door to my older sister and her four school-aged children. She loved having daily contact with them. She told me that she felt Dad smiling upon her as she was reunited with her daughters. She said that before he became sick, they had planned to move near the girls after his retirement in eleven years. Dad's death had reunited her with her daughters and grandchildren, but his early forced retirement could have led to the same result.

My initial sorrow at Dad's death was mainly from watching my mother and sisters grieving. I wanted to help them through it and protect them by being a substitute for that strong man who was now absent from all our lives. I accompanied Mom to California to find her a new house and I dealt with the realtor to sell the one in Manhattan.

It has been fifteen years since my father died, and I miss him most profoundly every holiday. I never miss a Christmas with my sisters and mother. My mother and sisters always come East to visit us for a few weeks each summer. We take a lot of photos and my children get to interact with their California cousins.

I am always sad whenever I think of that awful lone decision he made to end his life. It was probably a sudden desperate reaction. His oncologist friends tried to comfort us by saying that he might not have survived his disease for long. But even though his initial prognosis was grim, it would likely improve with ongoing progress in treatments. No one ever knows how well any one person with a given disease will do. Ironically, I learned that from my father.

I am certain that if I had said the right things to my father that night, he would not have taken his life. I regret that and I always will. He needed to hear that he had a significant and vital role in my life. I should have reminded him that he could benefit others by writing about his experiences and perspectives. His silence that night was a plea for us to say, "We know you will get through this because we need you and we love you." Why didn't I say that? It was not like our family to say the obvious. Until Dad died I never said, "I love you. I miss you. I need you in my life." Now there is seldom an interaction with my wife, my children, and the rest of my family without my saying that. I had always thought it was a little metro for a man to express those feelings, but not anymore.

I am often asked what I learned from this tragedy. It is simply, "State and discuss obvious concerns and problems with loved ones, and do not ever delay telling them that you love them and that they are important to you." It seems so simple. You might reply, "Of course they know I love them and appreciate them." My response is, "But they need to hear it. It won't hurt for them to hear it."

Not a day goes by that I do not email or call my mother. I tell her frequently that I love her and how much she means to me. I am the same with my wife and my three wonderful children. I remind them to talk to me about anything and everything. We share and we love. I talk to my father whenever I miss him and feel guilty about his death. I tell him that I learned the importance of directly discussing feelings of love and need too late to help him. However, because of him, I give generous doses of expressions of love and appreciation to the family he left behind.

CHAPTER 21

Loss of my father in a private plane crash
by Rachel Courtney

James Courtney III was a lawyer, private pilot and father of three.

I lost my dad in a plane crash when I was 26. We were very close. He was a lawyer, an avid fisherman, hunter, sailor and a private pilot. Flying was one of his favorite hobbies. He was flying to a hearing in Wisconsin from Minnesota. When he did not show up, the courthouse called his office and his office called the airport. They immediately tried to track him down.

My brother called me the day my dad's plane went missing, but I didn't get the message until the following day because I was traveling and did not have a cell phone. I was living in Washington DC, but was in California looking at a job and thinking about moving there. My brother had been desperately trying to reach me. Finally he had to leave a message on the phone. I checked my messages on a pay phone. In the message, he was very choked up and crying, "Dad's plane is missing and we can't find him, so you need to call me." When I heard it, I just froze. It was the first time in my life I felt such shock that I literally could not speak. I was with my boyfriend, and I had to hand him the phone to listen to the voice mail himself. Then I called my brother who reiterated, "Rachel, you need to come home. Dad's plane is missing." I just said, "Okay." Then I went further into a total state of shock and utter disbelief. At the same time, since they hadn't found his airplane, I had this overwhelming fear that he was injured and needed us. I went into autopilot mode. I knew I had to get home to find him, so for a while it was all about getting a plane ticket. That day I took a red-eye flight back to Minnesota.

I arrived in Minnesota at 6:30 in the morning and my brother picked me up at the airport. We went to the small private airport where my dad had taken off and where my stepmom and other family members and friends were waiting. We spent the entire day trying to get information about where his plane was going and what had happened. At the end of the day when the sun started going down, I remember going into a room by myself and having a meltdown. I just started sobbing. It was raining and I remember thinking that my dad was cold, but no one was helping him because nobody could get to him. I had an overwhelming sense of helplessness and inability to do anything. I was just really sad. My brother came into the room while I was sitting there. He sort of smiled at me. I looked up at him and I said, "What?" He said, "I sat here in this exact same seat doing the exact same thing last night."

My family was absolutely crucial in those initial moments. Everybody came together immediately to provide support. That was essential. My dad died with his legal assistant, so her family was there going through the same thing. It was really important that we all bonded together. All of us had the same interest in finding their plane and finding out what happened to them.

While we were stationed at the airport, we had to get our information from the Civil Air Patrol, which is an auxiliary branch of the Air Force consisting of private pilots. They had immediately stepped in. We needed information from his flight plan and from the last radar bleeps of his airplane in order to close in on his plane. After we narrowed down the area, we relocated to another airport closer to the place where we thought the airplane had crashed. We plotted out the entire 50- to 100-square-mile area where we thought the plane might be. We set up a volunteer branch there to walk through the woods to search the area.

James Courtney and his wife Marcia on their wedding day.

We spent a little over two weeks looking for the airplane. That experience was isolating because it didn't seem like anyone beyond us could understand what we were going through. I didn't think anyone else besides my family understood that feeling of not being able to find him and of not knowing whether he was alive or dead. My stepmom definitely gave me a lot of comfort. I could talk to her and hold her up when she was falling down, and she held me up when I was falling down. I remember feeling very helpless when my stepmom got really sad. She was very driven to find my dad, so when the Civil Air Patrol decided they were not going to look for him any longer, she had a real meltdown with crying and screaming. That was very difficult because she was always strong. Although it was right for her to break down, it was scary because she had been holding up everybody else.

We got a lot of support from the owners of the private airport and from the private airline community since my dad was very involved in it. The NTSB, the Civil Air Patrol and the sheriff were involved at different times

Chapter 21 Loss of my father in a private plane crash

and for different aspects, but there was a lack of communication among them. It was never really clear to us who was in charge, who was looking for the plane, and who was responsible for finding the body. We never knew whom to go to for information. It was very frustrating because there was no organized approach to finding my dad. We needed someone to take the lead and to coordinate the search efforts.

Because the plane crashed in the woods in the summertime, the ground was covered by greenery and virtually impossible to see. I remember calling the Air Force captain in charge of the Civil Air Patrol to ask him why they were calling off the search. He said, "We search only for survivors and we don't think your dad could have survived for more than eleven days." I asked the captain, "What would you do if you were in our shoes and this was your family member?" He said, "Honestly, I would wait until the leaves fall. Then you can find him." That was not a good answer for us. We asked volunteers to keep looking for him from the air and we paid for the gasoline. We asked others to keep searching for him on the ground. We had over 300 volunteers. The Salvation Army and the Red Cross were involved because he was missing for so long. The Salvation Army brought in a van to feed everybody at least two meals a day. That was really helpful. My stepmom and I gridded the maps around the flight path to determine where people had already looked and where they should look next.

Because the plane hadn't been found for a couple of weeks, the story of the missing airplane was in the media and the news. The public was asked to keep an eye out for it. A man named Bigz, who was a leader of an Indian tribe in Wisconsin, heard about it. He got up on the morning of August 21, gave a tobacco offering and asked a friend to fly him up to find this man he had seen on the news. He came to the airport where we were camped to see what we had done and what we knew about his flight. Then he headed out. Within only thirty minutes, he came back and announced that he had seen the plane. Bigz had only one eye and there had already been over a thousand flight hours logged in searching without success for the plane, but Bigz found it in less than an hour.

My dad's plane crashed on August 4, and we found him two days before his birthday on August 21. As soon as I heard that Bigz had found his plane, I knew in my heart and my head that my dad was dead. I knew there was no way he could have survived for three weeks in the woods. Despite knowing that, there was still a glimmer of hope because we didn't yet have the body or any remains. There might, by some miracle, be a chance that he had survived. I remember asking Bigz if the airplane door was open, thinking maybe my dad had just walked away. He looked puzzled and said, "I don't know." I could tell by his expression that the airplane had been totaled.

When Bigz returned, I was at the airport with my mom. I immediately called the sheriff's office with the exact location of the airplane. I also had to call my stepmom and my brother to tell them we had found the plane and that they needed to come back to the airport. That was really hard. When I reached my stepmom on the phone, I wasn't able to tell her. I couldn't talk, so I handed the phone to my mom to tell my stepmom, "We found Jim. We found Jim!" The airport was about three hours from the house. While my brother and stepmom were flying down, the sheriff went out to locate the remains of my dad and his legal assistant.

When the sheriff came back, he said, "We found them and we have confirmed that it is them and that they are dead." We had nearly three weeks to process it and to know that this would be the result, but it was still a total shock. All of us broke down. The sheriff asked my stepmom for dental records. She said, "Well, you can just check his wallet. It is in his pocket." They just stared at her, and finally said, "There is no body. The whole body was burned." Now we would never know, "Did he know he was going to crash? Did he know he was going to die? Was he afraid? Did he feel anything?"

Once we found his body, my sister, my brother, my stepmom and I planned his funeral. We had a big memorial service. The service provided me with so much comfort because all the people who came said wonderful things about him, his effect on their lives, and what a great person he was. I heard nice things about him that I would have never known otherwise. Some talked about how he was so proud of me. It was comforting that I had a good relationship with my dad and that the last thing I said to him was "I love you". That gave me a lot of peace.

James Courtney with his wife Marcia and two daughters, Anna and Rachel.

The most painful aspect of losing my dad was the realization that I would never see him again. He was not going to be at my wedding or meet my children. He was not going to be there when I would really need him. That realization was the hardest part. It was difficult seeing my little sister so sad. She was only ten when he died, so she wasn't going to have a dad in her life as she grew. That really broke my heart. As time went on, it was very hard to not be able to pick up the phone to call him as I had about all kinds of issues. I was used to just picking up the phone and calling him. I couldn't do that anymore. There were times when I thought about calling him. Then I had to realize once again that he was gone.

After the plane crash and after we found my dad, I left Minnesota and went back to work. I felt like I had been living in a nightmare and dream for a month. When I went back into the real world, I felt that everyone should have known what I had been through even though they had no way of knowing. It seemed weird to be walking down the street after being totally ensconced for a month completely immersed with thinking about and dealing with the plane crash and the loss of my dad. When the rest of the world just kept moving on, I felt very alone because I had just spent three weeks looking for my dad's body, finally finding it and having a memorial service. It had been like living in a separate dream world, but now I had to go back to work and into a semblance of normal life with people who had not experienced all that. I noticed a distance between me and my friends at work. No one was insensitive about it, but they really didn't know what to say. I felt very lonely.

Often people do not know what to say to someone who has just lost a family member, let alone a family member in a plane crash with a lot of publicity and delays in locating the remains. There was someone who worked down the hall from me that I didn't know. The first day I returned to work, he came down to my office and gave me a hug. He said that he felt terrible about what had happened to me and if there was anything he could do to help, he was just down the hall. There were many other acts of kindness. My company donated a thousand dollars to the charity fund to help pay for the gasoline to look for my dad, and the people I worked with donated hundreds of dollars as well. It felt very good that people were willing to help.

I definitely became closer to my stepmom, my brother and my sister when my dad died. We were the ones with the closest connection to him, and we really supported each other. A few months after the crash, I distanced myself a little bit from my brother. We just had very different views of my dad and how we were going to deal with the way that he died. We grew apart somewhat during that time, but eventually came back as close as ever.

In one of my first dreams about the crash, I was with a person who said he was in the back of the airplane when it crashed, so he knew what had happened. I kept begging him to tell me how the plane crashed, but he would not tell me because he thought I couldn't handle it. My dad was always alive in my dreams. I remember thinking how great it was to see him. In the first good dream I had about him, I saw him in front of me as I was walking down a hallway. I started running after him and yelling, "Dad! Dad!" When he got to the stairwell, he turned and started down the stairs. Halfway down the stairs, he stopped and turned to look at me with his bright blue eyes and wearing his bomber flying jacket. He winked at me and gave me the thumbs up. I remember just feeling so excited in the dream that I had seen him and that it felt so real. I ran down the stairs after him, but the hallway was empty.

My life is different without my dad in good and bad ways. In a bad way, I lost this person whom I really loved, looked up to and admired. In a good sense, it makes me try to be more like him by taking on those characteristics that I loved, valued and admired in him. It also makes me appreciate so much more the family I do have. Losing my dad so suddenly changed the way I think about the people in my life. Now I always leave on a good note. Every relationship counts for something.

I learned that it was important to talk about what had happened, how I felt and to keep his memory alive in a healthy way to make sure that he was still a part of my life. There is probably not a day that goes by that I do not think about him or that he does not pop into my mind. That happens mostly when I am trying to make a decision because I used to call him whenever I had decisions to make about work, relationships or just life in general. Now I stop and think, "If I could pick up the phone to talk to him, what would he say?"

One of the hardest things for me is going home to where we lived. We spread his ashes on an island outside of the house. When I look out onto the water, I can just see him on a boat or fishing. I remember what a wonderful life we had together and what good times we had, so it is really painful that he is not there anymore.

On the anniversary of my dad's death, I talk to my brother and my stepmom to be sure that they are doing okay. We remember him and sometimes tell funny stories about him. The rest of the day I make sure that I take care of myself and let myself feel sad and talk about him with whomever I want.

After my dad died, I left Washington DC immediately and moved to California without really thinking too much about it. It just seemed that the right thing to do was to fill my life up with a new job and new people. I tried to keep myself really busy. I wasn't taking the time to genuinely feel sad about what had happened. Rather than grieve about my dad, I became busy with new things so I didn't have to deal with it.

I contacted ACCESS about a year after my dad died because it wasn't until then that I started processing my grief. I found that the world was moving on while I wasn't in some ways. I looked for an organization with people who had gone through something similar. I came across ACCESS and searched their website. Heidi called me and made a connection. She put me in touch with a woman who had lost her father on a small Delta commuter flight outside of Atlanta. Just having someone else to talk to and connect with who had gone through something similar was a very important thing.

Later, I went to an ACCESS grief mentor training session. I became a mentor to a woman who had lost her father in a crash in Minnesota, which is where my father died. I also mentored a woman who had lost her father in a Colorado crash. I found it very rewarding to offer words of encouragement to another person going through the same thing I had gone through. I am pleased that I can offer a listening ear to others in a similar situation. I let them know that no matter how difficult it is, they are going to make it. When I meet others who have lost family members suddenly in air disasters, the most important thing I tell them is, "You are going to feel sad and there is no way around it. You will have to go through horrible pain, disbelief and shock. People can hold you and hold your hand and they can hug you, but ultimately you are the one who will have to get through it. The truth is, you will get through it, but it is going to be a long road and it's going to be a difficult road."

It has been so very helpful to me to be with others who have lost loved ones in air disasters because it feels like we are a community. We all know that shock of learning that people have been suddenly taken away from us, and we all know that period of not knowing what happened to them, and not really knowing whether they are dead or alive. It is comforting to talk to other people who have gone through that. That community is an ongoing supportive and meaningful network.

CHAPTER 22

Loss of my son on Pan Am 103
by Betty Capasso

My 21-year-old son Gregory was on Pan Am 103 when it exploded over Lockerbie, Scotland on December 21, 1988. He was an exchange student in London as a senior at Buffalo University in New York.

The day of the crash was the worst day of my life. My mother called to ask me which plane Gregory was on. She said that a plane had gone down. When I turned on the TV, I saw that the plane that had exploded was Greg's. My initial reaction was just absolute disbelief, "How could this be happening?" Yet I knew it was real. My husband was on his way home. I remember screaming out to him, "Greggy's plane went down! Greggy's plane went down!" He turned absolutely white and just stood there. He showed me a gift he had just bought for him. It was a cologne bottle with Greg's name engraved on the cap. We said, "What do we do? What do we do?" We started calling Pan Am. Then people began calling us to find out if Greg was on the plane. We kept calling Pan Am for any information, but we were unsuccessful. When I called Heathrow Airport, they told me they had his boarding pass, so I knew he was on the flight. Pan Am did not call me until 11 a.m. the next day. Their excuse for not calling sooner was, "Well, it was the middle of the night. We did not want to wake you." As if they could have woken me up! How could I sleep?

It became very apparent to me that I needed to speak to other people going through this. I asked everyone who called or came to my home if they knew of any other family members willing to talk about what had happened. I found out about a press conference being held at the Hyatt Hotel in Manhattan. I met other family members there and we planned a meeting at someone's home. That is when the Pan Am organization began. The group was my main source of comfort. Also, we had lost my brother fourteen years earlier when he drowned on his honeymoon. That was also very sudden and tragic. Because he died in Hawaii, we had to wait for his body. There were some similarities to what happened with Gregory, so my sister and my mother were well aware of my feelings. Some friends became closer and did not turn away. They could deal with my ups and downs. Others recognized that if it happened to me, it could happen to them. That possibility frightened them, so they distanced themselves.

I went back to work a little more than a month after Gregory died. I remember walking the streets of downtown Manhattan under scaffolding. I thought to myself, "Maybe something will fall and hit me on the head and put me out of my misery." I just wanted the pain to go away. The pain can be so excruciating. It is really hard to imagine unless you have experienced this kind of loss. The Pan Am organization was such a source of comfort for me because I met people with the same flashbacks, emotions and ups and downs. One woman said that she kept seeing planes exploding in the air. I said, "I do too." Having other people say that they were having the same thoughts was very helpful. I remember not being able to concentrate and jumping at every sound. Without the Pan Am group, I would have thought I was going crazy.

For the first year, I was very involved in the Pan Am organization and trying to find out what happened. I felt betrayed because Pan Am had warnings. We learned that when one employee reported that they were vulnerable to a terrorist attack, he was told, "Thank you very much for the information. You're fired." When the bomb was put on the plane, they were supposed to remove any luggage that did not match with a passenger, but there were seven pieces not matched to passengers, including the one that contained the bomb.

The airlines gave us a buddy. He was very nice, but I found it unnerving that every time I spoke to him he was typing away. He was upset with me when I did not want to fly on Pan Am to a memorial service. We were informed that Greg had been identified on the 28th of December. My brother-in-law went with the Pan Am buddy to accompany him back to the States. We had already scheduled Greg's memorial service while Greg's friends were all home from college on their holiday break. After Greg was returned in January, we had a very short service before he was cremated.

We went to Lockerbie for a dedication in a rose garden at the church near where the plane had fallen. The families there knew every victim by name and had everybody's picture up on a board. It amazed me. Two families took us out to eat. Another family invited us to their home for dinner. The Lockerbie people had even washed and ironed all the clothing from the crash.

I received Greg's tape cassette case. The case itself looked fine, but every cassette was cracked and dirt-encrusted. I still have that, and it is a reminder and a symbol of what happened to Gregory. We got one picture of Greg from his belongings when he was found. When I looked at that picture, I literally felt Greg come into my arms and that he was there with me. I will never forget that feeling. It took a long time to get some of his property back

Chapter 22 Loss of my son on Pan Am 103

because it was held for the criminal trial. After thirteen years, Greg's license and student photo ID card were returned. When I opened up the envelope and saw his picture on his two pieces of identification, it took me right back to day one.

I left Greg's things the way they were in his room for a very long time. I went in there periodically, but I did not really start to clean up for a long time. I gave his acoustic guitar to his very good friend who was a musician. I gave the little kids in the family his vast collection of stuffed animals. I gave his friends and his cousins what they wanted of Gregory's because it was very helpful for me that his things were cherished by others. We still had Greg's clothes when we moved nine years later, so I felt that Greg moved with us. His pictures are around the new house.

Having lost a sibling myself, I knew some of the feelings that my older son Andrew was experiencing. When parents lose a child, they become very focused on the child they lost, and sometimes lose sight of the needs of the surviving children. Andrew was already away at law school, but I recognized that he needed to be included in whatever decisions we made. I found myself becoming overprotective. I needed to know where Andrew was at all times. I told him, "Please bear with me. I am just scared that something's going to happen to you."

After the crash, my husband and I absolutely fell apart. We had individual therapy and the support of the Pan Am family group. The group was especially helpful because men and women do not always grieve the same way, and people who are married to each other do not necessarily grieve the same. I had the opportunity to talk with other mothers. My husband talked to other fathers. When we go to a dinner meeting, the men tend to sit together. My husband tells me that the men share feelings they would be unlikely to share with the larger group.

After the first year, society began telling us that we were supposed to be through the major part of grieving, but I wasn't. Then the second year was difficult, and the third year was very difficult. After many years, it got a little lighter. It was not so hard anymore. The Christmas holidays were especially still very hard because the crash happened so close to Christmas, but all the holidays were tough. I still take off Greg's birthday and death day because those are days that belong to him. I do not want to share them because I feel so awful on those days. The pain is still there, but not so intense all the time. It will never go away. To me, "closure" is a word that should be eradicated in discussions of grief. To have closure, I would need to have Gregory back alive. I have learned to live with it. I have learned to deal with it. My life is transformed into something else, but the pain is always there and the hole just never closes. It can be opened when even scratched at any time. When 9/11 happened, I instantly went back to the day of the Pan Am crash. Gregory would have been 33 and I wondered what he would be doing. How would he be different? Would he be married? Would he have a family?

I slowly began to revaluate my life. I had always wanted to be a social worker and a clinical therapist. Greg's death made it apparent that there was nothing that would make more sense. I finished my bachelor's degree and then my master's in social work. It was the most rewarding thing I have ever done. It makes me feel like I have a purpose and a function to fulfill. Greg would not have wanted his family to crawl into a hole and never come out. I know he is always looking down and thinking, "Mom, go for it!" He is always with me and part of who I am.

CHAPTER 23

Loss of my husband in a private plane crash
by Veronica Campanelli

Michael and Veronica Campanelli on their wedding day.

I lost my husband Michael on a small carrier flight on April 4, 2003. He was a designer and a furniture maker. We met at the Metropolitan Museum of Art where we worked as security officers. We were together for eight years before we were married. After two years of marriage, we were planning to start a family.

His work involved much traveling. The morning of the crash, he got up early to fly out to Martha's Vineyard. We made evening dinner plans because he was coming back in the late afternoon. He told me he loved me and we gave each other a hug. I watched him walk down the block and out of sight. I never saw him again.

He was not supposed to be on that plane. He had a long-standing dental appointment that day because he had been in a lot of pain, but his employer called the night before to ask him to go on the project because he did not want to go. I said, "Don't go. Go to the dentist." He said, "Well, my boss asked me, and I should really go." I said, "Yeah, but you really do not want to put this off for another week." Then I dropped it. Usually whenever he had to take these small carrier planes to his job, I would give him some resistance and vocalize my fear and anxiety. He would calm me down. This time I did not want to do that because he was already upset about missing his dental appointment. I thought I was doing him a favor, but looking back on it, I wish I had kept saying, "No, don't go. Go to your dental appointment. Please stay home!"

I was at work when his employer called. As soon as I heard his voice, I broke down because I knew something was not right. He told me the plane went down in the outskirts of Massachusetts and that there were survivors. At that moment, though I had some hope in the back of my mind, I just knew he was gone. I remember screaming "No!" and throwing the receiver at the wall in front of my desk as I fell to the ground. I was spread out there crying and sobbing uncontrollably. I remember screaming "No! No! No!" over and over again. I could not control it. I could almost hear my screams echoing throughout the gallery as if I were somehow outside of my body.

My father brought me to my parents' home. During the drive it was confirmed that Michael was dead. I was going in and out of awareness about this and remember asking, "How do you know? I want to know for sure." They said, "Well, we have his ID. We have his wallet." I kept thinking, "Okay, so maybe you have his ID, but maybe he is somewhere else. Maybe he was able to escape. Maybe he is still out there." I just wanted to get into the car to be with him and to find him somehow. Someone told me they were preparing his remains to be brought to me. The idea of his remains in the hospital or in the coroner's office seemed wrong. He was there all by himself. I just felt so guilty that I could not be with him that night. That was the first of many sleepless nights. I do not think I really slept for about a year.

It was surreal. One moment I was planning what to make for dinner or where we were going for dinner, and the next moment my mother was asking me, "Veronica, do you want a burial or a cremation?" I was 31 years old and had never thought about anything like that. We were thinking about our options for different types of homes to buy and planning a family. Then I had to make a decision about what to do with his remains. That night they showed his picture on the news. It was the picture from his driver's license. I felt violated in a way because in my heart I did not know for sure that he was really gone. It felt horrible and it just crushed my hopes.

I wanted to take my own life almost immediately after the accident. I went into the bathroom, locked the door and took whatever was in the medicine cabinet. I just lay down on the floor and cried. The next thing I knew, I was waking up in the emergency room. I was disappointed that I was alive and still had to live through this. It was one of the saddest feelings ever. I thought, "No! I cannot believe I woke up. I do not want to wake up." I wanted to be alone, did not want to get out of bed, and did not want to eat.

Michael just seemed so far away and so gone. I could not do anything. I was totally helpless. There was nothing I could do. One moment I was in complete denial, "This cannot be! This isn't happening!" The next moment I was angry, frustrated and utterly sad. Some of my anger was at the very person who called me when the plane went down because he was supposed to be on the plane instead of Michael.

Before Michael passed away, I felt very strong and content with him and with my work situation. I was in graduate school. My faith was at a huge high. Now there was anger at my religion because it did not seem fair. This "who gets to live and who has to die" did not make any sense. I felt very punished and took it personally. I thought, "How could God do this to me? How could he take this amazing person off the planet?" He was

Chapter 23 Loss of my husband in a private plane crash

After two years of marriage, Michael and Veronica Campanelli were planning a family.

the most sweet and gentle guy. He was the one who was so incredibly special. Why did it have to be him? Why couldn't it have been me? He had brothers in the fire department and the police department. His oldest brother is a pilot. I could understand if something happened to one of them because they are in high-risk jobs, but they are still here. Michael designed furniture, so why did he have to die in a plane crash? It just did not add up.

There were seven people in the plane including the pilot and copilot. The only survivor was a sixteen-year-old girl who lost her parents in the crash. She walked away with a sprained ankle. That was always such a challenge for me. It almost seemed like someone said, "Okay. You, you and you, but you're gonna stay." I felt sort of jealous and at once guilty for those feelings. After I met her, I realized, "My goodness! Think what she is going through and what she will go through for the rest of her life from that experience!" At the end of the day, she gave me much strength from her surviving the whole experience.

She said that everything happened quickly in those last critical moments of the flight. She was flying in the back of the plane and was nervous because she did not like flying and the weather had not been great. Michael made her feel really comfortable and even laugh. Knowing that he helped her, which was so typical of him, just made me love him even more. Then there was a lot of turbulence, so she was getting nervous again. Michael said something to make her laugh and smile again just as she heard her father say, "Oh, God!" And that was it. The next thing she remembers is walking out of the plane by stepping over her mother, who was upside down with her seat belt still on. Right after she escaped, the plane exploded and burned.

Michael's funeral service was in the same church with the same priest who had married us. A couple of months later, I drove to the crash site with my family on a beautiful sunny day. I had to see it to believe it and I had to spend some time there. There was still wreckage scattered around and a tarp over an area that was particularly burnt. I placed his picture and some flowers at the site.

My job was pretty high-level and stressful with a lot of responsibilities. I was very proud of those responsibilities and my boss missed me, so I went right back to work after two weeks. It was hard because that is where I found out about the accident. I was dealing with that first memory as well as the day-to-day challenges. Staying incredibly busy and feeling that I had a responsibility for myself and for others helped keep me going. Other people depended on me and needed me. I did not want to let anybody down.

After I returned to work, I had low points when I felt I was at the bottom of a well. Those feelings have dissipated to some degree over the years, but there are still times when I am in that well and just want to stay underneath the covers and not get out of bed. One of the things I have learned from being in that well so often is that it will pass. I realize, "Okay, I'm down in the well now and I will be there again, but it is not forever."

I did not realize that death, particularly a sudden tragic death, is very difficult to understand for those who have never experienced such a loss. Many did not know what to say or do. Some were scared to be around me, perhaps because they felt it was contagious or because they did not want to deal with it. Some of those people are not in my life anymore, which has been a sad additional loss for me. This crisis situation was very revealing. I found out who was truly there for me and truly in my corner. There were so many people who were so incredibly supportive. Their presence alone, their hugs, their going out for food and for walks with me, and just my knowing they were there for me were key to my survival. I did not say much and was probably just staring into space, but I knew they were there.

I did not really start to get on with my life until maybe about a year or two afterward with the help of family, friends and even some books. Maybe it was divine intervention, but I heard Michael tell me that he was still here supporting me. He assured me that I could go on. I realized he would never want me to live in such agony. At that point, I began really trying to help myself get out of that deep well of hopelessness. I sought help in any way, in any shape, and in any form I could. I sought out therapy, which proved to be incredibly helpful. It helped to talk about my experiences and my feelings with someone who was there just to listen. I joined a widows' support group. The experiences of others who had lost a spouse were critical because we shared a common pain and loss. Hearing stories of others who had survived similar losses helped me realize, "If they can do it, I can do it by learning from their experiences." Even now, whenever I need support, I call on friends from that group that are like family to me because they truly understand what I am facing. They never judge or criticize me.

I began writing about my thoughts, my memories and my dreams. Those writings helped me realize how much I loved him and he loved me. I looked at photographs of us together and remembered the things that we did together. I went to events that Michael and I had attended and places we had visited together to soothe me. We loved the Brooklyn Botanic Garden, so I walked through the Garden. We loved to bike, so I took my bike on paths we used to take together. I went to our favorite restaurants and our bookstores. I gravitated towards these places.

The main way I honor Michael is by taking on some of his wonderful

Chapter 23 Loss of my husband in a private plane crash

traits and going about my daily life as he did. He was a loving and gentle soul who was always nonjudgmental and almost fearless to pursue our life's dreams. I strive to be like him. I memorialize him by doing the things I know would make him proud of me in the midst of all the chaos since his death. Whenever I cook, make the house beautiful, and do the things he loved to do, I am memorializing him. When I completed my graduate degree, I dedicated my thesis to him.

Right after the accident, one of his pieces was featured on the cover of *Elle Décor*. He never saw his work come to fruition with that much public exposure. He didn't get the credit for it initially, so I wrote a letter to the editor and to the magazine to let them know about him and his work. In response, the following month there was an article in the magazine about his life and his work. Doing something to make others appreciate his work meant a lot to me.

Michael had a lot of belongings because he was an artist, a collector, and a furniture maker. For several months, I kept everything in the apartment exactly the way it was at the time of his death. I left his shoes in the middle of the living room floor where he had left them. I would just walk over them. When anyone came over, they would have to walk over them too. I kept it very shrine-like and very much a time-warp zone. After two years, I took all of his clothes to an organization for families in need. It felt good that someone would benefit from the clothes that he was so selective in choosing.

I first learned about ACCESS at work when I was organizing our files. I found a brochure in the nonprofit section. I read through it and looked at the website. I was so happy that it existed. I just felt so proud that Heidi, someone like me, could come away from this experience to influence and motivate so many other people to honor loved ones with the activity of being there for others in a similar situation. At last I did not feel alone in my type of loss. I felt, "Wow! People like me have a voice out there." I was still working and still processing what had happened to me, but I made copies of the materials and held onto them until I felt ready to be in a position to help others and could go to the volunteer grief mentor training.

After Michael died, everything just stopped. Even when it picked up again, it was at a slower pace with much more appreciation for so many different things. I see beauty in music and in common things, such as birds and the sun shining through the leaves in the morning. I had taken them for granted when I was just rushing through life. Now I live literally moment to moment. I just put one foot in front of the other in baby steps because sometimes I do not know what I am doing or where my path will finally lead. My dreams in life were really Michael's and mine together. Even though he was gone, I still had them. I still wanted a home in the area where we had decided to live, so I bought a beautiful home there. I know it is a place he would have loved. It brings me joy that I am still fulfilling a part of our dreams.

I call the anniversaries "mark dates". I always have a plan for his birthday, the holidays, and especially the day of the crash. I take that death day off from work to do something meditative and healing, such as going to a cathedral or walking in a park. Each year it is something different.

If we could relive our lives together, I would not sweat the small stuff. I realize that things that seemed really important or detrimental before Michael died weren't really significant at all. It was not really important to stay at work until nine or ten o'clock at night. I wish I had come home in time for dinner more often and I wish I had spent more time with him. I just thought we had all the time in the world.

For someone who is now just experiencing such a sudden and tragic loss, the greatest comfort I can bring is that I went through a similar experience and I am still here. You are not alone because so many of us appreciate the magnitude of what you are going through and are here for you as proof and reassurance that you can get through it too.

CHAPTER 24

Loss of my parents on Air France Flight 007
by Nina Crimm

My mother and father were killed in an airplane crash on June 3, 1962. I was ten years old and my brothers were eight and twelve. My mother was very involved in our synagogue as a volunteer. She was a gardener and loved to help people. My father was a transportation attorney. In building his own law practice, he worked long hours and traveled a great deal.

The accident occurred on a Sunday morning when my parents were returning from Paris on Air France. Their plane crashed and exploded at the end of the runway as it began to lift. At about seven in the morning, our sitter awakened my brothers and me without any explanation and shepherded us to the country club. We usually went there to swim. Since I had never been swimming at that hour, I knew something was awry. Then I remembered I had told my mother about a week before their trip that I had a premonition that they would not return. They were frequent travelers, but previously I had never had such a feeling. I had tried to convince my mother that they should not go, but she insisted that everything would be all right.

When we were brought to the county club that morning, I felt that the worst had already happened. As we sat there, we asked the sitter over and over again if we could go home to get prepared for our parents' return. My younger brother had just had his eighth birthday, so we were planning a small birthday and welcome home celebration with my parents. She repeatedly told us, "No, we cannot go home." Many hours later, an announcement came over the intercom requesting her to come to the telephone. I listened to her conversation but did not learn very much. We piled into her Ford Valiant and rode back to the house. I saw many parked cars as we approached our street, so I thought somebody was having some function. Then I saw several cars parked in our driveway. It gave me confirmation that something was wrong. As we got out of the car, the front door of our house opened. This was another sign that something bad had happened because we always entered through the kitchen door.

We walked into the living room and saw our pediatrician, our rabbi, a neighbor physician and an aunt. They said, "Come in. Come in." We walked in hesitatingly and sat down. The rabbi told us that something had happened to our parents. My older brother said, "Well, what has happened?" The rabbi responded, "Your parents will not be coming home today." My brother then asked, "When will they be coming home?" At that point, I was so frustrated and so upset that I just blurted out, "Don't you understand? They'll never be home. They're dead! They're dead!" My younger brother ran out of the living room and into my parents' bathroom. I ran after him and said, "Don't worry. I will take care of you." The rabbi did not tell us directly that our parents had been killed. He informed us only in this backhanded manner, and then we were sent off to our respective bedrooms. The pediatrician came in and insisted on giving each of us an injection of a sedative. Of course we fell asleep. When we awoke, we were each alone in our dark bedrooms.

I desperately needed to be told a little about what had happened and what to expect. I needed to be surrounded by loving relatives, such as my maternal aunt. It was awful to have a lot of non-family members who did not have an intimate interest in us watch our initial reactions to the news. It was just wrong at many levels.

I remember feeling very alone. A lot of adults I did not know came to our house. My own friends were not permitted there, so I felt very isolated. After a week or two, my brothers and I were informed that we would remain together in our home in Atlanta with a relative who would come to live with us. Days before the accident, my father had changed his will to appoint his unmarried sister as our guardian instead of our very sweet maternal aunt whom we all loved. Because there was some concern as to whether my father's sister would be the best guardian, my mother's family considered contesting the will. We were taken to the courthouse where the judge asked us if we wanted to live with our paternal aunt. I answered very honestly, "No, I don't want to live with her." I had no impact on the judge and she was appointed our guardian.

The three of us were orphaned and very lonely. Our aunt sternly instructed us to play quietly in our own rooms and occasionally in our yard. There was not much interaction with other children at our house. I believed that eventually we would resume a more normal life, but my aunt continued to keep us isolated. Since other children were not welcomed into our home, they stopped asking us to their homes and to other functions. My younger brother told me that he felt like a freak because he was now so different from the other kids. My aunt would summarily go through the list of my friends and tell me which ones I could not play with or visit. She would say that one was not a good person because of this or that, and another was a bad person because of something else. I wanted some interaction. I wanted somebody to love me. I needed somebody. My internal response was, "Well, Aunt, maybe you will treat me better if I do not have those people you do not like as my friends. Then maybe you will love me." Some of my isolation was from my trying to please my aunt.

It took weeks for my parents' remains to be returned. My understanding is that there was a memorial service for them, but my brothers and I were not allowed to attend. The first time I ever saw the graves of my parents was when I was a young adult. Many people did not know how to constructively express their condolences. About two months after the accident, the mother of one of my friends saw me in the front yard. She crossed the street to say that she was truly sorry about the accident, but she commented that the accident happened for a reason and that it would make me a stronger person. As a child, that is not what I needed to hear. I wanted to know that somebody would love me and be supportive and nurturing, not that I should put my chin up and become a stronger individual.

My aunt was very reluctant to acknowledge that my parents had ever lived, let alone died. For the most part, my brothers and I were not allowed to talk about them. Only one photograph of my parents was left up in the house. It was of my parents with my brothers and me taken probably two or three years before the accident. The photo remained in our den where we often sat to read. Except for that photo, my parents were wiped out of our lives, so it almost felt that the photo was of some other family of which I had never been a part. For about two years, I remember hoping that my parents just had amnesia and were finding their way back home. Whenever I walked out on the street or rode in a car, I would look to see if I could find them.

The most important comfort after my parents' deaths was growing up with my two brothers. We had a major bond which kept us close together. We cried on each others' shoulders and tried to cope with our difficult situation together. My isolation would have been overwhelming without them. To this day, we are closer than many other siblings because of our loss. Another comfort was our occasional travel to the home of our maternal aunt. We would spend a week with her, my uncle and my cousin in a very loving and supportive atmosphere. The dramatic change was a wonderful respite, but it was short-lived because we always returned to our home in Atlanta.

One of the greatest comforts for me was to curl up with my books to read. I tried to get lost in books to mentally escape to a better place. As time progressed, I assumed a survival attitude and developed skills on my own that I would need to get through my life. The message I received from my aunt was that I would not succeed in becoming an accomplished individual. To prove my aunt wrong and to prove to myself that I was not as bad as she made me feel, I immersed myself in my studies and grew determined I was going to succeed. I did well enough in my studies and was unhappy enough with my aunt to leave high school at the end of eleventh grade. I applied to colleges and was accepted to a couple of them without my high school degree. I was so glad to inform my aunt that I was going to college. I left home and that is what got me through.

My father made a big impression on my life. His legacy as a lawyer lived on when I became a tax lawyer, but my father worked very hard and had little time for pleasure. He died prematurely without enjoying his life as much as he could have. At one juncture in my life, after having been a practicing lawyer for a number of years and having worked fifteen-hour days, I decided that it was not the way I wanted to continue to live. Life is fragile. It is potentially very short. There are things to enjoy and other things to do besides work. As a result, I decided to balance my life better. I decided to enjoy it as much as I worked hard. I began to travel and to engage in outdoor activities that I had always liked but had never taken the time to enjoy.

The first time I talked with others beyond my family who were grieving was when there was a documentary film being made about my parents' fatal flight. I met up with others who lost people from that same flight. There were common threads. A number of the other people also had premonitions about the crash. Many had difficulties adjusting to their new lives and felt isolated in their mourning. There was a bond with its foundation in the trauma, sudden death and loss. There was a sense of understanding and knowing that same feeling from losing a loved one without saying goodbye and with so much unfinished business never to be completed.

If somebody had asked what I needed at the time of the accident, I would have said, "Someone to reach out to me, to be accessible to me, and to allow me to talk about my fears, about my loss and about how much I missed my parents." I wanted to hear from someone who had been through a similar trauma and to see with my own eyes that they were smart, fully functioning, and relatively happy individuals at a later time in their lives. ACCESS does this for people through its grief mentoring program. Through ACCESS, I connected with another woman who had also lost her parents in childhood and had been left with a life as disrupted and lonely as mine had been. There was a mutual appreciation for the hardships that accompanied our losses at such a young age. Our discussions of survival were especially meaningful because neither of us had ever before felt that we could openly discuss our losses, our responses to them, and their ongoing effects on our lives with another who could truly understand.

CHAPTER 25

Loss of my brother on Swissair Flight 111
by Jack Karamanoukian

I lost my eldest brother Serge aboard Swissair Flight 111 when it crashed off the coast of Nova Scotia outside of Halifax on September 2, 1998. He was an integral part of my daily life. We lived near each other in New York City and spent almost every day together. He was taking his annual trip from New York to spend his vacation visiting our grandmother in Geneva. That is an example of what a special person he was. He was the kind of person who did more for others than he did for himself.

Brothers Serge, Henry and Jack Karamanoukian.

I was just starting my own company. I had talked to Serge earlier in the day, and our discussion was about one of my company's jobs which he had arranged for us. I was on my way home when my best friend called to ask if I had heard the news about a Swissair plane going down. I learned from the radio that there were two flights every night to Switzerland, one to Zurich and one to Geneva. When I arrived home, I immediately turned on both the TV and the radio to find out which flight had crashed. Initially the media was not sure, but about midnight it was confirmed that the Geneva flight had crashed. I tried calling Serge's best friend because I was not sure which flight he was on. At about the same time, my father came home from dinner. He asked me if I had heard about it. I said "yes" and I called one of his friends to come over while my friend Will took me to the airport.

My initial reaction was disbelief. It seemed unreal. I just could not believe what was happening. For the first time in my life, I could not even drive a car because I was shaking so badly. I hoped that it was another flight and that maybe he had changed his plans or got bumped off the plane. The airport was pretty empty. They let us into the lounge and confirmed that he was on the passenger list. The CEO of Swissair came into the room at about 2 a.m. and told us that there were no survivors.

I was the first person in my family to find out, so I had to tell everyone else. I left the airport at 5 a.m. and arrived home to find my father sitting at the bottom of the stairs. I do not think I said anything. He sort of already knew. My brother Henry and my grandmother were already on their way to New York.

For the next couple of days, I imagined Serge safe and alive and possibly swimming to try to find land. Slowly I realized that was not the case. I do not think I slept for three days. I was busy trying to get the family together and to coordinate food, transportation and a memorial.

Swissair did a very good job making sure that the family of each passenger had someone dedicated to its needs. These representatives stayed in touch with the families for the first three weeks after the accident and escorted them to Peggy's Cove, which was the closest point to the crash site and near the morgue where DNA samples were collected and the remains were identified.

At the airport I heard a lot of stories about what other people were going through. This helped me understand that the way I was feeling was normal. I met people who lost entire families. This helped put things in perspective because, thank God, at least my whole family was not on the plane. There was a short general service at St. Patrick's Cathedral in New York City attended by Swissair executives and families that made me aware of the scope of the disaster to so many others.

I kept thinking that I needed to take care of my family, so that occupied my time. My father and brother helped me by giving me the opportunity to support them even though I am the youngest. They gave me a reason not to crawl into a shell or lose my mind. Without them, I would have. We are very close, so being together was the most important thing. Separately, we probably would have fallen apart.

A lot of phone calls were coming in from our friends and family. For a few days everyone came to the house to sit and talk and to make sure we knew that we were not alone. Especially for the first couple of weeks, whenever I had time to think, I had horrible thoughts about what had happened to Serge. I locked that away for three or four months until I could deal with it. My time was spent making sure that my family was okay. I planned a ceremony for Serge on September 11. With the help of friends, we wrote our own press release about what we wanted to share about Serge. It was important to have the church memorial service even before Serge's remains were identified because we did not want to wait two or three months. It was attended by 800 people and made me proud of my brother. It helped us realize that he had left his mark on so many family and friends.

Some people who came over knew the right things to do. They offered support in their silence. Without our asking, they helped around the house doing laundry, cooking or driving us places. Others tried to tell us what to do and wanted to control things that were more personal to us. Some offered to pack up Serge's room, close up his apartment and handle the funeral arrangements. That was too much. There is a fine line between what is welcomed and what is inappropriate.

The biggest challenge was getting my father out of bed and out of his room. He refused for the first three days. Many told me to tell my father to get out of bed. They would say, "You have to get him up. You have to let him come out to greet people." I did not have to do any of that. It is not what he wanted. I was there to make sure it did not happen, even though I knew that eventually it would help him to get outside and to be around his friends. A priest came to the house when my father was sleeping and not in the mood to talk to anybody. It was not the right time and it was very tough for me to say, "No, I am sorry. You cannot see him." I just let my father figure out what was best for him. I made sure he did not go overboard, but I did not tell him what to do for two or three days. Then I said, "Dad, I know it is hard, but you have two other sons here who need you. Whether you like it or not, you have to take care of us now." He did. The next day he sat down with my brother and me and said, "Thank you." We had taken care of him and now he wanted to take care of us.

After a month and a half, only fifteen or twenty people from the crash had been identified. On October 23, I was sitting in Serge's office when a man from the coroner's office called me to say they had identified Serge. He said the medical examiner would call me later and that someone should be with me when he called just in case there was something difficult to hear. I said, "No, I'm okay." He read the report and I immediately regretted it. I never felt that others needed to know that only part of his body had been recovered. We planned the funeral in Geneva about a month later. It was important for us to have his remains and to put him to rest.

Some of Serge's personal effects were released in January. This included his overstuffed wallet, his clothes, and other items. My father was really happy when they returned his belongings. I put a rubber band around Serge's wallet and gave it to my father. He smiled and just opened it, closed it and folded it. It made him happy and sad at the same time. Serge had cut out a horoscope from a magazine that he must have found while he was on the plane or in the airport that described the kind of person he was. It described someone caring and giving who was going through hard times. I just shook my head because his hard times were over. I cherished it, copied it, laminated it and put it in my wallet.

I moved back home to take care of my father for a while. Four weeks after the crash, my father said, "You have to go back to work." I asked, "Why?" He responded, "It's not good to sit here." I said, "All right. I'll go back to work if you go back to work." We both agreed and went back to work. It made us think about things other than Serge and the crash.

My grandmother gave me the most comfort. She was an 87-year-old woman whom Serge visited because she still had more life in her than anyone else we knew. As she came outside to meet me on her porch, she looked at me and said, "I'm worried about you." I said, "I know. I'm worried about you too." Then she said, "Well, we'll just have to keep an eye on each other." I responded, "Yeah, I think so." Knowing her strength gave me the power to know that I could get through this. She had lost her husband, her daughter and her grandson, but still had a very good outlook on life. It helped me to know that loss helps to make a person, not to kill him.

One of the hardest things was getting to the point where I could think about the crash and the loss of Serge while thinking positively. This took telling stories about him and remembering who he was, the comfort he gave me, and what he taught me. After he died, I learned about a promise that he and my other older brother had made years earlier when I was only five and my mother passed away. They had never told me that they had agreed that one of them would always live in New York to watch over me to support me emotionally.

Serge's death changed my life and helped me become more understanding, caring, and loving, and to not take things for granted. When I felt down or depressed, I wrote about how I felt. It helped to go back over those notes later to remember how my brother affected me, what he meant to me and what he still means to me. I realized I wanted to practice in myself a lot of his personal characteristics. Serge always remembered people's birthdays and would call them. I still have his calendar with everyone's birthday. Now I call practically every one of our friends on their birthdays. It is something that they love and cherish.

Sometimes it helped to think that Serge was near. One day the light in my office flickered. It was the only time I saw the light flicker. My secretary and I had been laughing about Serge, so when the light flickered I said, "Oh, he's there. He's right around the corner and he's watching us." I landed a big contract the day of the first year anniversary of the crash. I got the call in Halifax right after the ceremony. I looked at my father and said, "I bet you that was him." My dad just nodded his head and said, "Yeah." Then I said, "Well, he's looking out for me." It's something that I believe. I just know that he is looking down at me, and I always find myself looking up at him.

People handle things differently. Some people distanced themselves and others stuck around and got closer. My best friend was there to take care of my family, and it brought us closer. Another very close friend could not cope with my loss and did not want to deal with it. One of Serge's best friends did not go to his funeral and admitted a few months later that it was too hard for him.

During the first couple of months, I secluded myself and rarely went out. That was a natural instinct, but after a while I could no longer curl up into a shell and avoid doing things just because someone else was not there anymore. Now I play golf with Serge's friends because it makes us happy to laugh and to remember Serge.

My father has pictures of my brother and my mother in every corner of the house. He believes that having pictures of them that he can see from any angle in the house means they are watching over him. Whether we are walking down a hallway or in any room in his house, there is a picture of my mother and my brother looking over us.

My family never talked to people about their feelings and experiences. We did not know anyone who had lived through an air disaster related loss. A friend took me to an ACCESS event in May 2001. Being involved in ACCESS has given me the feeling of personally belonging and of identifying with others. It showed me and it shows others that they are not alone and that someone understands what they are going through. Through ACCESS, I have been able to help others feel better and even smile again.

CHAPTER 26

Loss of my father in a motor vehicle accident
by Andrew August

My father was a very gregarious and friendly guy. Everyone loved him. He was born in New York to parents from Poland and never graduated from high school. He went to work for his father who had a small printing company on the Lower East Side of New York. My father took over that business and ran it until he and my mom retired to Florida.

While I was growing up, the thing I remember most about my father is how hard he worked. We lived on Long Island. He would leave at six in the morning when a car pool picked him up, and he would come home at seven at night five days a week. I cannot imagine what it would be like sitting in a car with other grown men who smoked driving in and out of New York City in the heat, rain and snow. He did that for twenty-five years to provide for our family.

Andrew with his father who taught him to work hard and to value family above everything else.

Family was always very important to him. He always told me, and I have repeated it many times, that there are two things you have to do with family. You have to attend funerals and bar and bat mitzvahs because they are the things that happen only once by definition. Weddings, birthdays and dinner parties can happen more than once. Because of his advice, I make it a point to go to funerals and to every bar and bat mitzvah that I am invited to. That is a legacy from my father. I am extremely close to all of my family including my uncle and my cousins.

My adult life with him was a little tempestuous because early in college I sensed that I had a certain instinct and intellect that would carry me further in academics. My father did not value intellectual capacity as much as hard work. When I went to college in Upstate New York, my parents promised to send me to the University of Colorado if I did very well. I remember vividly driving out of the driveway to Colorado in that blue Ford Gran Torino packed to the gills. He bought it for me because he felt that my other car was not safe enough to drive across the country. He was extremely generous and always very concerned about me.

When I decided to go to law school, he realized I was very focused. He had a certain pride which really peaked after I graduated from law school. He was so proud when he came out for my law school graduation. After I passed the bar exam, my parents threw a party for me at their house in Boca. He hugged me and introduced me around saying, "Here's my lawyer." We got along very well for a father and son with strong personalities and wills.

He was extraordinarily proud when my son Adam was born. He said, "I always wanted a grandson." Although Adam was only five when my dad died, they forged a truly incredibly close bond. I have all kinds of videos of him playing with Adam. He would call to see how Adam was doing and talk with him on the phone. We spoke the day before he died. I can picture exactly where I was standing in the kitchen. He asked, "How are you doing? How's work? How are my kids?" It was one of those casual conversations when you say, "See you later. Talk with you later," and then there is no later. I had no idea it would be the last time I would talk to him.

It was Friday of Memorial Day weekend. My partner and I had to interview another lawyer at the Park Hyatt Hotel. All of a sudden my secretary ran in crying with a very horrified look on her face. She said, "Andy, your father was in an accident and you need to call your sister." I went to my office, but I couldn't reach my sister. I called her again from my car and was given a number at the hospital. She answered and said, "Mom and Dad were in a car accident and Dad died." I immediately asked about Mom because she wound up in the hospital. It was almost as if I were more concerned about her than the shock that Dad had died and what that meant. I just knew that he died in the car accident and that they were helicoptered away from the scene and that my mother was conscious. I started thinking logically, which is what I often do. I started thinking about the logistics of immediately getting down to Florida from California on a Memorial Day weekend. I didn't really lose it until I came into the house and saw Marsha holding Adam, who didn't know what was going on. That was when the meaning of "Dad died" began sinking in.

We had to get a sitter for our one-year-old son Corey, but Adam certainly understood that there was something going on that was not good. With professional advice, we decided to bring him to Florida. I flew alone the next morning, and Adam and Marsha joined us the next day. I remember being aware of staying conscious about what was happening. I was trying to be very cerebral. I made a checklist of items such as insurance. My brother-in-law picked me up at the airport, and we claimed all my parents' personal belongings from the Florida Highway Patrol. My sister had brought my

Chapter 26 Loss of my father in a motor vehicle accident

mother home from the hospital to my parents' house. When I saw her, we had a big family hug and cry.

I learned more of the accident. I learned that my parents were waiting in the grass median for the oncoming traffic to pass when they were broadsided by a kid who never slowed down. The three in the van were a young landscaping crew who had just finished their last job before a three-day weekend. There was probably more to be learned about the driver. He may have been drinking or talking to his friends. I regret not pressing the highway patrol to check the driver for alcohol. The idea that there was no beer or something else involved in the accident is hard for me to comprehend.

I was able to suppress my emotional reactions until a later time because I had business to manage. My sister, brother-in-law and my Aunt Rhoda and Uncle Bob lived nearby, so we all helped make the funeral arrangements together. I stayed at my sister's house the night before the funeral. I woke up in the middle of the night and all of a sudden I broke down. I was truly hysterical and at last I let it all go.

The service was really amazing. I was astonished that there were five or six hundred people there. He had a ton of friends and was president of the homeowners' and other associations. Everybody had great things to say about him. I wrote a eulogy that I felt I could not deliver, so one of his good friends read it. As far as funerals go, it was a good one. It was sad because it was too soon.

Though I had to go back to my job, Marsha and Adam stayed for my nephew's first birthday party which my sister had planned weeks earlier. When Marsha dropped me at the curb, Adam asked me if I was "ever going to be happy again and stop crying". On the first leg of the trip I was really sad and concerned about how Adam was reacting. The second leg of the trip was all about Joe Montana. Adam loved the 49ers and Joe Montana. He would put on a helmet and jersey and place a bobble head of the 49ers in front of the TV to set up a shrine to them before every game. When I boarded the plane in Dallas, Joe Montana was sitting in the front row. I asked the flight attendant if she would be willing to ask him for his autograph for my son. She said, "No, we are under very strict instructions to protect his privacy." I had post-its, the obituary and all the articles about the accident with me. I wrote Joe a lengthy note telling him what had happened to my dad, how my son loved Joe and the 49ers, and that it would really make him happy if he would write something. I used my post-its to label the articles just like I was writing a legal brief. I told the flight attendant, "Do me a favor and just read this, and if you don't think it's appropriate to give him to sign, I understand." She came back about a half hour later and said, "If he doesn't give your son an autograph then I will kick him off the plane." She returned about twenty minutes later with a note from Joe Montana saying, "To Adam, There will be happy days ahead." That was very nice. I was looking for the bright spots.

I was very absentminded for several weeks after I got back into the flow of things. I forgot things that would just be very natural for me to remember. After I missed a few court dates, I started taking notes to deal with this aspect of my grief. My mother had a much tougher time than I. She wouldn't drive on the highway although she was a fiercely independent driver before. When I was a kid, she would drive us into Manhattan or go by herself to meet my father for dinner. My sister was also more affected than I was because she had to drive by the scene of the accident day in and day out.

Everyone has their own way of dealing with grief and shock. I tend to hide my fears and emotions with humor. Marsha was great from the moment I walked into the house right after the accident. She was extremely understanding and very supportive of whatever we needed to do to deal with his death. Her father was also wonderful and stepped into the breach to become a father figure. I used my business as a kind of support system.

We incorporate my dad into our family in symbolic ways. He was very supportive and loving of Adam. Adam loves hot dogs the way my father loved hot dogs. Adam asks about my golf game just as he did. We have pictures of him all around the house. Adam has seen the videos of them together and remembers him.

To some extent, I am resigned to the fact that we are put on earth for a certain period of time and that some people have better and longer lives than others. My father did well for himself. I am glad that he had a good life and that he instilled in me a work ethic and family ethic. He left a legacy that I have adopted to work hard, have fun and to take care of my family.

There are extreme parallels between his life and mine now. I learned at times to burn the candle at three ends because he did. Because my father's life ended so suddenly and so unpredictably, it emphasized the whole notion that you have to live your life now in whatever way that means to you. For me, it was playing golf and making sure I went skiing with my kids on the weekends. It was working out of my house once the Internet enabled me to connect remotely with the office. It was important to me to be home when the kids got home from school. If I had had a different role model, I would not have stayed in a small law firm environment where I have more control over my daily destiny.

His most important legacy to me was the value of family. Family can be a blessing or a curse, but I go out of my way to make it a blessing. I never had the feeling that I didn't get to say anything to him that I should have. I am sure I didn't say "I love you", but I didn't have to say that. He was extraordinarily generous to me and gave me the platform I needed to become independent and a lawyer. We showed our love through actions rather than words, but knowing what I know today, I always make the effort to say "I love you". It takes on more and more meaning after you say it enough. Maybe that is why I say it to my kids all the time. I make it a point to say "I love you" whenever I talk to Adam and Corey. Last night Adam wrote me a text message saying, "Goodnight. Love you, Pops."

I have been working with ACCESS for many years. I see airplane disasters as especially difficult. It is important to know that life has tragedies. Not talking about them doesn't do anything to diminish them and they become the white elephant in the room. Death is an uncomfortable concept, and accidental sudden death is even more uncomfortable. I want to help people who are struggling with it.

The biggest lesson I learned from my father's death is to value family greater than I had before. Now there are certain family events that I will not miss, and I will not let them slide because the plane can go down tomorrow, the car can overturn tonight, and the heart can stop in an instant.

Surviving Sudden Loss: *Stories from those who have lived it*

CHAPTER 27

Loss of my daughter in 9/11 on American Flight 77
by Marion Kminek

Mari-Rae was passionate about gymnastics. On 9/11, she was going to California to become a gymnastics coach.

I lost my 35-year-old daughter Mari-Rae on American Airlines Flight 77 that crashed into the Pentagon on September 11, 2001. She was very passionate about life, and especially about gymnastics. After law school, she passed the bar and went into the Navy Job Corp. She was working for a private firm in DC for about a year when she decided to follow her passion for gymnastics. On 9/11, she was moving to California to coach gymnastics at the University of California in Santa Barbara.

Although Mari-Rae had lived away from home since she was eighteen, we spent much time together and she always called once or twice a week. I called her on the Friday before 9/11. She had to attend a wedding on Saturday and was worried because she was not completely packed for her move. I told her to go to the wedding anyway. She was glad she did because she saw all of her DC friends one last time. I left her a phone message on Sunday.

At about 7:30 a.m. on 9/11, I was lying in bed talking on the phone with a friend. She told me that a plane had crashed into the World Trade Center. When I asked if it was a private plane, she responded, "I guess," and we continued talking. I turned on the television and saw the second plane crash. I was totally confused as were the newscasters, but I was still not that concerned. I had to get ready for an appointment at 11 a.m., so I was doing the paperwork to prepare for it and having my coffee when I heard that a bomb had gone off in the Pentagon. I became a little concerned because my other daughter also worked in DC, and I was not exactly sure where she was. Then they said a plane from Boston crashed into the Pentagon. I knew Mari-Rae was starting work on Wednesday, but did not know if she had already flown out Monday night or had waited until that morning. I was thinking, "I hope she got out. She will be so upset if she gets stuck at the airport."

Then they announced that they had been wrong. It was an American Airlines flight from DC bound for California that had crashed into the Pentagon. Then I knew. I screamed and I knew. I felt this whoosh that she was gone. I still needed to find out for sure. I thought, "Well, maybe not." I tried to make phone calls, but I could not get through. I could not even get through to my other daughter in DC. Finally she called and I asked her if she had taken Mari-Rae to the airport. We learned that her friend Jim had taken her for an 8:00 a.m. flight out of Dulles early enough to definitely make the flight. So by 10:30 or 11:00 a.m., we pretty much knew she was on the flight. My family called the airlines. They said she was supposed to be on the flight, but that it was not confirmed. Later in the afternoon the airlines reasserted, "Well, it is not confirmed." I said, "What do you mean by not confirmed? Does that mean she had a reservation, but you do not know if she boarded?" They said, "Yes." Later I found out that they already knew, but were waiting for the disaster team to contact me. At about 6:00 p.m., when we already had a house full of people, one of my friends handed me the phone. I do not remember a thing they said, but American Airlines finally confirmed what we already knew.

The next day, two women from the airlines came to my house. They arranged for transportation to the memorial services and were helpful for that first year. After a year, they forgot who we were. It was like we fell off the radar. We were just supposed to be normal again.

I am not a person who cries in front of people. I have always held in my emotions. The day she died, I stayed busy calling people on the phone. People were calling me and coming over to the house. On the first or second day, I can remember my friends sitting at the kitchen table as I sat on the edge of the couch. All of a sudden, I totally lost it and put my face into my hands sobbing, "I cannot do this. I cannot do this!" I wanted to run away. I wanted to get into the car and drive to California. I did not know what that would solve, but my response was a desire to run. Even though we all knew she was dead, in my mind she was in California and we had just not talked to her for a while. She had always lived out of state, so I could imagine her just living in California.

My other daughter came home and was trying to take care of me even though she was grieving too. She tried to protect me by blocking some of my friends from reaching me on the phone. She did not realize that those calls were holding me together. During that first week after 9/11, we had people over every single night. It happened on Tuesday, and there were people there that afternoon. We had people come in from out of town, including one of

Chapter 27 Loss of my daughter in 9/11 on American Flight 77

my younger daughter's girlfriends who flew in from Hong Kong when not many planes were flying. It is pretty much a blur, but I remember we planned the memorial for that Sunday. I still do not know how we did it.

I wanted to talk to people. We gave our first interview to Mari-Rae's friend who was a reporter in Chicago. She had called and asked very nicely if she could do a story on Mari-Rae. Because I knew her, I agreed. She was very sensitive. After she came, I let other reporters in because the more I told my daughter's story, the better I felt. My other daughter kept reminding me, "You do not have to do this, Mom," and I would say, "Yes, I do because I have to tell everybody about her life." On every anniversary, they would call to do a follow-up because they knew I would talk to them. It was healing for me.

I was a real estate broker. After about two weeks I tried to show a house. I thought, "Well, I can handle this." I did not realize how raw my nerves were. I couldn't even drive. It was like I had this heavy bar across my chest. It was as if I had the flu. I could not keep anything down. I thought, "Wow, I did not know I could physically feel grief." Sometimes it was like I was standing on the sidelines observing myself. I had never been through anything like it.

I tried not to think about what I told my daughter to do before 9/11. I pushed it out of my mind because while I had given her the best advice, if I had given her different advice, she might be alive today. When she was hesitant to accept the job offer at UCSB because it was only guaranteed for a year, I told her, "Go for it. Life is short. Go for it." Then, to save money in moving, she wanted to drive to California from DC. I said, "Don't do that. It is too dangerous to drive across the country all by yourself. Get on a plane. It is so much safer." I talked her into it. I was right. What were the odds? I try not to let myself feel guilty about that, but I need to talk about it to keep it in perspective.

Mari-Rae was in the Navy Corps and was buried in Arlington Cemetery.

The first six months after 9/11 are a blur. A couple of weeks after 9/11, the Navy called to say they had found her remains. The Corps had her dental records on file, so that is how they identified her. I did not care that they had found her remains once I knew that she was on the plane. Later on, I felt guilty for not caring because I met people who had not gotten remains when it was terribly important for them. They asked me what I wanted to do with her remains. Since she was in the Navy, I had them buried at Arlington Cemetery. That is wonderful because anytime someone is going to Washington DC, I always tell them that Mari-Rae is there.

Since Mari-Rae was moving, the mover had all her

personal belongings. Her car had been shipped to California. Our biggest challenge was finding out who the mover was and who had shipped the car. I had her mail forwarded to me including the credit card bills that referred to the shippers. When I contacted the mover to explain what had happened, he was wonderful. He held her things for as long as we wanted and let us go to the storage facility whenever we wanted. My other daughter lived in DC and went out there right away to find her will. In October, they had the memorial service in DC. Our whole family was there, so we went through all her belongings as best we could. It was really hard. Each of us took what we wanted. Then the mover shipped the rest to three or four different places, including a women's shelter. The mover did all of that for us without any charge.

Before 9/11, I always went to funerals and felt bad for the people left, but never expressed my emotions. After 9/11, when I went to pay my respects, I would sit in the back of the church and sob or walk out sobbing loudly all the way to the parking lot. Funerals were triggers and I could not predict when I was going to start crying. It was a way of letting out my feelings. I could deal with it better each year. A few years ago I joined a bereaved parents group just before Christmas because I remembered how hard the holidays were. I thought that since it had been six years at that point, I could help others, and I planned to have them ask me questions. They asked me to tell them what happened and I broke down in the middle of it. I thought, "Wow, I guess those raw feelings never go away!"

The loss of my daughter in 9/11 changed our whole family. Mari-Rae was a pivotal part of our family because she was so passionate. There was no gray. Everything was black or white. She was hardworking, loyal and passionate about her beliefs. My youngest daughter went back to school for her master's degree because Mari-Rae had been so passionate about education. My other daughter who lived in DC became as politically active as Mari-Rae. My sons became closer and family became more important to them. My oldest boy, for example, has a wonderful family with four children, and he calls or contacts his siblings and me more often than he did before 9/11.

I had so much support and hundreds and hundreds of cards from many people I did not know. My high school English teacher looked me up and called me. Others from my high school years found my address and contacted me. That taught me something. I used to occasionally send a sympathy note to families I knew, but I did not realize how much it meant until it happened to me. Now I always send a card if I hear about the death of somebody I knew even back in high school, especially when the death is unexpected.

Some people whom I thought were good friends were not supportive.

Chapter 27 Loss of my daughter in 9/11 on American Flight 77

That was disappointing. Since 9/11, because I have so many wonderful people in my life and only so much time, I tend to move beyond those who did not really seem to care about me. It was a matter of priorities, not anger. A couple of years after 9/11, a friend of mine said, "It is time to put the past behind you." Though I could not believe she said that, when I thought about it afterward, I realized that she had never lost anybody, so she just did not know that the sorrow of losing a daughter never goes away. She did not say it out of meanness.

I immersed myself in managing a memorial fund for Mari-Rae. We had a charity event in March on the six-month anniversary of 9/11. We sold raffle tickets for donated items from all across the United States and had a big dinner dance downtown. I just kept doing things because that was how I kept my feet on the ground. I felt in control of something. Doing something in my daughter's name was the most helpful and healing thing for me. Every birthday and every Christmas I give money that I would have spent on her presents to a charity in her name. We bought bricks with her name on them to put on sidewalks, so her memory is everywhere.

Through the memorial fund and fundraising events, we donate money in her name to many gymnastics programs, which is what she would have wanted. There are awards at several colleges and gymnastics clubs. A lot of them are for the most improved or the most passionate gymnasts because she worked so hard at gymnastics. We have received emails from those who learned her story when they won the awards in her name.

I always felt blessed that if she had to die, she died in 9/11 because we got so much support and so much help. If it had been a single accident, everybody would have forgotten about it in a couple of days. In the very beginning, and for the first two or three years, the press and the news media focused on 9/11. For me that was healing because as I watched it over and over again, it deadened my reaction. I felt less each time. Others could not watch it at all.

My husband and I had talked about going to Florida after retirement. After a few years, when one of our close friends died, I took a deep breath and said, "We are going to Florida." 9/11 had already made me realize how short life can be. With our friend's death, I realized, "Hey, we need to do what we want to do." We retired to Florida and I am very glad we did. We never know what is going to happen tomorrow.

I went out to lunch with a friend of mine on New Year's Day 2002. He said, "What do you think you learned from 9/11?" A lot of people would have taken offense to that question, but we had a very close relationship. I thought for a minute, "What did I learn? This is still so raw at this point." Then it became so clear. I said, "I learned two things. I learned everybody is here on loan to us and that we cannot control anything." I used to try to control everything. I still wish I could, but I cannot. Realizing those two simple facts has been an important part of my healing. There would never be any closure. It would just be different. There is nothing I can do about it. I have come to accept that.

The concept and the creation of ACCESS were brilliant. It is so important to have contact with someone who has been through something similar to your experience. I learned what pinpoints the importance of ACCESS in October 2001. The Department of Defense brought all the 9/11 families involved in the Pentagon crash to Washington DC. We all stayed in the same hotel, and my adult children came too. One of my sons said, "My gosh! It is nice to be in a room where everybody has the same look in their eyes." And I thought, "Wow, I did not even think about that, but it was comforting to him to be among others with similar losses." We need that connection. Family tries to help, but they are grieving too. Friends try to help, but they have their own lives and they are not going through it.

After 9/11, a woman who had lost her daughter in a car accident several years before Mari-Rae died came over to my house. I talked to her about what she did after her daughter's death. It was very helpful. My other friend had lost her son to brain cancer many years earlier. She was helpful to me, but I felt really bad about how unhelpful I had been to her! I just did not understand before it happened to me. I have another friend who lost her husband in a private plane crash years before 9/11. She had little children. Six months after he died, I tried to get her moving forward with her life by taking her to a bar to meet men. While we were sitting there, she just started crying. She said, "I have to leave." I thought, "What is wrong with her? It has been enough time!" I did not mean anything bad by it, but it shows I just did not know.

When I meet other moms who have lost children, I just say, "I am so sorry." Before it happened to me, I never knew what to say. I thought I had to say wonderful things, but I have learned to just say, "I am so sorry, I lost my daughter too."

CHAPTER 28
Loss of my parents on TWA Flight 800
by Ned Brooks

My parents, Ed and Ruth Brooks, were passengers on TWA Flight 800 that exploded on July 17, 1996 off Long Island. My mom and dad were on their way to Paris for my mom's 80th birthday. They were retired and had lived in Edgartown on Martha's Vineyard for many years. They traveled around the world for three or four months out of the year and loved flying, especially on TWA.

Ruth, Ned and Ed Brooks.

I found out about the accident while I was getting ready for bed. It was roughly 9 p.m. when I flipped on the TV. My parents had stayed at our house in Connecticut the night before their flight and left from there for the airport. I did not know which flight they were on, so when I heard the news of an air crash, I thought, "My goodness! That is a shame!" Then the report said it was a TWA flight. I thought, "I'm sure it was not theirs." But the flight that crashed was going to Paris, and that is where my parents were going. Slowly over the course of about ten minutes, I put the pieces together enough to pick up the phone and call my sister who was listening to the same news coverage. There was a TWA flight from New York through Boston to Paris scheduled to leave roughly at the same time as the direct flight that crashed. One of my sisters convinced herself that my parents were not on the nonstop flight. She had a very good night's sleep.

It was impossible to get through to anybody at TWA. I spent about four or five hours calling various TWA lines. I was a broker and one of my favorite stocks at that time was TWA. I knew that TWA's top management had left for London that afternoon leaving no one in senior management in the States. At about 1 a.m., my sister and I drove to JFK Airport. It was a scene of confusion, but after we parked the car, we were escorted to a holding area and then onto a bus to a nearby Ramada Inn. At the Ramada Inn, there was a huge hall with people milling around with Red Cross and other volunteer workers. There was a stunning sense of being overwhelmed by the reality of something that we had spent the last four or five hours trying to deny. There were people wailing and others sobbing quietly. I noticed a lot of people sitting quietly just trying to absorb what had happened. I recall a sense of numbness and a sense that everything was going to be very different from here on out. A support worker stayed with us until Mayor Rudy Giuliani personally came over and asked us our names and the names of our loved ones. He then went through the manifest and said, "Yes, they were on the flight that crashed."

I think my sister and I absorbed the news relatively quickly, but we felt lost and out of touch with reality. I drove home in a state of shock. Dr. Joyce Brothers had gotten up at 4 a.m. to be on the radio for us. Her words were comforting and poignant. I marvel now at how strongly her words affected me. It was very kind of her to make the special effort to connect with us.

After arriving back home, I tossed and turned for ninety minutes. My wife and children were at my parents' Edgartown home. I called to let my wife know what had happened, and she started the phone tree to various friends. It was very difficult for the community because Edgartown is a small town in which everybody knew my parents for so many years. All of their various friends were very kind and solicitous of our children, who felt the loss very, very deeply. Grandma and Grandpa were particularly important figures in their lives.

After I called my wife, my brother-in-law and I drove to Edgartown. I was executor of my parents' estate, and I needed to figure out the legal viewpoint. I started gathering papers from my parents' house. My reaction was one of hyperactivity and a need to feel busy. I felt that all sorts of things were terribly important to accomplish immediately, but they really were not.

The next day our entire family gathered at my parents' house. We followed all the news broadcasts. We poured over every newspaper we could find to learn about what had happened to the plane. That went on for quite a long time. We needed some sort of touchstone. We needed some form of material confirmation. The details, even the small details, became very important. My mother's body was one of the first recovered. It was important for me to know that. She was sitting where the plane split. My father's body was not recovered for another two weeks. On a spiritual level, the bodies were completely unimportant, but I had a sense of having found my parents at some level when we had their remains.

I threw myself right back into my work within days of the crash. I told myself that I was strong and that everything was going to be okay. Five days after the crash, I had a business trip that I absolutely had to make. On the return flight, I had a crisis of sorts. I asked the stewardess if she could bring

Chapter 28 Loss of my parents on TWA Flight 800

the engineer back to me because I really wanted to know what my parents had experienced when their plane blew up. The engineer was remarkable. Once I could actually articulate my concerns, he responded, "I know exactly what you need to know." He went forward and brought back several books about death that described a person's immediate loss of consciousness from the decompression before death in that sort of air disaster. He really consoled me by explaining that my parents experienced no pain. That was very helpful.

About ten days after the crash, we had a very large memorial service before my parents' bodies were released. There were many remembrances. That was wonderful for us. There was a real sense of the whole community coming together to provide support and consolation to one another. We had a much smaller ceremony weeks later when we received their remains.

Over the course of the next weeks and months, I was disturbed by a lot of things that reminded me of my parents. I would be walking down the street and see somebody from the back and say to myself, "My God, it's Mom! My God, it's Dad!" When our children did something very well, such as getting a commendation or a good grade, I constantly reached for the telephone to call Mom and Dad because I knew they would be so proud. Then it was hard when I remembered they were not there. After the crash, holidays were all very hard. That first Christmas Eve, my wife and I were looking at the presents under the tree and admiring how pretty everything looked, but there was something wrong. I could not figure out what it was. I asked my wife, "Louise, what is wrong? Something is wrong with this picture. Why aren't there more presents?" She said, "Because your mom gave us so many presents."

I have a very supportive wife and felt I was strong enough not to need any professional counseling. Then three and a half years later, a series of events that had been building up slowly over time made me understand my need for counseling. My judgment became poor. It was hard to maintain an even keel and my patience became uncharacteristically very short. That was hard on everyone around me, so I addressed it with counseling. It would have been less prominent if I had sought counseling earlier.

One aspect of the terrible event that created a large wound for me was that the real cause of the crash took so long to determine. The other was not having the chance to say goodbye to my parents and to tell them for the last time how much I loved them. At least we had a very close relationship, so we did not have a lot of unresolved issues. As a father of three children, my loss had several dimensions. First, the children felt a huge hole in their hearts by the loss of their grandparents who had a way of handling them with such love and patience. Second, I missed my parents and I wanted very much to touch and hold them both just once more.

My eating and sleeping patterns were very disturbed. I did not eat well and lost a fair amount of weight. I would sleep for short periods of time, such as two to three hours, and then be up for the day. I had nightmares about exploding planes and bodies falling from the sky. My parents visited me in a dream about three months after the accident. They told me they were okay. It felt very real.

Things that people said to me were either helpful or hurtful. A very good friend of mine lost her husband about five years after TWA on September 11. She said, "Ned, when TWA Flight 800 happened, I did not understand what you were going through. It is only now that I understand." Nobody understands the experience without having been through it. It hurts when someone who has not been through a similar incident says, "I know exactly how you feel." They can help by just being there and saying "I'm thinking of you." That is probably the nicest thing that I heard over and over again.

For the first year after the event, I found people extremely sympathetic. Then there was a sense of, "Come on. It's time to get on with it." That attitude is understandable, but it can create rifts in relationships. I had permanently changed in some fundamental ways which made it difficult for my relationships to resume as before. That horrid word "closure" was supposed to apply to us after the cremation ceremony, but there was no meaningful closure for me. The concept of closure is overrated. In general, few understand how long it takes to get through the grieving process enough to restore even a semblance of normalcy. Normalcy after the loss is not the same normalcy as before the loss. There is a new sense of balance in life when you realize that bad things can happen when you least expect them.

I perceive the effect of a disaster, such as an airplane crash, very differently now than I did before. Prior to TWA, it was something abstract. It happened to other people. It was a great tragedy and a very sad thing, but I did not feel it viscerally. Since the TWA crash, I am brought back to the point when I first learned about my parents being killed whenever there is another large crash such as Swissair, EgyptAir, Alaska Air and 9/11. Those things, and even obscure references to them, can open up the wound again and bring back those emotions and memories. I was in Portland, Oregon on business on 9/11. Because of the flying ban, I was confined to my hotel room for three or four days before I could get back to my family. I was in hell. In monstrous proportions, I was brought straight back to what it was like in the first days after my parents were killed. I don't think I will ever be able to read about or watch TV coverage of an event like that without it bringing me back in a very real way to my own experience of losing my parents on Flight 800.

I am doing far more charitable work now and getting much more pleasure out of it than I ever thought possible. When I first heard about ACCESS and when Heidi first asked me about the possibility of my being a grief mentor, I was uncertain whether I had the proper skills. Now I consider my work with the ACCESS mentoring program to be one of the most truly meaningful contributions of my life. The act of meeting with or talking with somebody who has experienced a similar loss is powerful.

In my first role as a mentor to a woman who lost her parents on Swissair, I was very touched by the depths of the emotional bond that we achieved from our shared experiences. ACCESS does a spectacular job of pairing people with similar types of losses. The matching allows people to interact with each other in very profound and meaningful ways. I can provide a window into the future for those who are in a state of shock. They are trying to grapple with not only what they have been through and what they are going through, but also what they might experience in the near term. I can provide them with some perspective. Being a mentor is a little bit like taking a friend for a tour through a town that you have known all your life. As you escort them around, you see the town through their eyes. The experience becomes fresh again. I can help others understand what the next steps and reactions may be. We can also compare notes on the first traumatic experience of learning about the loss, dealing with family members' difficulties, the holidays, the birthdays and reactions to comments from other people. There can be a discussion of these experiences and how to deal with them. I am greedy enough to say that the exchanges benefit me as much as they do the people I have had the privilege and pleasure to mentor. It is wonderful and meaningful to give back to others what I received from those who consoled me.

Surviving Sudden Loss: *Stories from those who have lived it*

CHAPTER 29

Loss of my daughter in 9/11 on United Flight 175
by John Titus

On September 11, 2001, I was sitting at the head of the conference table leading a staff meeting and talking about what seemed to be matters of consequence at the college where I work. Someone burst into the room and excitedly yelled, "Turn on the TV. A plane just crashed into the World Trade Center." Within five minutes, I witnessed the scene that would play over and over again in my mind. The horror of that scene still haunts me unceasingly.

Initially I did not know that Alicia was working aboard United Flight 175, the plane that exploded into a fireball in front of my eyes as it crashed into the South Tower of the World Trade Center. I did not find out definitively until several hours later. The panic that set in during those timeless minutes was overwhelming. Suddenly my greatest conceived fear was there in my face. I remember praying, "Dear God, how can I go on?" as reality tried to supplant the surrealness and the protective veil that enshrouded me in the initial moment of shock. How on earth were we going to deal with this? Why did this have to happen to the sweetest person in the world? How could we cope with such a loss?

Early on I would awake sobbing from the horror of what had happened. I soon realized that taking care of my basic needs and those of my family were critical to survival. I continued to force myself to run, eat, sleep and meditate. I also cried when the tears longed for release. I processed my feelings and innermost thoughts through prayer, writing in a journal, and regularly holding profound conversations with empathetic friends. I would retreat into the forest or sit along the river for hours in deep thought and meditation. I could not stand to be among people who were concerned with what seemed inconsequential and mundane to me. I could not focus on anything but my pain and the pain of my loved ones.

People from all over the world reached out to us. We received cards, letters, emails, hugs, loving words and other acts of compassion. Thousands of people offered their love and support. We attended memorial services in Ohio, Michigan, Boston, New York and San Francisco. We flew all over for various events, spoke in front of groups, and were interviewed on TV and quoted in newspapers all over the world. People sent us money from fundraisers and donations in a heartfelt effort to help. Special mementos came to us from an ironworker at the World Trade Center site, from quilt-makers in Nebraska, from caring people in Australia, and from the flight attendants' union, which held fundraisers. Early on, the airlines provided us with a supportive and caring woman to help us make funeral arrangements. Government officials sent words of sympathy, and loving friends and family reached out to us in countless ways. All of this helped, but it still felt like a bad dream. All we wanted was to have our daughter back. All I wanted was to hold her in my arms and to tell her how much I loved her. There would be no more joy, hope, laughter or life as it was before for a long time and maybe never.

As a former counselor, I had encountered many situations of hopelessness and despair. I had dealt with suicide and death of friends and family. I grieved the tragic loss of my nephew in a car crash. I knew the stages of grief. I had coursework in death and dying. I had a strong faith in a loving God. All of that seemed for naught. The theoretical understanding gave me some insight, but the feelings just did not manifest as smoothly and predictably in real life. One can never be prepared for such a tragic loss. Having our precious child murdered was just unfathomable. Society doesn't really give us a road map to recover from such a painful loss. The norm is to take a few days off from work, get yourself together, and immerse yourself in busywork to take your mind off it. I cannot put such powerful feelings of heartache and sadness aside as if all is well in my daily life.

Grief is such a personal journey that no one else can go through it for you. There is no escape. The only way through grief is through the very heart of it. There are no shortcuts. There is no release from the incessant bombardment of feelings that threaten to consume you. There are resources available to guide you and there are compassionate people who willingly provide comfort, but the burden is still on you and you alone. It is a desolate journey.

During those first weeks, it seemed I was making progress in my grief. I cried daily, I prayed often, I wrote whenever I could, and I spent time with family and friends. I knew that it was going to be a long journey, but I rationalized that if I could make it through that first year of birthdays, holidays and anniversary reminders, I would be well on my way to healing. I realized around Christmas that the full impact of my loss was really just beginning. The days dragged on and the burden got heavier. I could not concentrate, I could not sleep and I could not laugh. Life was oppressive. Some days I did not want to go on, although I knew that I somehow had to continue on for my family, my friends, for myself and for Alicia. I had gone back to work, but I did not want to be there. The daily tasks of supervising a staff of forty and dealing with the day-to-day problems of the many students we served were overwhelming. I wanted to run away, but there was nowhere to run.

Months after 9/11, I talked with the president of the college. I needed some time off to heal and to be with my family. He agreed without hesitation, so I took a five-month sabbatical. I wrote extensively during those months. I sought counseling. I spent time with my family and friends. My wife and I traveled and I ran the *San Francisco Chronicle* Marathon in Alicia's honor with my daughter and her fiancé. A little more than a year after 9/11, I returned to work to a newly created position with the same status but fewer headaches. It all seemed so well planned, but the pain did not go away. I had a long way to go. It felt as if my world would always be painful and bleak.

People treated us differently. Some reached out to us with empathy and love. Others stayed away for reasons they must have rationalized. After that initial designated grieving period that society dictates, we felt all alone. My wife Bev and I found ourselves becoming socially isolated. We found it hard to return to normal life and avoided crowds like the plague. We longed for some evidence that caring others still thought of us in our time of despair. Some did, but many did not, so that really hurt. Perhaps they could not deal with it. Perhaps it was just easier to retreat into their little world and avoid the hurt and pain. We really got a clear picture of who were truly compassionate friends and family in our hour of need. Tragedy brings out the best in those special souls. Although I have fewer superficial contacts with people, my true friendships and familial bonds have grown and flourished.

One sunny afternoon, Bev and I went for a ride in our convertible. As usual, we went by a beautiful little lake surrounded by a collage of hardwoods and evergreen trees to watch the sunset. This was the last place I had taken Alicia during the summer of 2001 for her birthday. Now we noticed a sign for a house for sale pointing to a remote area along the lake. The next day we looked at it and made an offer. Now it is the place where we go to run away.

It has been years since Alicia died while working aboard United Flight 175. Since that fateful day my heart has ached more than I thought humanly possible. The pain is still incomprehensible and life without my beautiful daughter is still almost unbearable. She is always on my mind and in my heart. Sometimes I can feel life starting to trickle back into my longing soul, but the void is vast and deep. I am slowly learning how to cope with this burden, but at times the load is heavy. My little grandson helps me retain a sense of hope in times of despair, a glimpse of joy through the veil of sadness and a sense of wonder in times of stark reality. He seems to know what we need and comes running to me with a greeting, "Hi, Papa! Will you come and play with me?" To see the world through his eyes is a gift from God.

Alicia was and is a shining star with a smile to measure all other smiles against. She would light up a room. She still visits me in times of need and confirms that love, truth, joy and hope are real and that she too is still very much alive in another dimension. I diligently strive to make the most out of the here and now because there are no promises for any of us about longevity or life as we know it.

CHAPTER 30

Loss of my wife on TWA Flight 800
by Stewart Mosberg

Stewart's wife, Rosie Braman.

I lost my wife Rosie who was a flight attendant for TWA. The morning of the crash, she had an international flight to Rome so she was sleeping late. Before I left for work, I asked her which flight she was on and told her to have a safe trip. She said, "Okay." I said, "Come home safely." She responded, "I always do," and I went off to work. Later that day she called to say her flight to Rome was canceled, but TWA was deadheading the crew to Paris. She loved Paris, so she was happy with that. Tomorrow they would pick up the return flight from Rome back to New York.

We had gotten a new kitten for her birthday. We had the best time trying to come up with names for it. The night before the crash, the kitten was running around, playing on our laps and playing with toys. While watching the kitten, I suggested, "Why don't we call him Gonzo or Speedy Gonzales?" We laughed about that. The next day when she called to say the flight plan had changed, I asked, "Well, how do you like Gonzo instead of Gonzales?" We laughed again and agreed to talk about it when she returned.

I learned about the TWA crash watching CNN news. When the announcement was made that there was a crash, they mentioned the flight number. I knew immediately and sensed that all was lost, even though it was early. I just did not have a lot of hope, although I hadn't yet been informed by the airline. Rosie had been flying for a long time, so we had talked often about this possibility.

The first few hours were really awful. It was like being in a tin can. I would hear sounds and see things, but they did not register. I was in total shock. I was fortunate to have the support of my brother who had introduced me to Rosie. He immediately came to my aid. He drove out from Long Island to spend time with me, and he helped get me through the first night. Then, within a couple of days, my daughter flew in from California. Even though

I surrounded myself with friends and family, I was really still somewhat removed from it. Mentally I was in my own little space. Everything seemed blurry and murky. I do not even remember if something really happened or if I just thought it happened. It was a pretty awful time. Sometimes I had lucid moments and sometimes I did not. I stayed home during the days after the crash. I had no desire to go anywhere. I insulated myself for quite some time even after the memorial service. My daughter was very helpful to me. She got me out running again in the mornings. It was extremely beneficial to get out of bed and to exercise.

Because Rosie was part of the crew, I had access to more information than the general public. Nonetheless, notification of her death took quite some time. It is difficult for me to remember exactly whether it was within an hour, two days or a week, but I think it was a couple of days after the crash. I was contacted by a TWA special services volunteer, a flight attendant herself, who became my escort and was extremely supportive by helping me in any way she could. Besides providing emotional support, she was instrumental the rest of the summer with paperwork, contact with TWA, funeral arrangements and whatever else needed to be accomplished.

TWA provided a crisis support counselor within a couple of days. He would come to the house and spend as much time with me as I needed. He was a shoulder to lean on. He did not tell me what to do, but he was there to listen and to let me bounce things off him. When I talked about what I was feeling, there was no judgment about whether I was doing things right or wrong. He was an enormous help. A man called me who had lost a child in the crash of Pan Am 103. He offered his support and inquired if I needed anything. I never met him, but he called me almost every single day just to make sure I was okay. I got to a point where I looked forward to hearing from him. He had a gentle voice and had experienced a similar type of loss of a loved one and was just there to lend support and an understanding heart. That was very beneficial to me.

Within the first couple of weeks there was a memorial service at the TWA hangar for TWA employees and families of the lost flight attendants and crew. It was a rather large gathering of a few thousand people. I did not want to go because I did not feel like publicly displaying my emotions. However, Rosie's parents had flown in and I felt an obligation to share that experience. As I expected, it was extraordinarily painful. The hangar was a place in which I had been with Rosie on a number of occasions. TWA operations were there, so she would go there to schedule her flights. I would often go to the hangar with her if we were flying together, so it was very hard being there without her for the memorial service. There was an impromptu wall of photographs and mementos put up by the flight attendants who had lost their friends. Seeing that wall of photographs and mementos was especially devastating because it reflected the number of people killed.

Although TWA had set up a crash command center at the JFK Ramada Inn, I spent no time there. I did not feel the need to be surrounded by strangers and to grieve with others. It was a year or more before I looked at the list of other passengers on the flight. When I looked at who else was killed, it just hit me like a truck. I suddenly realized that I was not alone in this tragedy. There were 229 other people on that flight who had left grieving families, children, husbands, wives, brothers, uncles, and parents. Realizing that I was not alone was the beginning of the healing process. That feeling suggested to me why people went to the Ramada Inn after the crash and to the memorial services at the beach.

After Rosie was cremated, my brother and I had a very small private funeral service for her with just my brother, his wife and my daughter because that is the way I wanted it. Her parents lived too far away to travel for that service, but they were an integral part of the memorial service I held a couple of months later for friends and family as a tribute to her.

Initially after the crash, sleeping without Rosie was not so different from before the crash because her flight schedules sometimes kept her away from home for several days. Then I realized she was never coming back from this trip. It was not just a layover or an international flight. She was just never coming back. I had an especially hard time sleeping after that.

Because I could not go through Rosie's closet and drawers and dispose of her personal belongings immediately after the crash, I asked her girlfriends to move all of her clothing. In retrospect, I did it too soon. It was counterproductive to discard some of Rosie's personal effects from our home so soon after the crash.

When I was told that a copy of the autopsy report was available to me, I refused to see it. I was trying very hard to avoid thinking about the actual incident itself. It was terrible thinking about the moment of the explosion and crash and how frightening it must have been for her in the fire. One day I said something to her mother about it. She said that she had read the autopsy report which showed that Rosie died immediately and before she hit the water. That helped me so much.

Immediately following the crash, I was looking for some papers. I came across a videotape from one of Rosie's interviews at TWA when she first applied for an international travel position early in her career. She had shown it to me once, and I remember we had a good laugh about it. I had forgotten about it. On the first viewing, its emotional impact was very strong. Eventually, when I watched it a second time, I noticed her animation and listened to her voice. At that point, I had enough distance from the time of the tragedy that in watching it I felt a great fondness for her and could smile instead of feeling sad and crying.

I do not think there is anything that anyone could have said or done differently to make my grieving process better. It just was what it was. Because the TWA Flight 800 crash was such a public event, I received letters and cards from total strangers. The amazing outpouring of public sentiment touched me. I received letters from my senator to call her if I needed assistance, and I received a letter and flowers from Mayor Rudolph Giuliani. It was remarkable how she impacted people's lives and how they felt about her. She had touched so many people in ways I had not known. The theme was that she was an extraordinary person who made people feel happy with her smile and the joy that she brought to her work and her life. On one hand it made it worse because I realized that her loss impacted not only me, but so many others as well.

There are different types of responses to people suffering after tragedy. Some respond overzealously and do too much. They become overbearing. They do not let the survivor grieve. Some say things which may seem insensitive or callous although that is not their intention. They might say, "Oh, don't worry about it. You will feel better soon. You will get used to it." When Rosie's body was recovered, a dear friend of hers asked me for a lock of Rosie's hair. I almost went ballistic. I said, "I do not even know if she has hair!" I probably said it in a way that was hostile, but she loved Rosie so much that she just wanted to have something to remember her by. It felt thoughtless to me at the time. Other people were embarrassed or ashamed that they did not know what to say, so they do not say anything. Some people gave me books to read on the grieving process, and I knew they meant well.

I felt at fault about what happened to Rosie. We had some heated discussions about her retiring or quitting on a number of occasions. I always feared for her. She would always say that she was safer flying in an airplane than walking on the streets of Manhattan. I always felt that was not the case. I had a premonition, but I did not try hard enough. Some ultimatum might have made her stop flying. I now accept that I could not have protected her. No one knows what is going to happen, but there is still a part of me that feels I did not try hard enough to keep her alive.

Whenever I saw couples, I realized that I was not part of a couple anymore. I was the third wheel or the fifth wheel. I felt extremely bothered when, after a period of time, people began to try to fix me up. I was not ready for it. People were doing it because they were trying to help, but they were pushing me prematurely. I needed to say, "No, I'll do it on my own when I am ready."

I went back to my office to let everyone know that I was okay. I told them that I appreciated their condolences. I went back to work two to three weeks later for a couple of hours a day to answer mail and phone calls. The old routine became a very positive and important force for me. Nonetheless, it was difficult because I was not working at full capacity mentally. Over time, I was able to focus better. I wound up putting a lot more time into it and became more productive. Success was bittersweet because I could not share my accomplishments with Rosie.

At her funeral service, I turned to my brother and asked him if he would have introduced Rosie to me if he had known it was going to end this way. He said, "You two had more life in your years together than most people have in a lifetime. You did so much together and had a relationship that was so powerful! How could you not want that? How could you not be happy to have that? Of course I would introduce you again!" Only recently can I look back on it and remember how glad I am that I met her and that we had what we had together.

For a very, very long time, I did not allow myself to think about the actual accident itself. I had refused to read newspaper and magazine accounts. I totally avoided them. I was not in denial because I was quite aware that Rosie was gone. Having said that, the pain and realization came at different times in waves. For example, for years after the crash, it was always painful to hear our song on the radio. There are still things which bring tears to my eyes. A smell, a sound or a sight can cause that to happen. Finding personal effects of Rosie's that I had forgotten about or that were lost in the shuffle was extraordinarily painful. The pain has varied. There have been mental anguish and physical illness as part of my grieving.

After two years, I went to the TWA Memorial in Long Island. I went by myself. That was part of the cathartic process I needed to go through. The timing was right for me. It was a very personal experience and I felt close to Rosie. Maybe it has something to do with paying homage to her by making the pilgrimage there. It is a beautiful spot with a park, gardens, and a walkway made of bricks with the loved ones' names on them. Seeing the bricks was poignant. The first thing I did was to find the one with Rosie's name because I remembered the message I put on it about missing her.

The experience caused me to grow closer with some of Rosie's friends. Feeling close to someone whom she had been close to was beneficial. Also, I became closer to Rosie's family. We now correspond regularly and spend time together when it is feasible. That closeness provides grounding to survive as we remember her and continue to miss her.

CHAPTER 31

Loss of my family in a private plane crash
by Richard Stanley

Kathleen and Richard Stanley. Kathleen died in the air crash with their son, daughter, and son-in-law.

Lisa Stanley Shaw with her husband Scott. The couple died with Lisa's mother and brother in the plane crash.

Kevin Stanley with his wife Diane and daughters Ashley and Kathryn.

I lost my 53-year-old wife Kathleen, my 31-year-old daughter Lisa, my 29-year-old son Kevin, and my 31-year-old son-in-law Scott in a private plane crash in Florida on January 18, 2003.

My wife was a very devoted soul and a mother to even her own mother. She was the glue that held the family together and did everything for everybody. She helped all three of our daughters and our son participate in gymnastics and many other activities.

Lisa was a carbon copy of her mother. She worked for the federal government and spent a lot of time volunteering. She started a program for seniors, worked with the police and sheriffs' departments, and volunteered in the schools. If there was a public program that she could start, she started it. She was bilingual and had learned many Spanish dialects by studying in Ecuador, Mexico, Spain and Peru. She used that to her advantage after high school and college. She translated in clinics when she became an EMT and then a physician's assistant. She won accolades for her work everywhere she went. Everybody loved her.

My son Kevin was a racecar driver and mechanic with his own shop. He befriended my son-in-law Scott, let him drive his vehicles, and took him to the drag strip. Scott had always wanted to be a pilot, but had been too busy working his way up to personnel manager at his work. I asked him, "Why don't you become a pilot?" He decided to do just that. When Scott and Lisa married, they moved to Florida so he could go to flight school. He accepted a flight instructor position for Delta Airlines. To celebrate his promotion, he took my son, daughter and wife up in one of the planes. It basically fell apart in the air.

I went to work at 6 a.m. on the morning of the crash. About noon, I was thinking, "I bet they are out there flying around and having a good time." As I drove home, I was thinking about them again. When I put the key into the back door, all of a sudden it was as if someone hit me on the head with a sledgehammer. I went down on my knees to the ground in pain without knowing why. I couldn't focus. The pain was excruciating. I crawled through the door and up the stairs as I tried to figure out what was wrong with me. I went into the medicine cabinet and took five aspirin. Then I slid back down the stairs and crawled onto the couch. I was tossing and turning. I was nauseated and I could not believe the pain. It was like when I was injured in the service. At that time, the intensity of the pain was so unbelievable that even the air hurt. I had no idea what was going on. I had no idea that the whole ordeal began at the moment of the plane crash which took away my wife and two of my children. I was feeling something that I wasn't even aware of yet.

Finally, when my eyesight began to come back, I could see that it was three o'clock. I had told everyone I would be back at 2:30 p.m. When I arrived back at work, someone said, "Dick, you look awful." I did my work. It was brutal because everything was so painful. By about six o'clock, most of the pain and the headache were gone, but I was still just feeling bad. At about 6:30 p.m., I was at home sitting in front of the television thinking, "That was a terrible ordeal. I never want to go through that again. Tomorrow my wife will be home. All of this will be behind me and everything will be back to normal."

Ten minutes later, my daughter-in-law was on the phone saying, "They are gone! They are all gone! They took a flight and they are gone!" I asked, "What are you talking about?" A man picked up the phone and identified himself as the sheriff. I asked him what was going on. He said, "Well, there has been an accident and there are three fatalities." I replied, "Three fatalities?" and he responded, "Yes, three fatalities." Diane had said there were four people on the plane. I ran the various scenarios about who had died and who had survived through my mind. I wondered whether it was my daughter, my son or my wife who had survived. "Which one survived? If my wife survived, but our daughter died, my wife would be like a vegetable. If my son died, my wife would be a basket case. Any way I looked at it, she would be destroyed if she survived." I thought, "What should I do?" I was helpless. Being in New York while this had happened in Florida was like being in the middle of nowhere. I was trying to get confirmation from a sheriff who did not even know who was aboard the plane. So the nightmare

Chapter 31 Loss of my family in a private plane crash

began.

I called the sheriff's department back. They did not return my calls or pass on any more information to me because of concerns with disclosures and releases. At 11 p.m., I learned there were four fatalities. I did not know the reason for the increase from three to four. I did not know if someone else had just died in the interim or exactly what had happened. It was hell on earth! Absolute hell on earth! I was completely in shock. I tried to go through the mechanics of what to do in this situation. It was to convey information, which I did. I called our relatives. I called Scott's brother first. In the back of my head I was thinking, "My life is over. It is gone. It is done." I did not sleep for three days.

Reporters were parked in front of my house. Everybody wanted to interview me. I thought, "Go away! Go home and kiss your wife. Buy her flowers. Just get away from me." I had to leave for four days to escape them.

I heard my wife come home several days later. I heard her drive into the driveway, get out of the car and come through the back door and up the stairs. When I turned all the lights on, she was not there. The next morning I heard the TV downstairs. She used to watch the weather report every morning, and now I could hear that it was the weather. I ran downstairs. She was not there, but I could feel her presence in the house as I shut off the TV.

There was confusion about exactly how the accident took place. I tried and tried to get information. I also had to make a decision, "Is it going to do me any good to go to Florida? Am I going to be able to help? The answer was "no". I was not going to get any more information by being there than by staying home. I was just going to make phone calls there, and I could make them just as well from home. I just wanted to know what had happened. I asked when the state of Florida would release the bodies. The answer was, "They have to be autopsied." I thought, "This is what they do to human beings? They take them to look for drugs and something to blame them for the accident." I was outraged, absolutely outraged. There was a lot of anger, a tremendous amount of anger. There was no place to release the anger. There was no one to turn to and no place to go to find out what had happened.

Eventually I went to Florida. I picked up their personal effects. The people were so impersonal at the sheriff's office. They had me sign and just handed me a bag. That was it. They did not say or do anything and were as cold as they could be.

We went down to the water's edge where they had brought the bodies in. We had ceremonies there with the children. We had to go through my daughter's house in Florida to decide who was going to get what. Since nothing could bring anybody back, I didn't care. I was concerned about the four people I lost. Here in New York, we had to use a gym as a makeshift funeral parlor because over a thousand people came. If you had met me in the funeral home when I lost four loved ones, I would have told you, "Oh, my God! Life is over." I was ready to step into a box next to them. I didn't know anything else to do.

Early on, one woman advised me, "You have to do things that make you feel good. You should concentrate on doing those things no matter what anybody else says. Everybody is going to have some opinion of what you should be doing." Everybody did have an opinion about what I was supposed to do. I had to make up my mind that I was not my son, I was not my daughter, not my son-in-law and certainly not my wife. I was not going to do the things that they would have done if I had died. I had to learn who I was now. I had a very good idea about who I was before the loss, but now I was different. I kept wishing this had never happened and hoping that it would change, but they were not ever coming back.

Everybody says, "Life goes on." Anybody who is in the middle of grieving will not hear that and find it insensitive. A grieving person knows what is going on, but cannot control it. There is no training in our society for grieving. There was nobody to talk to. Those people like my wife, whom I would have talked to about all this, were gone. I really wanted to tell people about my experience, so I did. It did not bring them back, but just made it palatable. Now I have a deeper understanding of the process. I realize I have emotions for a reason and that is what makes me human. I had to experience all of the downside emotions, and that was very difficult. It is very difficult to cry if you are a man. It is very difficult to be accepted if you cry if you are a man. I learned that when I have an emotional crisis, I give into whatever I am feeling. It gives me a handle on this grieving process, but it is still very tough.

CHAPTER 32

Loss of my mother in childbirth
by Kiersten Stevens

Kiersten with her mother, father and brother Parker.

Jennifer Miller on her wedding day with her son Parker and daughter Kiersten.

My mother, Jennifer Lynn Miller, died giving birth to my baby brother when I was twelve. Her life revolved around us kids. She loved being a mom and had more enthusiasm and devotion to motherhood than most others. She had a wonderful voice and I remember her playing the Bryan Adams song, *Everything I Do, I Do It for You*, on the piano after school. She was an aerobics instructor and taught first grade for a few years. I had so much fun going to her classroom to help out. She was involved in every aspect of my life including mother-daughter teas.

My mother was expecting my baby brother, so we were planning baby showers, decorating the baby's room and picking out names for boys. Once when we were standing in the baby's room, I suddenly had an overwhelming feeling that my mother might pass away. I asked her, "Do people often die while having babies?" My mother assured me that this was not the case, but that memory has forever stayed in my mind.

My mother's labor had to be induced. My grandma and my brother and I visited her in her hospital room. She smiled, but I could see she was in pain. She asked my grandmother to get the nurse because she wasn't feeling so well. We didn't realize the significance of her complaint and headed down to the cafeteria. While we were eating, I heard my mother's hospital room being called out. When I mentioned it to my grandmother, she dismissed it as being another room. Then they clearly announced her room number as they summoned all available doctors to come. We rushed back upstairs. We knew something was wrong and were told to go to the waiting room. I was twelve and my brother was nine, so no one told us anything. We felt like animals in a zoo as they stared at us and whispered about us.

A hospital worker took us back to the cafeteria and offered us anything we wanted to eat. His job was to distract us while they were working on my mother. We were not told that they were trying to operate on her, but we knew something was wrong. I've always associated him with my mom's death.

Then we were taken to a tiny room near my mother's hospital room. It was full of relatives who were all in tears. I can't even remember if my dad was there yet. I don't remember who told me, but I heard the worst news of my life in words said very slowly, "Your mom has passed away." As I looked at my little brother's face, I knew that nothing was ever going to be the same. I felt that I needed to protect him. We were no longer little kids.

I remember my father walking with me down the stark white halls of the hospital to see my mother. I did not want to go. Reluctantly, I squinted from eyes that were clenched shut against that scene to see my mom dead under a white blanket. I took off running as fast as I could down the hallway. I never wanted to see that sight again. I hate hospitals to this day.

They moved us into a larger room so we could notify our friends and family. I remember my stepdad calling his family in North Dakota and screaming into the answering machine, "Jennifer's dead!" It was horrible.

When we went home, my brother and I slept with my dad. We all needed each other. My baby brother Matthew was still in the NICU, so we were still crossing our fingers that he would be okay. My mother died from an amniotic fluid embolism, but my brother somehow lived and was normal despite prolonged oxygen deprivation before birth. My parents were divorced and we had been living with Mom and our stepdad. We moved in with my dad that day and never slept in our old house, my mother's house, again. We met there only to talk about the funeral.

Our family friend and hairdresser did my mom's hair and makeup for the viewing. I remember them crying. I have a vivid memory of the smell, touch and feeling of my mother. Everything smelled like gardenias, so I have a distinct association with my mother attached to them. I even had a gardenia tattooed on my back to remember her. I remember touching my mom's hands and finding them incredibly cold and hard. Then my dad cut a piece of my mom's hair for me to keep. I didn't stay long in the viewing room. I didn't feel that my mom was there. Her body was there, but her entire life had been removed from her. I was hopeful that she was someplace that was beautiful.

Her funeral was at the church where she had taught Sunday school. The church was overflowing with friends and family. It was overwhelming to see so many longtime friends including past teachers, friends from school

Chapter 32 Loss of my mother in childbirth

and family from around the country. She had clearly made an impact on everyone around her. We asked family and friends to bring photos of them with her to bury with her. One family friend brought a little Valentine's bear my mom had given her. We eventually buried her, but I don't like to visit her grave. I'd rather connect with her spiritually than visit a hole in the ground. I like to be with her on a higher level because I know she's still out there.

For quite a few months after my mother's passing, the hospital sent us loads of diapers, formula and toys. It was a nice gesture, but it didn't bring my mother back. For about two years, my family was involved in a lawsuit with the hospital over my mother's death. There were many cases of amniotic fluid embolism in which the women survived, so the hospital should have acknowledged that they did something wrong that day. We eventually put the case to rest because we needed to move on with our lives.

I was in junior high, so my immediate friends could not fully relate to my loss, but I always had a tight support group around me. Their way of dealing with me was to go out of their way to compliment me with comments such as, "Kiersten, your bangs look so cute!"

My whole family attended a bereavement group. I really liked it because I talked with kids my own age about our losses. Some were having a hard time and doing poorly in school. I went back to a second session because it was a safe place to talk about my feelings. Though I was sad, I could see the larger picture of life and kept moving through it. It was definitely not easy, but I knew my mother wanted me to keep smiling.

I missed my mother especially around the holidays. A few things bothered me because of her loss such as seeing friends being disrespectful to their mothers. Mine was gone and I always envied them. Luckily I have an amazing father who did things with me that moms often do. He even braided my hair. We made it through the hard times together.

My father remarried, and his new wife brought her son to join our family. As we rebuilt our lives together, I was lucky to have a very tight family and supportive friends. My family has always been very open about my mother's death, so there was never anything that went unspoken. For example, every time we have a family dinner, we light the "Jennifer Candle", a tradition my Uncle Justin began to remember her.

It has been thirteen years since my mother died, and despite all the early turbulence in our lives, we are all making it. My eyes were opened when my mother died. Through her death, I acquired a profound respect for my life and for those around me. I don't take things for granted and I realize life is too short to sweat the small things. I never leave my house mad at someone, and I remember to say "I love you" to those around me. I have an amazing relationship with my father in part because of that awful experience of losing my mother. We managed to find the good in the bad. As the years have passed, I've gotten even more comfortable about having honest conversations with my friends and loved ones about my loss. I still cry when I talk about her and remember that awful day when I lost my mother.

Appendix

The Mission of AirCraft Casualty Emotional Support Services

At AirCraft Casualty Emotional Support Services (ACCESS) we devote our resources to working with those who have lost loved ones in air disasters and to pairing volunteer grief mentors who have lost loved ones in years past to callers with similar relationships lost. Although grief in the setting of sudden death is nearly universal and everyone who has experienced it can appreciate its scope, our support is specialized in its focus to be especially appropriate to each individual's particular situation. We match our callers to the most suitable grief mentors according to specific relationships lost.

While grief affects those left in the wake of sudden loss of loved ones regardless of the cause, ACCESS concentrates on air disaster related tragedies because there are typical common logistics confronted in the aftermath of air disasters. For example, there are frequently delays in confirmation and notification of the loss, and the remains may be absent or incomplete. If they are found, their identification and release is often delayed. These logistics can profoundly impact the grieving process by raising special concerns that need to be addressed.

The distinguishing feature of ACCESS bereavement support is that it is provided by volunteer grief mentors who themselves have previously suffered similar losses. It is the only organization dedicated to connecting those who have survived or lost loved ones in air disasters in years past to individuals who have lost loved ones in more recent air disasters. All of our professionally trained mentors have acquired credentials through their own pain, sorrow, and grief. A special type of comfort is gleaned from talking to others who have been through it before. This common factor establishes a foundation of communication and trust that other support systems may not. Most importantly, since all of our volunteer grief mentors have survived their losses, they are models of hope when the grief-stricken find their lives impossibly painful. They are living proof that others can survive this type of loss. They are nonjudgmental and compassionate listeners who provide emotional support by offering our callers a safe and confidential place to express emotions.

In addition to the common bond of sudden loss in air disasters, ACCESS recognizes that even closer ties exist between those who have lost a similar relationship. For example, a mother who has lost a teenaged son may relate more to another who also lost a teenaged son than to a woman who lost her husband. For the mother, there is the immediate focus on her son's room and belongings, and there is loss of watching the child grow, graduate, marry and have children. For a woman losing a husband, there are different issues to confront and different manifestations of loss in a future without him.

Another distinctive feature of ACCESS is that the scope of its emotional support is not limited in time. ACCESS helps grieving individuals through their losses from the moment a plane goes down for as long as they need our help. Immediately following an accident, it is important that acute crisis responders meet the logistical and bereavement needs on site, but a corollary to this care is the responsibility to provide information about continued resources from ACCESS or other easily accessible entities that specialize in emotional support. This makes the bereaved feel less abandoned when the disaster teams disband and they return home to begin their lives without their loved ones and find it difficult to cope with their pain. Many of our callers wish they had known about ACCESS before they returned home. For example, one of our grief mentors lost his mother and was dealing with his own and his elderly father's grief. While the initial acute care teams were helpful, when he and his father returned home, they had to scramble to find any emotional support, and what they found fell short of their specific needs.

ACCESS is distinct from the other organizations because we provide a seamless transition to grief support that is always available and easily accessible from any location. After she left the TWA grief site, Heidi Snow had no place to turn for support as the shock of the tragedy gave way to unremitting intense grief and anguish. She felt isolated and desperately wanted to talk to someone who could relate to what she was going through. This need is what inspired her to found ACCESS.

Since its founding in 1996, ACCESS has grown exponentially. The organization has a 24-hour hotline and more than 250 grief mentors. Airlines, disaster response agencies and many other entities throughout the country, and as far as the Middle East and New Zealand, use its guidance in training first responders and others interacting with the grief-stricken. Heidi and other ACCESS representatives have spoken about surviving loss to many groups including clinicians and disaster response workers. Heidi was the New Yorker of the Week on the NY1 news channel in New York City. She and others have represented ACCESS on many networks and shows including *Larry King Live,* CNN, CBS, NBC, ABC, FOX and A&E and in many magazines and newspapers including *The New York Times*, *Life Magazine* and *People Magazine* in the aftermath of major air disasters including 9/11. The ACCESS advisory board includes New York Mayor Rudy Giuliani and Governor George Pataki, as well as Rabbi Harold S. Kushner and San Francisco Mayor Gavin Newsom. Resources enabling ACCESS to grow have come through grants, capital campaigns, and charity events, as well as contributions from hundreds of individuals, corporations and foundations nationwide.

ACCESS Sensitivity Training for Airline Crisis Responders and other Disaster Response Teams

Southwest Airlines crisis response team training session. They recognize that it is important that some of the training for these teams is by those who have personally experienced the loss of a loved one in an air disaster.

Some of the most important work of ACCESS begins before an air disaster occurs. Through our extensive firsthand experience, we have perspectives that uniquely qualify us to train crisis response teams to successfully navigate the delicate interactions with the grief-stricken following an air disaster and to provide the greatest possible comfort and care. We conduct sensitivity training workshops for the airlines, disaster response organizations, and other entities who come in contact with the victims' loved ones. We teach the sensitivity and crisis communication skills necessary to address the labile emotional state of the bereaved following sudden loss. This outreach is consistent with our mission to provide emotional support to those left unexpectedly in the wake of air disasters. It is important that some of the training for those interacting with the grief-stricken is presented by those who have experienced it because we truly appreciate what it feels

Appendix

like and we share this information to help those who assist the bereaved following an air disaster understand how it feels. We introduce the trainees to a number of individuals who have lost loved ones in air disasters by telling our own personal stories and by presenting our ACCESS video.

Heidi Snow at a crisis response training session for Qatar Airways. Heidi Snow and others have brought the message and experience of ACCESS to train crisis responders and disaster response teams across the country and around the world.

Our sensitivity training materials are based on our cumulative experiences and stories from our volunteers and callers from hundreds of disasters. We at ACCESS have learned so much the hard way through our own experience and pain. We have a larger body of feedback and collective experience than any other group because we have accumulated it from hundreds of individuals who lost children, nieces, nephews, parents, siblings, colleagues, spouses, fiancés, partners, friends, aunts, uncles and others. This has given us unprecedented insight into responding to the grief-stricken after sudden loss. We have compiled these insights from those who have lived it to prepare first responders at airlines and other agencies to best serve the grieving in the aftermath of an air disaster as they are notified of the incident, receiving remains and personal affects, and planning memorials.

In our workshops, we review in detail the common reactions of individuals immediately following an air disaster and the responses documented to be optimal from our extensive experience. We present how to best deal with the full range of reactions that they will encounter such as shock, anger and guilt.

Besides the traditional overview regarding loss, we provide guidelines to avoid pitfalls and to optimize relationships with the grief-stricken. What to say, how to say it and what to do is not enough. What not to say and what not to do is also important. An instructive and helpful guide in dealing with the grief-stricken is our ever-evolving list of the most hurtful and most helpful comments compiled from people involved in ACCESS. It is surprising to most of our trainees that well-intentioned and seemingly supportive common remarks can be very hurtful. For example, one well-meaning comment our population has found hurtful is, "I know exactly how you feel." Telling individuals that you already know what they are feeling implies that you do not want to hear what they are feeling and that what they are feeling is not important. This is the most significant event in their lives and no one could possibly know what they are feeling. This comment does not change what they are feeling. It dismisses their feelings and denies them any comfort they might derive from expressing their grief.

ACCESS has provided sensitivity training to personnel from a wide variety of organizations including JetBlue Airways, Southwest Airlines, SkyWest, Air New Zealand, Qatar Airways, Heritage Aviation, the American Red Cross, the National Transportation and Safety Board, the New York City Medical Examiners Office, the New Jersey Self-Help Clearinghouse, Embry-Riddle Aeronautical University Aviation & Law Insurance Symposium, American Association for Justice, Dombroff Gilmore Jacques & French, Travelers Aviation, National Structured Settlement Trade Association, and the American Bar Association.

Testimonials about Grief Support through ACCESS

AirCraft Casualty Emotional Support Services (ACCESS) has helped hundreds and hundreds of individuals. Some of the comments we have received include:

"The grief was immense. It was the worst thing that could have happened to me and my sons. I kept feeling like I was going downhill with no way out. But ACCESS never quit. I'm convinced that my mentor has to be one of the most wonderful people in the world. From the care I received I knew that I wanted to be involved with ACCESS and to help others."
- Mary Conklin, Capron, IL, lost her husband John in a private plane crash on 7/8/00

"When I first found out about ACCESS I didn't feel alone anymore. I am so happy that ACCESS exists. I feel so proud that people like me have a voice out there and that someone like Heidi could come away from an experience like this and influence so many others. Now I feel I am also in a position to truly be able to help others."
- Veronica Campanelli, Nyack, NY, lost her husband Michael in a private plane crash on 4/4/03

"ACCESS is a safe place for those who feel all alone in their grief. To have an outlet, just someone to talk to who understands, can mean so much and can help a person heal in their journey through pain and darkness. ACCESS offers hope to those who otherwise have nowhere to turn to express their feelings."
- Shari Miles, Colbert, WA, lost her father Robert, 42, in a private plane crash on 5/22/76

"I appreciate the sincerity and caring of ACCESS. My mentor Helen lost her twin daughters and has helped me work through this. I am stronger than I was last year. It helps knowing that I am not alone."
- Mary Louise White, Port St. Lucie, FL, lost her daughter Elizabeth, 27, on United Flight 93 on 9/11/01

"The help and kindness I received from ACCESS during the most despairing time of my life not only comforted me but helped me learn how to help others that have gone through a similar experience."
- Shari Gemmill, Tuscon, AZ, lost her mother Barbara and stepfather James on EgyptAir 990 on 10/31/99

"It was important to have someone to listen, and even more important to have someone who understood."
- Rachel Courtney, San Francisco, CA, lost her father in a private plane crash on 8/4/98

"ACCESS provides me with an opportunity to focus on healing through helping others, which at the end of the day helps me too."
- Daniel Winchester, Tallahassee, FL, lost his brother Gus in a private plane crash on 3/3/03

"It is impossible to explain your grief and shock to someone who has not experienced this kind of loss. ACCESS put me in touch with Marion who lost her daughter in an airline disaster. She had already walked this painful road and listened compassionately to my story."
- Marilyn Kausner, Clarence Center, NY, lost her daughter Ellyce, 24, on Continental Flight 3407 on 2/12/09

Surviving Sudden Loss: *Stories from those who have lived it*

"From an airline emergency response perspective, ACCESS has invaluable insight in helping us to create a program that will ensure that our employees treat passengers affected by an airline disaster with the appropriate level of respect and care."
- Sandy Nelson, Southwest Airlines Family Notification Coordinator

"The ACCESS volunteer grief mentor training conference gave me the knowledge and tools to help me with my work. As delicate as it is to talk to someone going through grief, it is vital to be trained in order to help. Thank you, ACCESS!"
- Lisa Kokal, Libertytown, MD, lost her fiancé Kevin in a private plane crash on 6/23/00

"At the top of my list of volunteer organizations is ACCESS, and recently I had the honor of training their volunteer grief mentors. Heidi and the ACCESS mentors provide unprecedented emotional support in the aftermath of an air disaster. The ACCESS mentors are an exceptional group whose hard-earned knowledge comes through their firsthand experience as survivors. I left their training program deeply inspired by the dedication and genuine caring of this powerful volunteer army."
- Dr. Ken Druck, Founder, The Jenna Druck Center, lost his daughter Jenna, 21, in a bus accident on 3/27/96

"One of the most difficult things for me is telling people my story. I lost my entire family, so when people ask 'does your family live here?' or 'do you have any siblings?' it's sometimes overwhelming for them. But it's not something I can hide inside because it is such a big part of my life. ACCESS gave me a chance to let who I am on the inside be who I am on the outside, and has helped me realize that sharing my story and my experience is valuable and helpful to other people."
- Elizabeth Norton, Colorado Springs, CO, lost her father Kendrick, 48, mother Belva, 45, and brother Jeffrey, 18, in a private plane crash on 3/22/90

"I can accomplish more through ACCESS than I could anywhere else. ACCESS is a great organization for understanding individual circumstances and what the grieving process is all about. We are all a work in process. ACCESS is amazing."
- Richard Stanley, Bowmansville, NY, lost his wife Kathy, son Kevin, daughter Lisa and son-in-law Scott in a private plane crash on 1/18/03

"My dad always described the pilot community as a community of people who are brought together by their common love of flying. He described the AOPA as a place for people within that community to share stories, experiences and further their knowledge of flying. When my dad was killed in a plane crash, my family and I were forced to join a different community, one of people brought together by our common grief and sadness over having lost a loved one in a plane crash. Fortunately, there is an organization called ACCESS which provides my family with a place to share our stories and experiences with others who are grieving in a similar way. I am thankful to have ACCESS to help get me through this tragic time. It is important for the pilot community to have the AOPA, and it is instrumental for me, my family and those in our situation to have ACCESS."
- Robin Freeman, San Francisco, CA, lost her father James in a private plane crash on 8/4/10

"It is so important to have contact with someone who has been through something similar to your experience. I learned the importance of ACCESS in October 2001. The Department of Defense brought all the 9/11 families involved in the Pentagon and American Airlines to Washington, D.C. We all stayed in the same hotel and my adult children came too. One of my sons said, 'My gosh, it is nice to be in a room where everybody has the same look in their eyes.' I think we need that connection and so the concept of ACCESS is brilliant."
- Marion Kminek, Cape Coral, FL, lost her daughter Mari-Rae, 35, on American Airlines Flight 77 on 9/11/01

Testimonials about Grief Support through ACCESS

"If somebody asked what I needed at the time of the accident I would have said, 'Someone to reach out to me, to be accessible and to allow me to talk about my fears, about my loss, and about how much I missed my parents.' ACCESS does this for people through its mentoring program. There is a sense of understanding, of knowing the feeling of losing a loved one without saying goodbye. There is a bond and a mutual appreciation for the hardship that accompanies life after our respective sudden losses."
- Nina Crimm, Jamaica, NY, lost her parents on Air France Flight 007 on 6/3/62

"One of the main benefits of ACCESS is having a nonjudgmental third party person you can speak with who has been through this type of loss. No one can tell another how to feel or whether a feeling is right or wrong. ACCESS mentors know this and do not try to control or judge a caller's feelings and actions. By mentoring another person through ACCESS, I have gained a new understanding of my own experience. For those of us who have been through an air tragedy to be able to listen to someone else talk about their experience is of great benefit. As mentors, we are not going to relieve or eliminate another's loss or grieving, but we can be the person who says, 'I am here. I care,' and that means an awful lot."
-Dr. Larry Gustin, Tampa, FL, lost his mother Anne on TWA Flight 800 on 7/17/96

"ACCESS is a necessity. We are learning through these tragedies that providing emotional support to the families and their loved ones is such an important component of the grief process. There is something unique and touching at any stage of grief, whether it is a day after the crash, months after the crash, or years after the crash. I will always be thankful for the opportunity to connect with others who have gone through similar experiences. The airlines should all get involved with ACCESS because they are not able to offer the insight and sensitivity that a mentor from ACCESS can. Being a part of ACCESS and helping another person who is going through a similar situation to the one that I went through is a privilege."
- Lyzbeth Glick Best, Hewitt, NJ, lost her husband Jeremy on United Flight 93 on 9/11/01

"There is more comfort in sitting silently in a room with someone who has been where you are than hours of someone else talking to you and trying to comfort you. That is what ACCESS is for air crash survivors. It is built on that very foundation that someone who has been down that road and is further along than you has so much light to shed. From the loss of my Eddie, I acquired wisdom that I did not ask for and did not want. Knowing that I have something to offer and then helping other people who are grieving have been without question the most rewarding things I have ever done."
- Julie Rudd, New York, NY, lost her fiancé Eddie in a gas explosion on 6/11/92 and called ACCESS to mentor those affected by 9/11

"I consider the ACCESS mentoring program to be one of the most truly meaningful contributions of my life. The act of meeting with or talking with somebody who has experienced a similar loss is powerful. I can provide those who call ACCESS with some perspective, not only on what they have been through, but also what they can expect in the near term. ACCESS does a spectacular job of pairing people with similar types of losses. The matching allows people to interact with each other in very profound and meaningful ways, and the exchange has benefited me as a mentor as much as it did the people I have had the privilege and pleasure to mentor."
- Ned Brooks, Norwalk, CT, lost his parents Edwin and Ruth on TWA Flight 800 on 7/17/96

"A friend took me to an ACCESS event in May 2001. My family had never talked to people about their feelings and experiences. We did not know anyone who had survived an air disaster related loss. Being involved in ACCESS has given me the feeling of personally belonging and identifying with others. It helped me take time to help others and to show them that they are not alone and that someone understands what they are going through."
- Jack Karamanoukian, Englewood Cliffs, NJ, lost his brother Serge on Swissair 111 on 9/2/98

Photo credits

Life Magazine: p 68. Used by permission of *Life Magazine*. Photographers Harry Benson, Denis Reggie and David Turnley, Nina Russo Photography, Herman Leonard Photography and Dilbert © Scott Adams. Used by permission of Universal Uclick and Iconix Brand Group. All rights reserved.

People Magazine: pp 44-5, 52. Used by permission of AP and *People Magazine*. Photographers Harry Benson, Susan Ragan and Bebeto Matthews. (Kerri Strug 1996) Image ID: 96072301420 - AP Photo/Susan Ragan (Flight 800) Image ID: 96072202064 - AP Photo/Bebeto Matthews. All rights reserved.

*We would like to extend a special thanks to our
ACCESS Angel Sponsors
for their help in making this book possible*

Aviation Lawyers ★ Houston, Texas

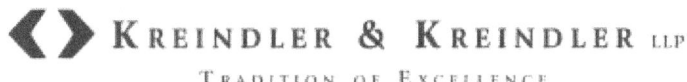

SPEISER, KRAUSE, NOLAN & GRANITO
ATTORNEYS AT LAW

www.ingramcontent.com/pod-product-compliance
Lightning Source LLC
Chambersburg PA
CBHW051806230426
43672CB00012B/2649